PRAISE FOR
The Route 66 Cookbook

"The magic of a memory-making Route 66 odyssey is the people met along the way, the time-capsule diners, and the meals shared with friends and fellow adventurers. . . . *The Route 66 Cookbook* [is] a delightful blending of history, trivia, and the special recipes that have transformed some Route 66 treasures into must-stop destinations. . . . It is the ultimate souvenir for the Route 66 enthusiast or armchair traveler that wants to bring a bit of the Route 66 magic into their kitchen."

—JIM HINCKLEY, author of *Route 66: 100 Years*

"One of the great joys of cruising Route 66 is experiencing local culture—and that includes food! Linda Ly has crafted a culinary journey that is about more than stereotypical diners and classic roadside fare—it's an exploration of the American Dream by way of small businesses and vibrant cuisine, couched in the stories that make them special. You'll want to make every recipe in here, then set out on your own to see what else you can find."

— RHYS MARTIN, author of *Lost Restaurants of Tulsa*

"Linda Ly . . . showcases a ton of really great eateries and tasty recipes. . . . *The Route 66 Cookbook* is, without a doubt, a book that should be . . . added to your collection."

—BRENNEN MATTHEWS, author of *Miles to Go: An African Family in Search of America along Route 66* and editor-in-chief at *ROUTE Magazine*

THE Route 66 COOKBOOK

THE BEST RECIPES from EVERY STOP ALONG THE WAY

Linda Ly

PHOTOGRAPHY BY WILL TAYLOR

HARVARD COMMON PRESS

Quarto.com

© 2025 Quarto Publishing Group USA Inc.
Text © 2025 Linda Ly

First Published in 2025 by The Harvard Common Press, an imprint of
The Quarto Group, 100 Cummings Center, Suite 265-D, Beverly, MA 01915, USA.
T (978) 282-9590 F (978) 283-2742

EEA Representation, WTS Tax d.o.o., Žanova ulica 3, 4000 Kranj, Slovenia. www.wts-tax.si

All rights reserved. No part of this book may be reproduced in any form without written permission of the copyright owners. All images in this book have been reproduced with the knowledge and prior consent of the artists concerned, and no responsibility is accepted by producer, publisher, or printer for any infringement of copyright or otherwise, arising from the contents of this publication. Every effort has been made to ensure that credits accurately comply with information supplied. We apologize for any inaccuracies that may have occurred and will resolve inaccurate or missing information in a subsequent reprinting of the book.

The Harvard Common Press titles are also available at discount for retail, wholesale, promotional, and bulk purchase. For details, contact the Special Sales Manager by email at specialsales@quarto.com or by mail at The Quarto Group, Attn: Special Sales Manager, 100 Cummings Center, Suite 265-D, Beverly, MA 01915, USA.

29 28 27 26 25   1 2 3 4 5

ISBN: 978-0-7603-9363-5

Digital edition published in 2025
eISBN: 978-0-7603-9364-2

Library of Congress Cataloging-in-Publication Data

Names: Ly, Linda, 1980- author | Taylor, Will photographer
  Title: The Route 66 cookbook : the best recipes from every stop along the
    way / Linda Ly ; photography by Will Taylor.
Other titles: Route Sixty-six cookbook
Description: Beverly, MA, USA : Harvard Common Press, 2025. | Includes bibliographical references and index. | Summary: "The Route 66 Cookbook shares recipes for the must-try breakfasts, lunches, dinners, and desserts from restaurants all along the Mother Road"-- Provided by publisher.
Identifiers: LCCN 2025008322 | ISBN 9780760393635 | ISBN 9780760393642 ebook
Subjects: LCSH: Cooking | Restaurants--United States Highway 66--History | LCGFT: Cookbooks
Classification: LCC TX714 .L925 2025 | DDC 641.5973--dc23/eng/20250319
LC record available at https://lccn.loc.gov/2025008322

Design: Kelley Galbreath
Photography: Will Taylor

Printed in Guangdong, China TT 062025

For Gemma Lumen and Ember Luna,
THE COOLEST PEOPLE WE KNOW.

You fed wild burros, walked through millions of years of history in a petrified forest, spray-painted cars in the middle of a desert, swam with turtles in a creek, explored a cave system in the Ozarks, One-wheeled and biked on miles of original Route 66 pavement, earned Junior Ranger badges at five new national parks, rode a tram up the tallest monument in the country, went to your first drive-in movie at the oldest original drive-in on 66, and even camped overnight at that drive-in. But in the end, when we asked what your favorite parts of the trip were, you both declared, "The water parks!"

Always hold on to that sense of wonder and adventure.

We love you to infinity.

Contents

Introduction	8
Kitchen Standards	12
Route 66 Map	16
Where Did Route 66 Really Begin?	18

ONE • ILLINOIS   20

Grilled Thick French Toast: *Lou Mitchell's Restaurant & Bakery*	22
Apple Strudel: *The Berghoff*	24
Dátiles con Almendras: *Mercat a la Planxa at The Blackstone*	26
Smoke-Filled-Room Cocktail: *Mercat a la Planxa at The Blackstone*	28
Sautéed Chicken Livers: *Dell Rhea's Chicken Basket*	30
Crispy Chicken Adobo Wings: *Lola's*	32
Morel Mushroom Pie: *Maldaner's Restaurant*	34
Docs S'mores Sundae: *Docs Just Off 66*	36
Strawberry Whipped Cheesecake: *The Ariston Cafe*	38
Butter Spritz Cookies: *Jubelt's Bakery & Restaurant*	40
Weezy's Coleslaw: *Weezy's Route 66 Bar & Grill*	44

TWO • MISSOURI   46

Heavenly Hash: *Crown Candy Kitchen*	48
Heart-Stopping BLT: *Crown Candy Kitchen*	50
Curly-Q Dog: *Carl's Drive-In*	52
French Onion Soup: *Historic Big Chief Roadhouse*	54
Cream of Chicken and Wild Rice Soup: *Weir on 66*	56
Cucumber and Onions: *Missouri Hick Bar-B-Que*	58
Beef Rub and Rib Rub: *Missouri Hick Bar-B-Que*	60
Blackberry Wine Cake: *St. James Winery*	62
Bang Bang Burger: *Hoppers Pub*	64
The Vernon—The Ultimate Route 66 Burger: *College Street Cafe*	66
Mom's Yeast Rolls: *Rise & Grind Coffee Station*	68
Beans and Corn Bread: *The Carthage Deli*	72

THREE • KANSAS   74

Goulash: *Streetcar Station Coffee Shop*	76
Roast Beef Sandwich: *Nelson's Old Riverton Store*	78
The Voodoo Child Pizza: *Bricks & Brews Woodfire Grill & Pub*	80
Egg Cream: *Monarch Pharmacy and Soda Fountain*	82

FOUR • OKLAHOMA   84

Calf Fries: *Clanton's Cafe*	86
Chile Colorado: *El Rancho Grande Mexican Food*	88
Chef's Special Pastel: *Doctor Kustom Bistro*	90
Poor Man's Pecan Pie, a.k.a. Oatmeal Pie: *Rock Cafe*	94
Späetzle: *Rock Cafe*	96
Root Beer Bread Pudding: *Pops 66*	98
Green Chile Grit Cakes: *Classen Grill*	100
Posole: *Green Chile Kitchen*	102
Green Chile Apple Pie: *Green Chile Kitchen*	105
Onion Fried Burger: *Sid's Diner*	106
Lucille's Jalapeño Fried Pork Chops: *Lucille's Roadhouse*	108
French Silk Pie: *Country Dove Gifts & Tea Room*	110

FIVE • TEXAS **112**

Mashed Potatoes: *The Big Texan Steak Ranch*	114
GoldenLight Cafe Chili: *The GoldenLight Cafe & Cantina*	116
When You're Here, You're Almost There	**118**
Bobby's Egg Custard Pie: *Mama Jo's Pies & Sweets*	120
The Elvis Ugly Crust Pie: *Midpoint Cafe*	122

SIX • NEW MEXICO **124**

Del's Rellenos: *Del's Restaurant*	126
New Mexican Posole: *Silver Moon Cafe*	128
Chiles Rellenos de Camarón: *La Plazuela at La Fonda on the Plaza*	130
Tattooed Lady and Sonoran Dog: *Clowndog Hot Dog Parlor*	134
Super Burger: *Western View Diner & Steakhouse*	136

SEVEN • ARIZONA **138**

House Salsa: *Brown Mug Cafe*	140
Halibut Ceviche: *The Turquoise Room at La Posada Hotel*	142
Pork Wiener Schnitzel: *Westside Lilo's*	144
Rack of Raccoon: *The Roadkill Cafe*	146
Greek Sandwich: *Rutherford's 66 Family Diner*	148

EIGHT • CALIFORNIA **150**

Albert's Ham Sandwich: *Roy's Motel & Cafe*	152
Strawberry Margarita Pie: *Chiquita Rosita's*	154
Chocolate Malt: *Fair Oaks Pharmacy & Soda Fountain*	156
Smoke and Peaches: *La Cuevita*	158
Sticky Short Rib Noodles: *The Formosa Cafe*	160
Wok Fried Rice with Pork Belly: *The Formosa Cafe*	163
The Route 66 Pup: *Tail o' the Pup*	164
Grandma's Chicken Soup: *Mel's Drive-In*	166
KHEE to My Success: *The Lobster*	168
Seared Mushrooms with Scallion-Ginger Drizzle: *The Lobster*	170
Grilled Maine Lobster with Lemon Garlic Herb Butter: *The Lobster*	172
Ahi Tuna Crudo with Kohlrabi: *The Misfit*	174
Spicy Seafood Soup: *The Albright*	176
Where's the Real End of Route 66?	**180**

Acknowledgments	183
About the Author and About the Photographer	184
Contributors	186
Route 66 Associations	188
Index	189

INTRODUCTION

THE FABLED ROUTE 66—often called the longest Main Street in America—was established in 1926 as the first federal highway, linking Chicago (and all the small towns and big cities in between) with the Wild West. In the last hundred years, this once-vital thoroughfare has lived many lives: as an east-west escape route during the Dust Bowl and Great Depression, a military road during World War II, and a leisure highway in the 1950s, luring newly minted motorists with the promise of adventure on the open road.

This was the heyday of Route 66: the age of roadside attractions, neon signs, gas stations, and lunch counters. But as the era of interstate highways dawned, the Mother Road (as John Steinbeck dubbed it in *The Grapes of Wrath*) became a victim of its own success: improved roadways and greater efficiency eventually led to its decline, and finally its decommissioning. But almost as soon as it was decommissioned, it was also revived—as an experience for those willing to persevere and follow the old route through.

The highway's still out there—just a little harder to find these days. And the highway itself has become a living museum, a yearning for a time when the great American road trip was more about the journey than the destination. It's a road not so much for tourists as it is for *travelers*—travelers seeking a slice of Americana in a country that is quickly becoming homogenized. They're drawn to not only the nostalgia but also the impermanence of the structures, landscapes, and communities that dot the highway.

Like all great road trips, Route 66 isn't just about the drive or the destination. It's also about the people, their stories, and the pit stops you make along the way—particularly for food.

Think: the snacks scooped up at the corner store; the meals devoured in a greasy spoon; the celebratory drinks and desserts after a long day on the road. Food connects us to new cultures and leaves long-lasting impressions after we come home, flush with that post-vacation glow.

And while the mention of Route 66 conjures up images of diners and drive-ins that haven't aged a day since 1954, the mythic road has adapted over time, shaped by changing demographics and tastes along its 2,400-something miles (3,862 km).

The diners are still there, many of them continuing to serve up old-school recipes that generations of visitors have come to know and expect. But tucked between these local gathering spots and landmarks are newer establishments where chefs have reimagined classic dishes with their own modern twists; where farm-to-table movements have brought back traditional cooking and local ingredients; and where each cuisine—in the eight states the highway meanders through—embodies each region's roots and unique identity.

When I signed on to write a book about America's most iconic road food, I imagined drinking my weight in milkshakes and sitting in chrome-trimmed cafés with swivel stools and sticky menus. Would it be burgers and corn dogs and soft serve, day in and day out? (Hey, my kids had no complaints!) But the farther along I got on my journey, I realized Route 66

ROUTE 66
LITCHFIELD
JOLIET
BLOOMINGTON
STAUNTON
SPRINGFIELD
HISTORIC
ILLINOIS
US
66
ROUTE
ILLINOIS
US
66
IllinoisRoute66.org
Reisch
BEER

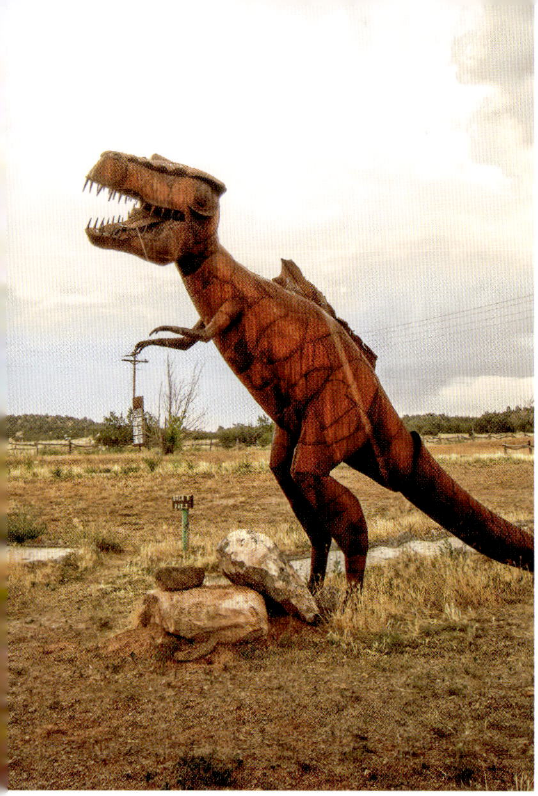

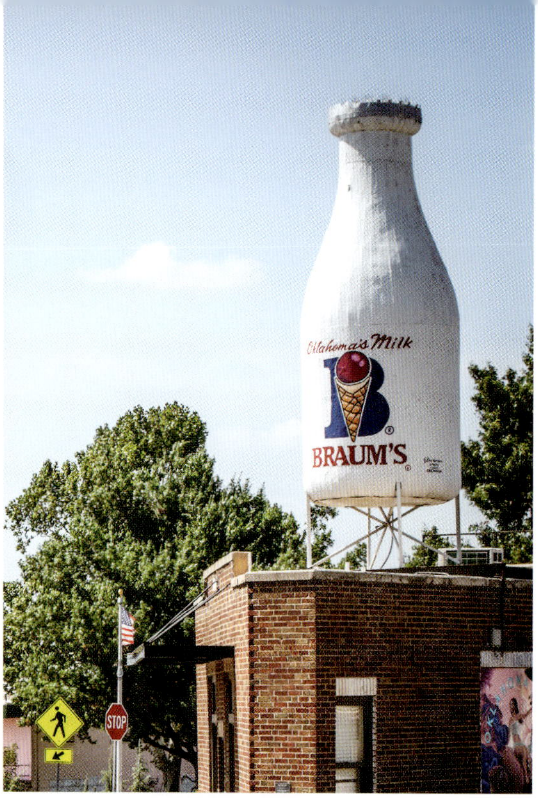
Oklahoma's Milk
BRAUM'S
STOP

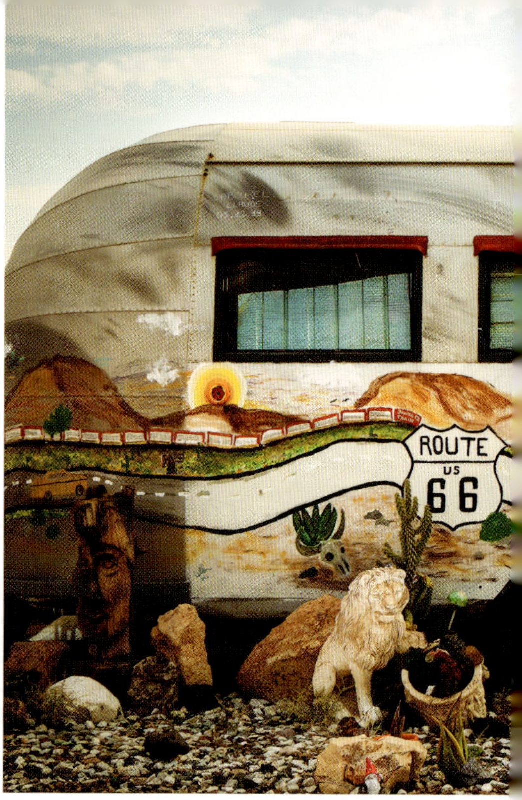
ROUTE
US
66

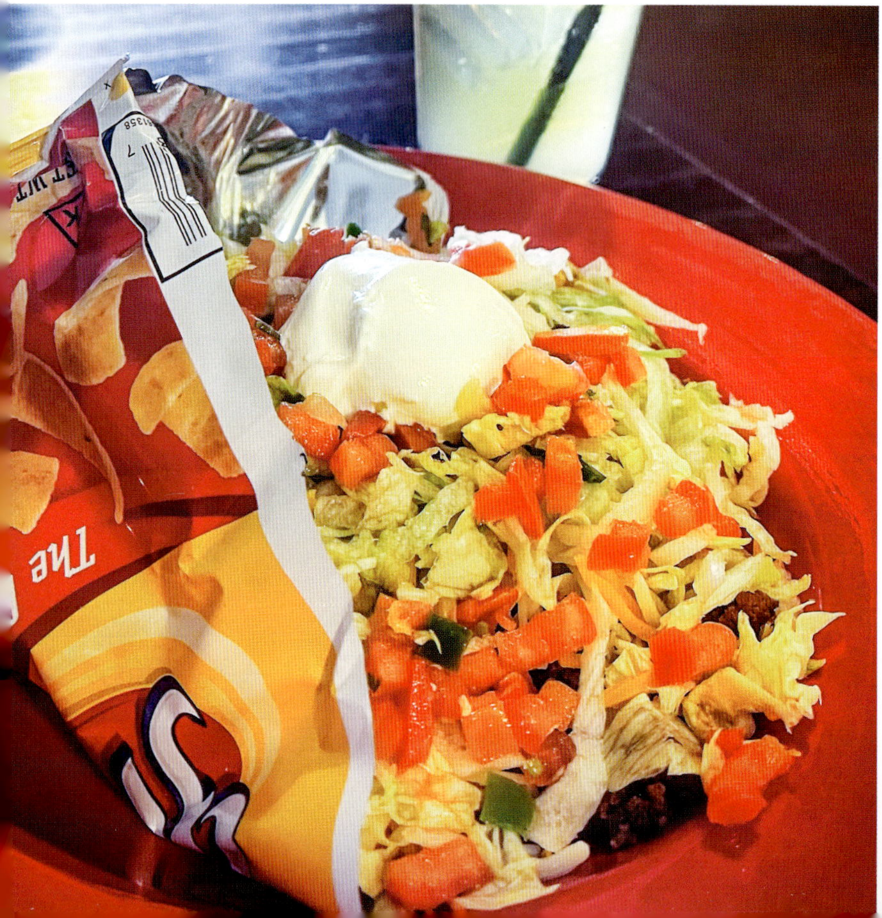

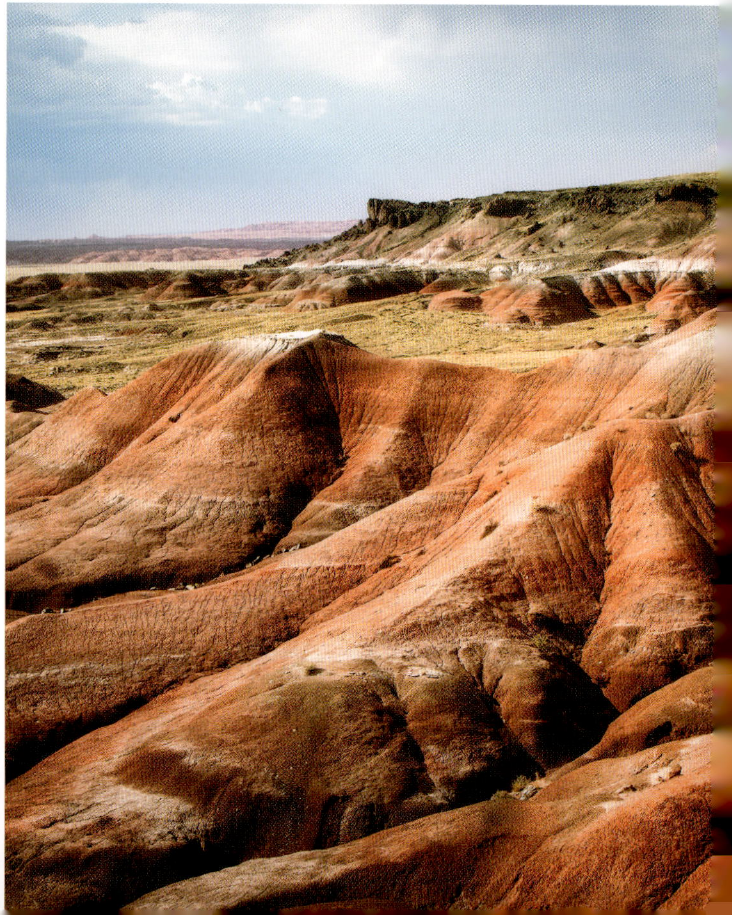

truly encapsulates the quirky eats and regional specialties that are deeply influenced by Indigenous foodways and our country's history of settlement.

Every type of eatery exists on the Mother Road, from old-fashioned soda fountains and new-school breweries to century-old sit-down restaurants and fine dining at original Harvey Houses. And each of these places along the way reflects the country's cultural patterns. The early entrepreneurs—from Mexico, Germany, Italy, Greece, Spain, and elsewhere—migrated in all directions and started diversifying their menus, blending new ideas and flavors from their adopted homeland into the food they grew up eating. The result is a delicious tapestry of multicultural cuisines that make up what we now consider Americana.

Follow the food on Route 66, and you'll find that every stop has a story. The journey is both a step back in time and a glimpse of the future, which is a great reminder that nothing stays the same forever. Like all the realignments of the original road, the restaurants and their proprietors continue to evolve and alter their histories. Some places will flourish as others fade away. Even while writing this book, and very likely after it's published, a few of the restaurants in these pages will change hands or disappear completely. But their stories—and even some of their recipes—will remain as a snapshot of the most famous highway in the world.

Here's to getting off the interstate and *going somewhere*.

INTRODUCTION | 11

KITCHEN STANDARDS

YOU DON'T NEED A COMMERCIAL KITCHEN to whip up delicious meals like a chef.

The Route 66 Cookbook was written with the home cook in mind, adapting high-volume restaurant recipes to scaled-down versions suitable for a family. That means you can use the same tools and ingredients you've always used—no unusual gadgets collecting dust after one meal or warehouse-size jugs to buy and store. This chapter outlines how I approach measurements and what I use and recommend throughout the book.

TECHNIQUES

Herbs and spices: If you don't have fresh herbs available, you can generally substitute dried herbs. A good rule of thumb is 1 teaspoon of dried equals 1 tablespoon of fresh. Dried herbs and spices do have an optimal shelf life, so if yours have been sitting around for a while, you may need to use a little more to get good flavor.

Measuring flour: If a recipe calls for cup measures, flour is measured without sifting it first. I use the "scoop and sweep" method: scoop a heaping mound of flour in the measuring cup, then sweep a straightedge across the cup to level it. Do not tamp down on the flour or tap the cup on a surface to settle it. If your flour has been compacted at the bottom of a bag or canister, lightly fluff it with a fork before scooping.

Salting: Certain recipes don't list an exact amount of salt to use, as it's open to personal preference. I recommend starting with a good pinch or two of salt, then taste and add more at the end of cooking as needed.

TOOLS

STANDARD COOKING VESSEL SIZES

	Saucepan	Skillet
Small	1 to 1½ quarts (946 ml to 1.4 L)	8 inches (20 cm)
Medium	2 to 3 quarts (1.9 to 2.8 L)	10 inches (25 cm)
Large	4 quarts (3.8 L)	12 inches (30 cm)

A stockpot should hold 6 quarts (5.7 L) or more, and a "large pot" is generally wider than it is deep. For recipes that call for deep-frying, use any heavy pan (such as a sauté pan, rondeau, or braiser) that's at least 3 inches (7.5 cm) deep.

Sheet pan: Sheet pans are also known as rimmed baking sheets. The best ones are made of heavy-gauge aluminum that doesn't warp under high heat, like the Nordic Ware brand. I recommend a "half sheet" size, 18 x 13 inches (45 x 33 cm) with 1-inch (2.5 cm)-tall sides for more versatility.

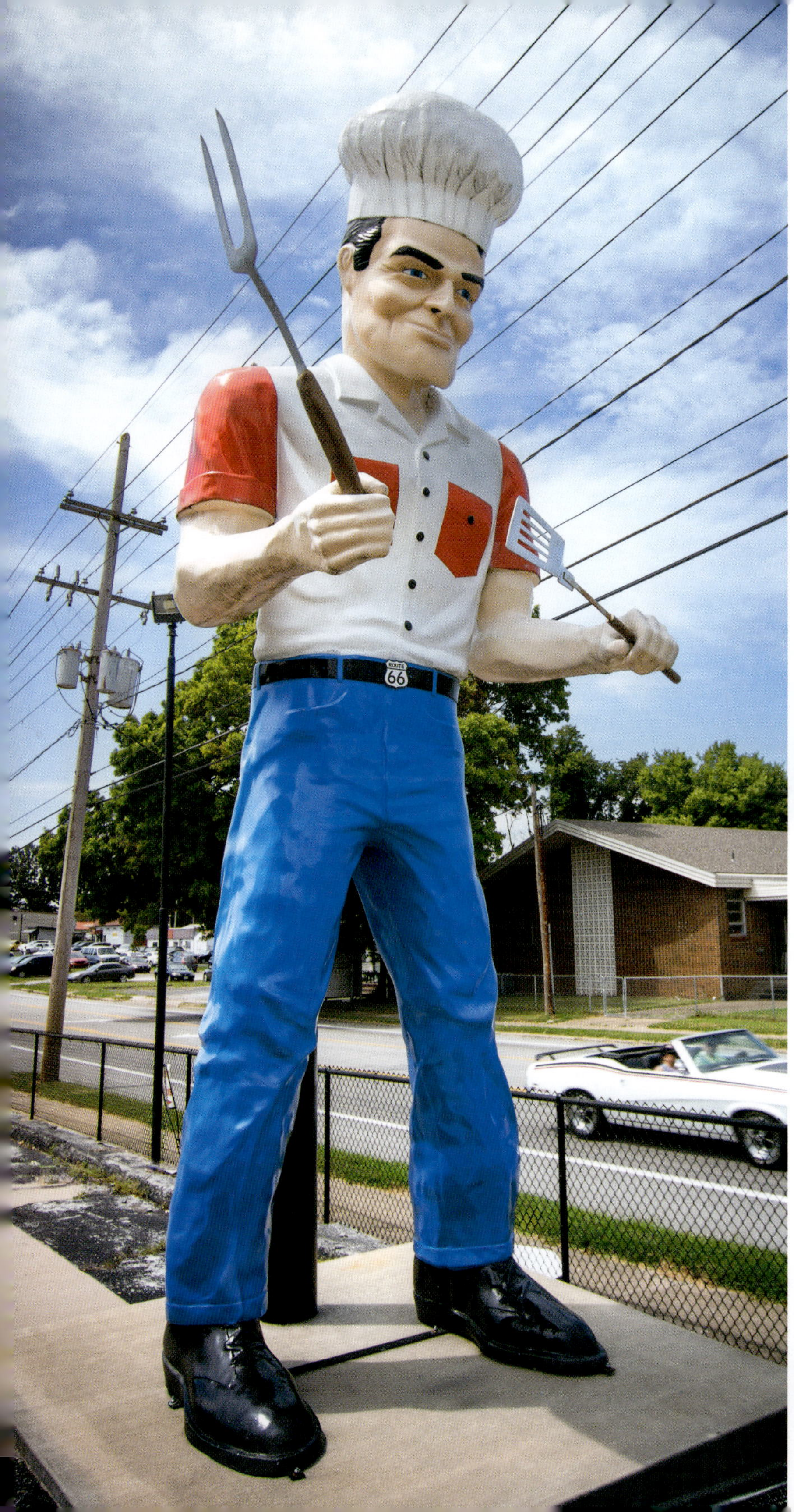

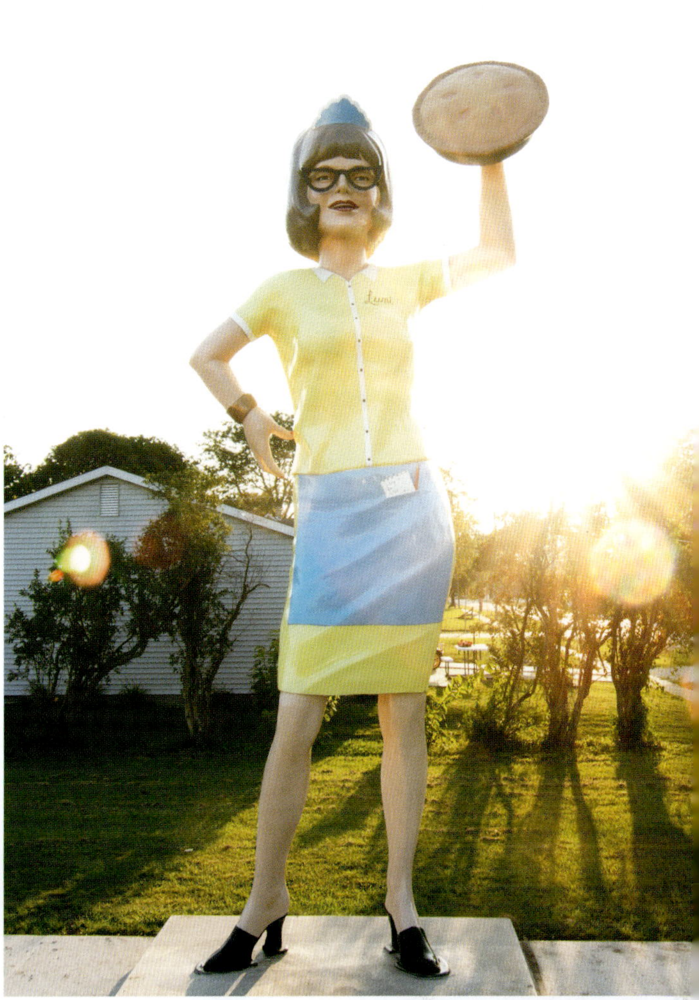

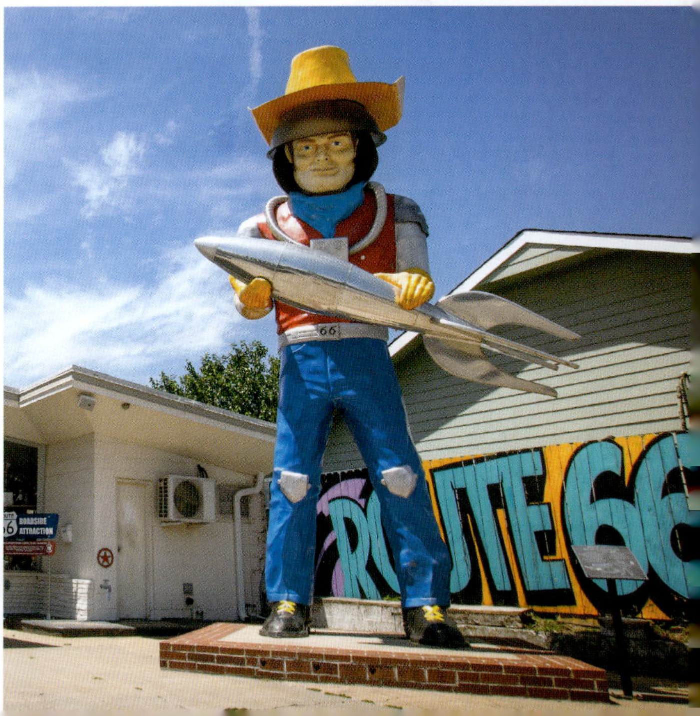
ROUTE 66

Pie pan/plate: Unless specified otherwise, the recipes in this book use a standard 9-inch (23 cm) pan size.

Stand mixer: Certain recipes call for a stand mixer, but if you don't have one, your next best option is a handheld mixer with interchangeable attachments for mixing and whipping. You can also mix, whip, and knead by hand, but doing so will take a bit more strength and stamina.

Kitchen scale: Some of the baking recipes in this book measure ingredients by weight. I recommend a compact digital food scale that weighs in pounds/ounces as well as kilograms/grams and has a capacity up to 11 pounds (2 kg). The Escali brand has been a workhorse in my kitchen for years.

Thermometer: For deep-frying, a digital instant-read meat thermometer or candy thermometer should be used to determine oil temperature. My go-to is the Thermapen from ThermoWorks.

INGREDIENTS

Some chefs call for specific brands in their recipes, and where possible, I list alternatives in case you can't source them. For common pantry ingredients, I list exactly what I use for consistency in taste and measurement. When working with your own preferred brands, use your best judgment and keep in mind important things like the size of the grain, amount of salt, level of sweetness, or fat content that may alter how your dish turns out.

14 | THE ROUTE 66 COOKBOOK

Broth: In recipes that call for broth, it's assumed your broth or stock is already well-seasoned. If it isn't, you may need to add more salt than the recipe specifies.

Butter: You likely won't taste the difference in salted versus unsalted butter if using a small amount, but if the recipe calls for ¼ cup (55 g) of butter or more, I recommend using unsalted butter and adding more salt in the end as needed.

Chicken or beef base: Unless otherwise specified, all chicken or beef bases are in paste form. Since different brands have varying salt content, you may need more or less salt than the recipe calls for.

Eggs: Unless otherwise specified, egg size is always large.

Flour: Unless otherwise specified, all recipes that call for flour use a middle-of-the-range, unbleached all-purpose flour (such as the Gold Medal brand, found in most grocers). Keep in mind that different brands of all-purpose flours have varying gluten content, especially across regions, so use your best judgment if you feel your dough needs more or less liquid to hold its shape.

Milk and other dairy: Milk is always whole and other dairy products, such as sour cream or cream cheese, are full-fat. Using skim or low-fat dairy may affect the outcome of recipes that rely on the fat content for proper results.

Nonstick cooking spray: I recommend an avocado oil spray, as it's a healthier alternative to traditional cooking sprays and has a neutral flavor and high smoke point. I like the Chosen Foods brand, which is available in most grocers.

Neutral oil: Neutral oil is specified in recipes that require an oil with a high smoke point and/or little to no flavor. I prefer avocado oil or high-oleic expeller-pressed sunflower oil for deep-frying, pan-frying, and stir-frying, but feel free to use your favorite type of oil.

Olive oil: For day-to-day cooking, I recommend an inexpensive, light and fruity extra-virgin olive oil sold in a dark bottle. My favorite brands are California Olive Ranch and Kirkland Signature (Costco), as the oils are always fresh and flavorful.

Salt: Most chefs use table salt, so in their recipes, I specify this as fine salt (you can use your favorite brand). If you prefer to use a coarse or flaky salt, refer to the measurement as a starting point when seasoning your dish—you will need a little more salt than the recipe calls for, but always taste as you go along. A few recipes call for kosher salt, and I recommend Morton Coarse Kosher Salt.

Sugar: Sugar is specified as granulated sugar (I use a table sugar like C&H Pure Cane Sugar, found in most grocery stores), brown sugar, or powdered sugar (also known as confectioners' sugar). Using another type of sweetener in place of granulated sugar, such as organic sugar, raw sugar, or sugar substitutes, may alter the flavor.

Wine: When a recipe calls for white wine, any midrange dry white wine will do; I prefer Pinot Grigio. Never use a bottle labeled "cooking wine," as it's bottom-of-the-barrel wine to which salt has been added. Using a wine you like to drink will always make your recipes taste better!

STOPS Along THE WAY
ROUTE 66
Sleep in a WIGWAM
Highland Park
West Hollywood
South Pasadena
SANTA MONICA
End
Barstow
Amboy
Kingman
Seligman
Winslow
SANTA FE
Tucumcari
ALBUQUERQUE
Santa Rosa
CALIFORNIA
ARIZONA
NEW MEXICO
SANTA MONICA
YACHT HARBOR
SPORT FISHING ★ BOATING
Cafes
ROCK SHOP
HISTORIC U.S. 66

CHICAGO
Willowbrook
Pontiac
Illinois
HISTORIC
ILLINOIS
US
66
ROUTE
BEGIN
SPRINGFIELD
Girard
Litchfield
Hamel
Brentwood
ST. LOUIS
Wildwood
CUBA
Waynesville
St. James
Miller
SPRINGFIELD
Carthage
Vinita
GEMINI GIANT
MISSOURI
Riverton
Galena
MISSOURI
KANSAS
Baxter Springs
KANSAS
OKLAHOMA
KANSAS
-Way
AFE
OKLAHOMA
TULSA
Stroud
Arcadia
Adrian
AMARILLO
Elk City
El Reno
Vega
Weatherford
Yukon
OKLAHOMA CITY
TEXAS

ROUTE
66
CHICAGO ROUTE 66
START OF THE TRAIL
HISTORY OF ROUTE 66
"THE MAIN STREET OF AMERICA"

Where Did Route 66 Really Begin?

Route 66 moved around quite a bit from its inception in 1926 to its decommissioning in 1985, and that also holds true on the eastern terminus of the highway in Illinois. Today, the "Begin Historic Illinois US Route 66" sign is on West Adams Street and South Michigan Avenue, just across the street from the Art Institute of Chicago.

But if you're heading east on Route 66, the "End Historic Illinois US Route 66" sign is one block south, on East Jackson Boulevard and South Michigan Avenue. Why? Turns out, this intersection was *also* the original start of Route 66 until the mid-1950s, when changes in traffic patterns moved the westbound alignment to Adams Street.

So where should you begin? If you're walking around the city, explore both alignments!

And if you really want to make sure you cover all your bases, continue east on Jackson Boulevard along the two-block stretch called Jackson Drive (not confusing at all, right?) to US Route 41—better known as Lake Shore Drive. Yep, Lake Shore Drive was the actual endpoint of Route 66 from the mid-1930s until 1976. While there's no official sign there, going all the way to the waterfront makes for a pretty great ending to your eastbound trip.

CHICAGO STYLE
CHICAGO WELCOMES
DNC 2024
Democratic National Convention
BEGIN
66

One

ILLINOIS

THE LEGENDARY MOTHER ROAD BEGINS in Illinois and takes road-trippers on a three-hundred-mile (483 km) journey from Chicago to East St. Louis. Some of the oldest establishments on Route 66 are found in the Prairie State, and these early eateries offered simple homestyle cooking with the type of Midwestern heartiness and down-to-earth hospitality you would expect. As the highway opened up a constant flow of travelers to and from the region over the last century, the local food scene also evolved, melding American comfort food with new ideas and flavors from our Greek, German, and Italian heritage—as well as beyond.

CHICAGO

GRILLED THICK FRENCH TOAST
Lou Mitchell's Restaurant & Bakery ★ MAKES 4 SERVINGS

---

5 eggs

3 cups (700 ml) milk

6 tablespoons (90 ml) imitation vanilla extract

1½ tablespoons (11 g) ground cinnamon

8 tablespoons (115 ml) clarified butter, divided

1 loaf white bread, cut into 1½-inch (4 cm)-thick slices

Powdered sugar, for serving (optional)

✳ *At-Home Tip*

To keep your French toast warm as you make it, set a wire rack inside a sheet pan and place in an oven heated to 200°F (93°C). Transfer the French toast to the rack in a single layer as you finish cooking each batch.

When most people depart on their Mother Road adventure, one of their first stops is Lou Mitchell's. William Mitchell opened the classic breakfast joint in 1923, naming it after his son, Louis W. Mitchell, who later partnered with his father and built the business into the Chicago icon it is today. In 1949, the thriving restaurant moved across the street to its current location, which is now listed in the National Register of Historic Places.

It's said that Lou Mitchell's invented the hearty American breakfast. They were the first restaurant in Chicago to serve breakfast all day, and some of their signature menu items—such as eggs served in a skillet—are now hallmarks of the American breakfast diner. "Uncle" Lou, as the second-generation owner was affectionately called, introduced their now-famous freshly baked donut holes in 1958. (To this day, every diner is offered a free plate of them after being seated.)

When it was time for Uncle Lou to retire in 1992, he sold the restaurant to his niece Kathryn Thanas—but she wasn't related by blood. In Greek, these types of relatives are called *koumbari*, meaning "better than blood," because they made a choice to join the family. And like a true family, Kathryn and her children, Nick and Heleen, continued the menu and traditions that were established by the Mitchells. Now five generations in, Lou Mitchell's remains family-owned and operated, serving the kind of comfort food and bottomless coffee that get Chicagoans and travelers through their day.

INSTRUCTIONS

In a large bowl, whisk the eggs. Add the milk, vanilla extract, and cinnamon and whisk until thoroughly combined.

Heat 2 tablespoons (28 ml) butter in a large skillet over medium heat. Soak 2 slices of bread in the batter until the bread is saturated, then remove the bread and gently squeeze them over the bowl to drain excess batter. Place the soaked bread in the skillet in a single layer and cook, swirling the butter occasionally, for about 3 minutes, or until browned on the bottom. Flip the bread and continue to cook, swirling occasionally, for 3 minutes longer. Repeat the soaking and cooking process with the remaining slices of bread, using 2 tablespoons (28 ml) butter for each batch.

Before serving, cut each piece of French toast on a diagonal. Sprinkle with powdered sugar if desired.

SELECTED NO 1
BREAKFAST
& LUNCH
RESTAURANT
AMERICA
Lou Mitchell's
Serving the worlds finest COFFEE
SINCE 1923
BREAKFAST • LUNCH • CARRYOUT • CATERING
BAKERY

CHICAGO

APPLE STRUDEL
The Berghoff ✶ MAKES 6 TO 8 SERVINGS

1¼ cups (285 ml) apple juice, divided

2 tablespoons (16 g) cornstarch

1½ pounds (680 g) Granny Smith apples, peeled, cored, and sliced ¼-inch (6 mm) thick (about 5 cups)

½ cup (75 g) dark seedless raisins

3 tablespoons (39 g) granulated sugar

1 teaspoon ground cinnamon

⅓ cup (37 g) chopped pecans

4 sheets (14 x 18 inch, or 36 x 46 cm) phyllo dough

All-purpose flour, for dusting

⅓ cup (75 g) butter, melted

3 tablespoons (21 g) fine dry breadcrumbs

Powdered sugar, for garnishing

Vanilla ice cream, for serving (optional)

The story of Berghoff begins with beer. When the World's Fair came to Chicago in 1893, German immigrant Herman Joseph Berghoff (who ran a brewery in Indiana) set up a stand in the Midway Plaisance to sell beer to people entering and exiting the fair. His success led him to open a saloon in Chicago in 1898. At the time, a beer at The Berghoff cost a nickel (with a free sandwich on the side).

When Prohibition hit, Herman saw it as an opportunity to branch out. He started producing "near beer," root beer, and a line of Bergo sodas and expanded into a full-service restaurant. After Prohibition was repealed in 1933, Herman obtained the city's first liquor license (a tradition that's been honored by Chicago every year since) and opened The Berghoff Bar alongside his restaurant.

Following Herman's death in 1934, his children, Lewis Windthorst and Clement Anthony, added a casual basement café in 1939. After Lewis and Clement retired in 1960, ownership passed to a succession of family members, including fourth-generation Pete Berghoff, who runs the restaurant today.

After more than a century, the menu has lightened up but still offers many Old World German favorites, like this strudel adapted from *The Berghoff Family Cookbook*.

INSTRUCTIONS

In a small bowl, combine ¼ cup (60 ml) of the apple juice with the cornstarch. Set aside.

In a large saucepan over medium heat, cook the apples with the remaining 1 cup (235 ml) apple juice, raisins, sugar, and cinnamon for 8 to 10 minutes, until the apples are tender. Stir the cornstarch slurry and add it to the apples, stirring constantly until smooth and lump-free. Simmer for 1 more minute, then remove from heat and cool. Stir in the pecans, cover, and refrigerate until ready to use.

Preheat the oven to 450°F (230°C, or gas mark 8). Line a sheet pan with parchment paper.

Lay 1 phyllo sheet on a lightly floured surface. Brush with melted butter and sprinkle with 1 tablespoon (7 g) breadcrumbs. Repeat the process with 2 more layers of phyllo, butter, and breadcrumbs. Top with the remaining phyllo sheet. Spread the apple mixture evenly across the phyllo, leaving a ½-inch (13 mm) border on all sides. Roll into an 18-inch (46 cm) log, folding the edges at each end under the log, and brush with melted butter. Carefully place the log on the prepared sheet pan, seam-side down.

Bake for 15 to 18 minutes, until golden brown. Remove the strudel from the oven and cool for 15 minutes before cutting into 2-inch (5 cm) slices. Sprinkle each slice with powdered sugar just before serving. Serve plain or with a scoop of ice cream.

THE BLACKSTONE

CHICAGO

DÁTILES CON ALMENDRAS
Mercat a la Planxa at The Blackstone ★ MAKES 8 SERVINGS

DATES
40 pitted dates
40 fried Marcona almonds
20 slices cooked bacon, cut in half crosswise

LA PERAL FONDUE
½ cup (112 g) European butter
1 shallot, finely chopped
½ cup (120 ml) white wine
2 cups (475 ml) heavy cream
1 pound (455 g) La Peral cheese, crumbled (see sidebar)
1 tablespoon (14 g) kosher salt

GARNISH SALAD
1 pound (455 g) green cabbage, julienned
2 red onions, julienned
½ cup (15 g) chopped parsley

✳ *At-Home Tip*
La Peral is a creamy, lightly blued cheese from Spain. If you can't source it, you can substitute an Italian Gorgonzola for the fondue.

Built in 1910, The Blackstone hotel was named for Timothy Blackstone, a notable Chicago politician and railroad executive whose mansion once sat on the property. After his death, his wife sold the mansion and it was demolished to make way for construction of the storied hotel. Celebrities, socialites, heads of state, and even notorious gangsters Al Capone (who held meetings while getting his haircut in the hotel barbershop) and Charles "Lucky" Luciano (who hosted the first-ever organized crime convention in the hotel ballroom) flocked to The Blackstone to hobnob.

After the Wall Street Crash of 1929, The Blackstone went through a series of owners and changes, as did the surrounding neighborhood. Only two rooms were preserved during its most recent restoration: the legendary "smoke-filled room" on the ninth floor and the original Presidential Suite on the tenth floor. The theater was converted to a bar and restaurant, Mercat a la Planxa, known for Spanish tapas like *dátiles con almendras* ("dates with almonds") and The Blackstone's famous Smoke-Filled-Room Cocktail (page 28).

INSTRUCTIONS
Prepare the dates: Steam the dates for 2 minutes until soft. Stuff each date with an almond, wrap with a bacon strip, and secure with a small wooden skewer.

Make the fondue: In a small saucepan over medium-high heat, melt the butter. Add the shallot and cook for 1 to 2 minutes, until soft. Pour in the wine and cook until slightly reduced. Add the heavy cream, bring to a simmer, and simmer until reduced by a quarter. Stir in the cheese until smooth and well blended. Stir in the salt, remove from heat, and let cool.

Make the garnish salad: In a large bowl, toss the cabbage, red onions, and parsley until combined.

Serve the salad alongside the stuffed dates, with individual bowls of fondue for dipping.

CHICAGO

SMOKE-FILLED-ROOM COCKTAIL
Mercat a la Planxa at The Blackstone ★ MAKES 1 SERVING

- ¾ ounce (21 ml) Bodegas Tradición Brandy de Jerez
- ¾ ounce (21 ml) High West Double Rye
- ¾ ounce (21 ml) Priorat Natur Vermouth
- 1 barspoon Licor 43
- 2 dashes Angostura Bitters
- 2 dashes Peychaud Bitters
- Rosemary sprigs (optional, for smoking cabinet)

The Blackstone is widely known as "The Hotel of Presidents" for good reason: It's hosted a dozen consecutive U.S. presidents from Taft to Carter, and the walls around the Presidential Suite were hollowed out to create a hidden passage, allowing the president to exit through the hotel's eastern stairwell unnoticed. (Rumor has it that the Secret Service snuck Marilyn Monroe into President Kennedy's suite this way!)

But the room that got the most attention—and became a part of American political parlance—was Suite 915, infamously known as the "smoke-filled room." It was here that cigar-smoking Republican power brokers and "Old Guard" leaders secretly met on the night of June 11, 1920, and agreed to force the Republican National Convention to nominate Warren G. Harding as their presidential candidate. Thus, "smoke-filled room" entered the lexicon as a reference to the intrigue and corruption of party bosses.

The three-room suite was preserved during the hotel's restoration, and yes, you can stay there—although ironically, it's now smoke-free.

INSTRUCTIONS

In a mixing glass, combine all the ingredients with ice and stir to chill. Strain into a double old-fashioned glass.

If using a smoking gun, turn an old-fashioned glass upside down and use the hose to fill the glass with smoke. Pull out the hose to trap the smoke in the glass. Serve tableside by flipping the glass with smoke over and quickly straining the cocktail into the glass.

If using a smoking cabinet or cloche, strain the cocktail into an old-fashioned glass and place the glass in a smoking cabinet. Add a few sprigs of rosemary and fill the cabinet with smoke. Once the cocktail has been exposed to the smoke for at least 1 minute, serve the drink immediately.

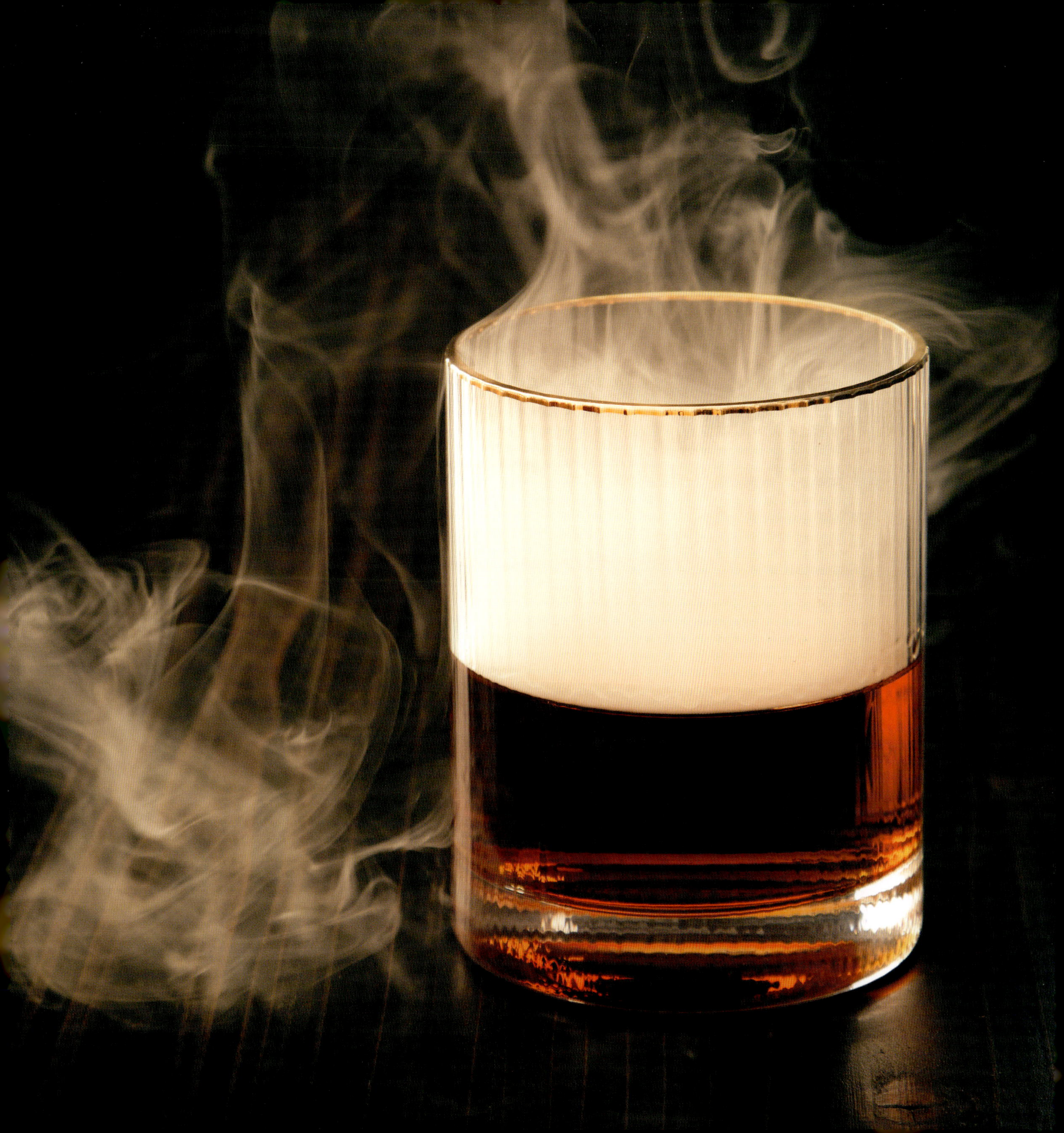

WILLOWBROOK

SAUTÉED CHICKEN LIVERS
Dell Rhea's Chicken Basket ★ MAKES 2 SERVINGS

- 2 cups (240 g) all-purpose flour
- 1 tablespoon (6 g) ground black pepper
- 2 teaspoons garlic salt
- ½ teaspoon fine salt, plus more for seasoning
- 12 ounces (340 g) chicken livers, rinsed, trimmed of fat, and patted dry
- 2 tablespoons (28 g) butter, divided
- ½ onion, sliced crosswise and rings separated
- 2 tablespoons (28 ml) dry Marsala wine

In the late 1920s, Ervin "Irv" Kolarik ran a humble lunch counter in a service station along Route 66. Legend has it that one day, two women came in and overheard Irv complaining about running the service station, as he preferred selling food. They offered to share their secret fried chicken recipe with him if he agreed to buy chickens from their farm, and to sweeten the deal, they even offered to make the chicken. The nationally famous Chicken Basket was born, and it was an instant success. The restaurant quickly outgrew the lunch counter, so Irv converted the garage bays in the service station into dining rooms.

By 1946, the restaurant outgrew its space again, prompting Irv to build a full-service restaurant next door. One of his marketing ploys to draw customers in winter was to flood the flat metal roof of the restaurant and hire locals to ice-skate on top of it! Business was booming, but by 1956, under the Federal Aid Highway Act, traffic was rerouted onto the interstates; the struggling Chicken Basket eventually went under foreclosure in 1962.

The restaurant, however, managed to escape the fate suffered by other mom-and-pop businesses when Delbert "Dell" Rhea, a prominent Chicago businessman, bought the restaurant in 1963. Dell (and later his son Patrick) turned things around by aggressively advertising the business to travelers and to Chicago's expanding suburban population. The classic brick building and freestanding neon sign were added to the National Register of Historic Places in 2006, cementing the Chicken Basket's legacy.

In 2019, the Lombardi family purchased the restaurant with the promise to continue Irv and Dell's traditions (minus the ice-skating, that is) and keep the original recipe intact. While the fried chicken is still a secret, this recipe is not and is one of many homestyle meals that make the restaurant famous.

INSTRUCTIONS

In a small bowl, combine the flour, pepper, garlic salt, and salt. Toss the chicken livers to coat.

Melt 1 tablespoon (14 g) butter in a large skillet over medium heat. Add the onion rings and sprinkle a pinch of salt over. Cook for about 10 minutes, stirring frequently, until caramelized. Transfer the onion to a plate.

In the same skillet over medium heat, melt the remaining 1 tablespoon (14 g) butter and arrange the chicken livers in a single layer. Cook for 3 to 4 minutes per side, until the livers are browned on the outside and slightly pink inside. Return the cooked onion to the pan and stir in the Marsala. Reduce the heat to low and simmer for 1 minute.

Divide the livers, onion, and all the liquid between 2 plates and serve.

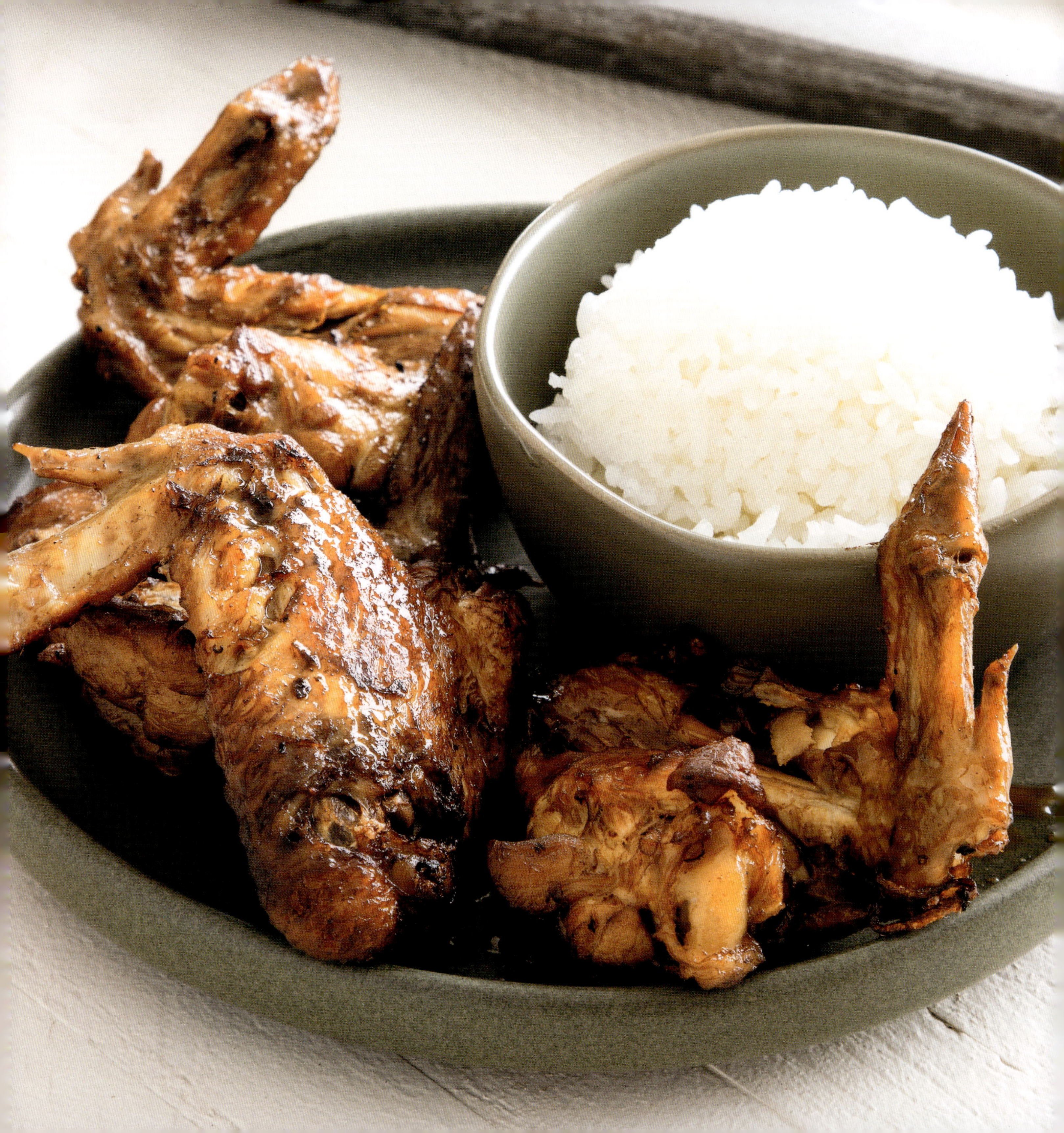

PONTIAC

CRISPY CHICKEN ADOBO WINGS

Lola's ★ MAKES 4 SERVINGS

- 1 tablespoon (15 ml) plus 2 cups (475 ml) neutral oil, divided
- ½ yellow onion, sliced
- 1 tablespoon (15 m) garlic puree
- 1 tablespoon (5 g) whole peppercorns
- 4 bay leaves
- 5 pounds (2.3 kg) chicken wings
- 1 teaspoon Filipino sea salt (see sidebar)
- 1 cup (235 ml) Silver Swan soy sauce
- 1 cup (235 ml) Datu Puti vinegar
- 1 cup (235 ml) water
- Steamed white rice, for serving

✱

Pantry Substitutions

This recipe calls for several Filipino ingredients that can easily be substituted. For the sea salt, Chef Anna suggests using any large flaky salt. Silver Swan soy sauce leans more toward the savory side, so it's most similar to tamari or a Chinese-style soy sauce (such as the Wan Ja Shan or Lee Kum Kee brand). If you can't find Datu Puti vinegar, you can use rice vinegar instead.

Most travelers pass through Pontiac on Old Route 66, a bypass that was built in 1945. But if you follow the original 1926 alignment (now called North Ladd Street) into town, you'll find a unique eatery with a menu full of savory, tangy, authentic Filipino street food.

Lola's opened in a former office space on the edge of downtown in 2022, but the owner's name isn't Lola—it's Anna Hoerner, and *her* lolas were the inspiration for her restaurant. *Lola* means "grandmother" in Tagalog, and Anna's recipes are based on the Filipino comfort food she grew up eating. The owner and chef received her culinary training in Chicago, but her first training started much earlier—in childhood—cooking with her mom (now a lola to Anna's own kids).

Since home-cooked Filipino food had always been a big part of her upbringing, Anna decided to open her own restaurant—something that was new in the community, yet close to her heart. There isn't another place like it in Pontiac or for many miles around, and it's a truly different and delicious evolution of Route 66.

INSTRUCTIONS

Heat a large wok over medium-high heat and drizzle 1 tablespoon (15 ml) oil. Add the onion, garlic, peppercorns, and bay leaves and cook for about 1 minute, or until fragrant. Add the chicken wings and cook until very lightly browned. Sprinkle with salt and pour in all the liquids. Stir and reduce the heat to a simmer. Cover and cook for about 40 minutes, or until the chicken is tender. Remove the wings from the liquid and dry completely. Strain the sauce and set aside.

Line a platter with paper towels. In a deep, heavy saucepan, heat the remaining 2 cups (475 ml) oil to 350°F (180°C). Fry the wings in batches until crispy and transfer to the prepared platter to drain.

Ladle the reserved sauce over the wings and serve with white rice.

ILLINOIS | 33

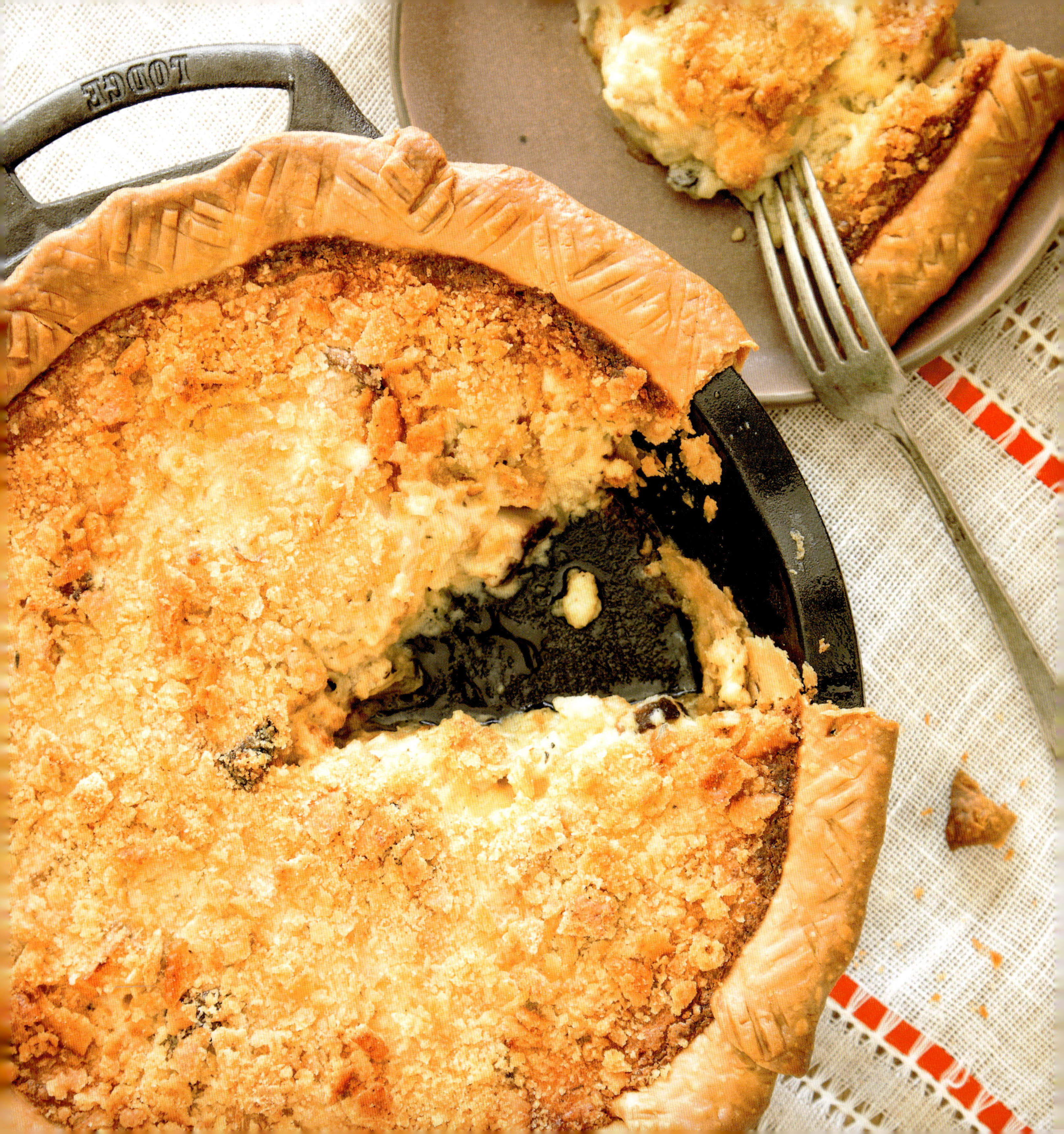
LODGE

SPRINGFIELD

MOREL MUSHROOM PIE
Maldaner's Restaurant ✶ MAKES 6 SERVINGS

- 1 prepared 9-inch (23 cm) pie crust
- 2 tablespoons (30 g) Dijon mustard
- 1¼ cups (125 g) grated Parmesan cheese, divided
- ½ cup (112 g) butter
- 1 Vidalia or other sweet onion, thinly sliced
- ½ pound (225 g) morel mushrooms, cleaned and chopped (see sidebar)
- 2 cups (475 ml) heavy cream
- ½ teaspoon dried thyme
- 2 eggs, lightly beaten
- Salt and ground black pepper
- 1 cup (72 g) cracker crumbs

✶
No Morels?
You can try this savory pie with a combination of fresh wild mushrooms instead.

Maldaner's is a rarity on Route 66, as it's one of the few still-operating restaurants that predates the historic highway by more than forty years. In 1884, pastry chef John Maldaner started his business as Confectionaries and Bakers at 216 South Sixth Street. It moved several times before finally settling in at its current address in 1898. After Maldaner's death, the restaurant underwent several ownership changes, renovations, and restorations to bring back its turn-of-the-century architectural features.

The current owners, Michael and Nancy Higgins, purchased the restaurant in 1994 after co-managing Maldaner's for twelve years. Chef Michael has kept a few Springfield standards on the menu but has also introduced new dishes over the years with a focus on seasonal local and regional ingredients. One of these is the highly anticipated, fresh-picked morel mushroom pie that he makes every spring using locally grown morels.

INSTRUCTIONS

Prepare the pie shell: Preheat the oven to 350°F (180°C, or gas mark 4). Line the prepared pie crust with heavy aluminum foil, pressing it against the sides. Fill with dried beans or pie weights and partially bake the crust for 10 to 12 minutes, until the edges are light brown. Remove the foil and weights. Brush Dijon mustard all over the crust and sprinkle ¼ cup (25 g) Parmesan across the bottom. Return the pie crust to the oven and bake until the cheese just melts. Remove from the oven and set aside. Leave the oven on while you prepare the filling.

Make the filling: In a large skillet, melt the butter over low to medium heat. Add the onion and cook until soft and translucent, stirring occasionally. Add the morels and cook until soft and half the liquid is reduced. Stir in the heavy cream, thyme, and remaining 1 cup (100 g) Parmesan. Bring to a simmer, then slowly stir in the eggs. Season with a few pinches of salt and pepper.

Pour the mixture into the prebaked pie shell and top with cracker crumbs. Bake at 350°F for 30 to 40 minutes, until the top is lightly browned and the custard is set. If the edges are getting too brown before the custard is done, cover the edges with foil or use a pie protector. Let cool for about 10 minutes before serving.

ILLINOIS | 35

GIRARD

DOCS S'MORES SUNDAE
Docs Just Off 66 ★ MAKES 1 SERVING

2 scoops chocolate ice cream
Marshmallow cream
Chocolate sauce
Crushed waffle cone
Whipped cream
Cherry

Located just a stone's throw from Illinois Route 4, the original alignment of Route 66, Docs Just Off 66 was once known as the "white drugstore" because it was the only white storefront on Girard Square. The century-old building opened in 1884 as Deck's Drug Store, at a time when no special training was required to be a pharmacist. A soda fountain was added in 1929, becoming the weekend hangout where locals could find an assortment of penny candy, phosphates, milkshakes, and hand-drawn sodas.

Three generations of Decks operated the drugstore for 117 years until Mike and Patty Makuta (the first owners who did not belong to the family) purchased the building in 2001. Unfortunately, this chapter didn't last long—the Makutas closed the business in 2003, leaving the town of Girard without a pharmacy for the first time in its history.

In 2007, Deck's Drug Store changed hands again, and new owners Bob and Renee Ernst revamped it as Doc's Soda Fountain. But history was not lost: The Deck family loaned them their vintage pharmacy collection, including old-time remedies and early medical equipment, to put on display.

Though the building underwent renovations after Steve and Casey Claypool took over in 2021, the pharmacy relics remained—as did the original marble-top soda fountain, where soda jerks still sling sodas and ice cream. Docs Just Off 66 may have a new name and larger restaurant space now, but the nostalgia is still high when you walk through its doors.

INSTRUCTIONS
In a tall sundae glass, layer the ice cream, a dollop of marshmallow cream, and a drizzle of chocolate sauce. Sprinkle with a handful of crushed waffle cone and top with whipped cream and a cherry.

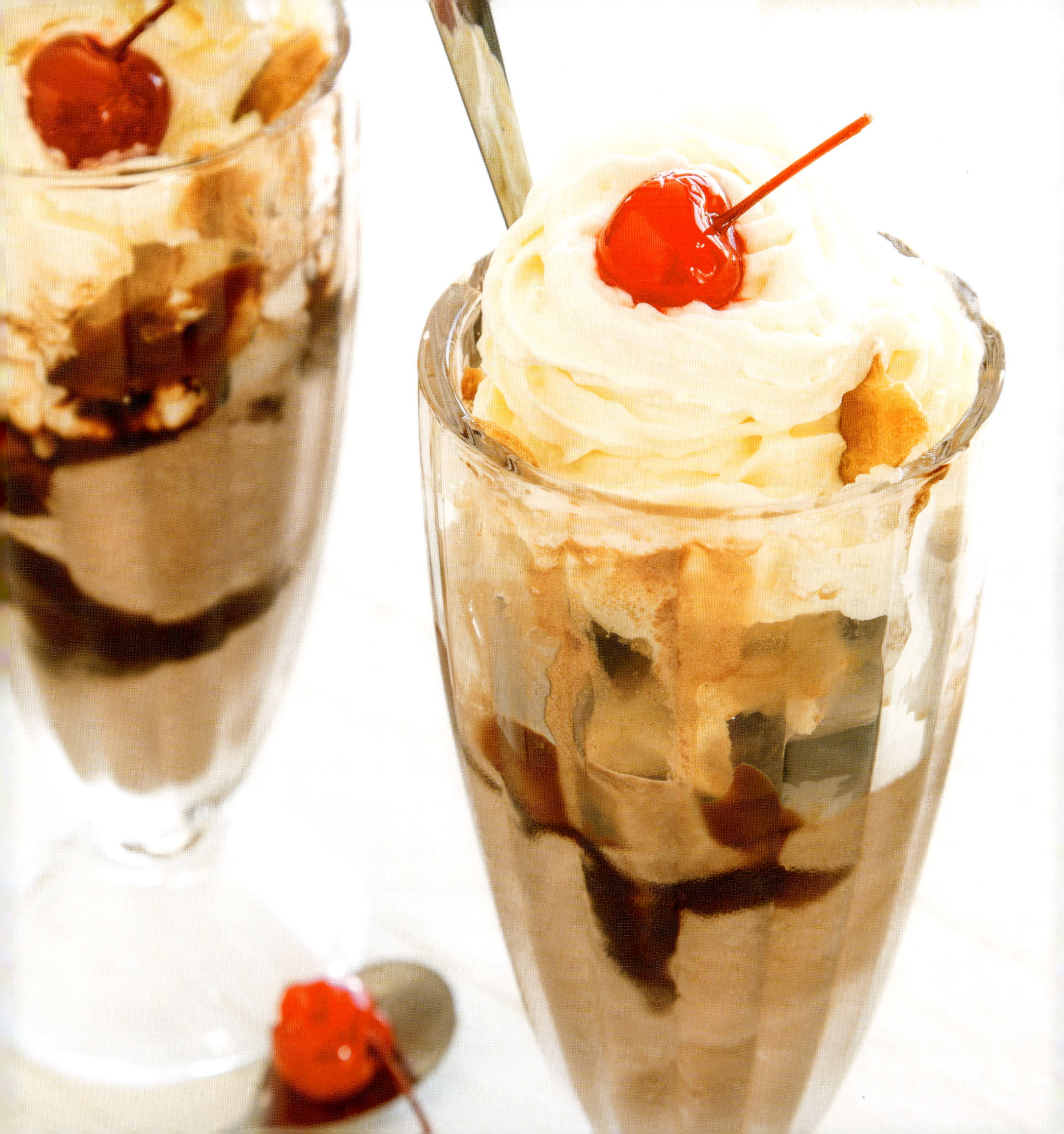

LITCHFIELD

STRAWBERRY WHIPPED CHEESECAKE
The Ariston Cafe ★ MAKES 12 SERVINGS

CRUST

2 cups (240 g) all-purpose flour

½ pound (225 g) margarine, softened

Chopped pecans

FILLING

2 pounds (910 g) strawberries, hulled and sliced

2 cups (400 g) granulated sugar

2 tablespoons (28 ml) lemon juice

2 cups (240 g) powdered sugar

16 ounces (455 g) Philadelphia cream cheese, softened

2 containers (16 ounces, or 455 g each) Cool Whip

15 ounces (425 g) sour cream

In 1924, Pete Adam and Tom Cokinos opened the original Ariston Cafe in nearby Carlinville on Route 4 (the predecessor of Route 66). After the highway was realigned through Litchfield, they moved the restaurant to its current location. Starting a business in 1935 during the depths of the Great Depression may have seemed like a foolish move, but the heavily trafficked highway helped The Ariston Cafe thrive. The owners installed two gas pumps in front to attract more customers and served a full-service menu that included a glass of Budweiser for 15 cents and a porterhouse steak for 85 cents.

After Pete's death in 1966, his son Nick and Nick's wife, Demi, took over for the next fifty years. During their time, The Ariston Cafe was listed in the National Register of Historic Places. They sold the business in 2018 to the Law and Steffens families, who continue the restaurant's long tradition.

While the gas pumps are long gone, dining at The Ariston Cafe is like taking a step back in time. Original neon signs decorate the front facade, and inside you'll find the 1935 acoustical tile ceiling, light fixtures, chrome stools, and Art Deco wall cabinet still intact. Few people leave without ordering one of the restaurant's homemade desserts—in fact, the café sells desserts to 98 percent of its diners, and on any given day, it usually has more desserts than diners, as many order multiple treats to take home.

INSTRUCTIONS

Make the crust: Preheat the oven to 300°F (150°C, or gas mark 2). In a medium bowl, combine the flour and margarine with a fork or pastry blender until a pliable dough forms. Press the dough evenly across the bottom of a 9 x 13-inch (23 x 33 cm) baking dish. Bake for 20 minutes, then let cool. Top the crust with a generous sprinkling of chopped pecans.

Make the filling: In a large saucepan over medium heat, combine the strawberries, sugar, and lemon juice. Bring to a boil, stirring constantly but gently to avoid smashing the berries. Boil for 3 to 5 minutes, until the mixture is thick. Remove from heat and let cool. Transfer the strawberry filling to a bowl, cover, and refrigerate.

Using a stand mixer fitted with a paddle attachment or an electric hand mixer, whip the powdered sugar, cream cheese, Cool Whip, and sour cream until smooth and well blended. Spread the mixture evenly over the prepared crust and chill for about 4 hours.

Top the whipped mixture with your desired amount of strawberry filling (you may not use all of it). Refrigerate any leftover strawberry filling (for up to a week) and reserve for another use. Cut the cheesecake into 3-inch (7.5 cm) squares to serve.

Jubelt's Bakery & Restaurant

Since 1922

DRIVE-THRU

LITCHFIELD

BUTTER SPRITZ COOKIES

Jubelt's Bakery & Restaurant ★ MAKES 7 TO 8 DOZEN COOKIES

---

1 cup (225 g) butter, softened
¾ cup (150 g) granulated sugar
3 eggs
1 teaspoon vanilla extract
½ teaspoon almond extract
3 cups (360 g) cake flour
½ teaspoon baking powder
Green food coloring (optional)
1 to 3 tablespoons (15 to 45 ml) milk, divided
Red sprinkles (optional)

The small town of Litchfield is home to not one, but *two* Mother Road landmarks next door to each other: The Ariston Cafe (page 38) and Jubelt's Bakery & Restaurant, which has sat on Route 66 for over forty years but has a long and tangled history going back more than a century.

In 1922, three brothers (Paul, Fred, and Albert Jubelt) bought an existing bakery in Mount Olive and began to bake bread. When Albert died in 1929, Paul and Fred opened a second bakery in Granite City. The brothers' partnership dissolved by 1935, so Paul continued to run the Mount Olive bakery by himself. His son John joined the family business in 1949, and shortly thereafter, John and his wife, Iris Dawkins, opened the original Downtown Litchfield location in 1952. Over the next several decades, the Jubelts opened more bakeries and started offering lunch—a pivot that would ultimately save them.

The next chapter brought historic changes to the family business. John and Iris's son Lance joined Jubelt's in 1977. As commercial activity in Litchfield began to shift to the west side of town, the Jubelts decided to look for a larger space and took the plunge on an old Burger Chef building on Route 66. They opened their new (and current) location in 1982 and survived industry turmoil in the 1990s when many independent bakeries folded.

In the early 2000s, Jeanmarie Jubelt returned home from Chicago (where she'd been living and working) to help her father and brother—both in declining health—run the family business. After John's death in 2003 and Lance's death in 2007, Jeanmarie and her mother made the tough decision to close all but one of their locations.

Jeanmarie eventually purchased Jubelt's from her mother in 2008 and is now the third-generation owner of a thriving business that welcomes but does not rely on Route 66 tourism. When asked what has kept the bakery and restaurant afloat through the years, Jeanmarie said it was their ability to innovate. For the past seventy years, Jubelt's has constantly adapted to keep up with changing lifestyles, and she believes that embracing these changes has been key to their success.

ILLINOIS | 41

BUTTER SPRITZ COOKIES
CONTINUED

INSTRUCTIONS

Preheat the oven to 400°F (200°C, or gas mark 6). Line three 13 x 18-inch (33 x 46 cm) sheet pans with parchment paper and set aside.

Using a stand mixer fitted with a paddle attachment, cream the softened butter and sugar together on low speed. Gradually add the eggs, vanilla extract, and almond extract. Mix on medium speed for 2 minutes. Scrape down the bowl with a rubber spatula and mix for 1 minute. Gradually add the cake flour and baking powder and mix until all ingredients are incorporated. Scrape down the bowl and mix for 1 minute. Add a few drops of food coloring (if using) and mix for 1 minute. Scrape down the bowl again, add 1 tablespoon (15 ml) milk, and mix for 1 minute. You want the dough to be creamy and pipeable (but still thick), so add up to 3 tablespoons (45 ml) milk as needed to reach that consistency. Keep in mind that the more milk you add, the more the cookies will spread, so freezing the dough before baking (as suggested in the sidebar) is highly recommended.

Scoop the dough into a large pastry bag fitted with a ½-inch (13 mm) star tip (such as a Wilton 8B or similar large piping tip) and pipe the dough onto the prepared sheet pans. Top with red sprinkles (if using) and bake each sheet for 6 to 8 minutes, until golden and very lightly browned on the edges. (Baking one sheet at a time ensures the heat is evenly distributed.) The cookies should not be brown, but should also not have a "doughy" look. If your oven runs hot, turn it down to 375°F (190°C, or gas mark 5).

Remove the sheet pan from the oven and let it cool for 2 minutes before transferring the parchment paper to a cooling rack to cool completely (and prevent the bottom of the cookies from browning).

At-Home Tip

From personal experience, I've found that the best way to keep the cookies from spreading is to freeze the dough before it goes in the oven. After piping your cookies, place the sheet pans in the freezer to set for 15 to 20 minutes. This helps the cookies hold their shape during baking.

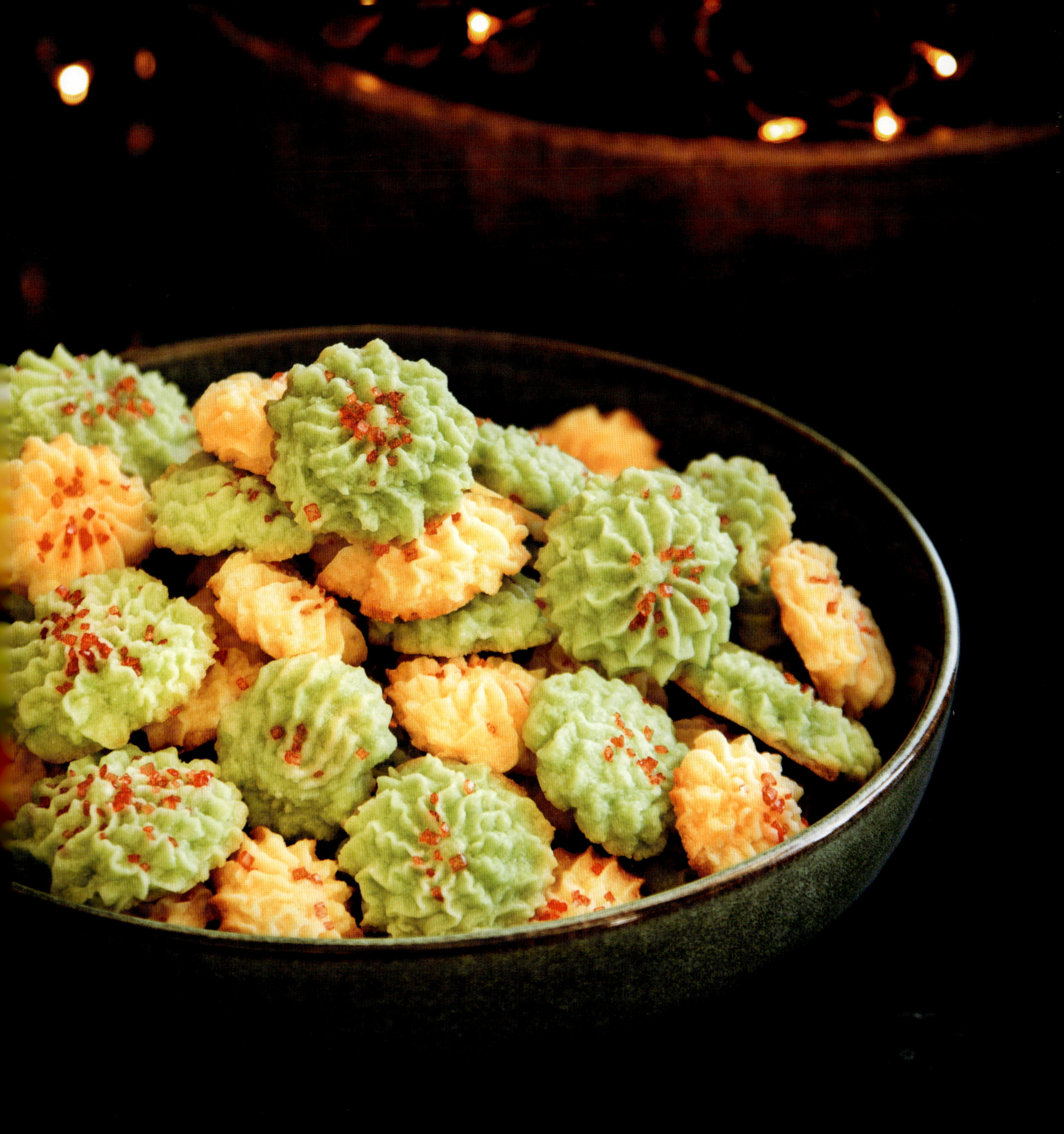

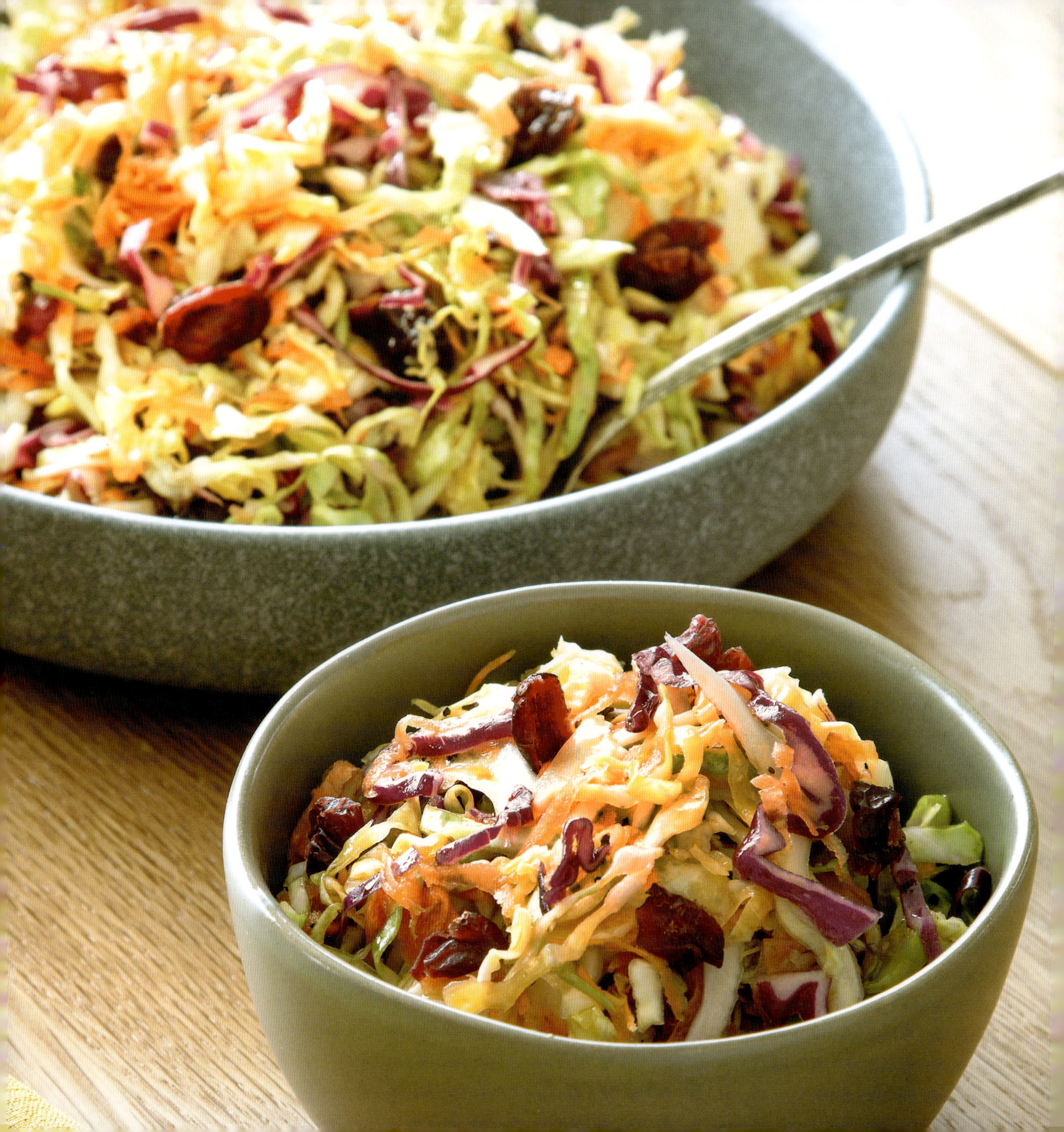

WEEZY'S COLESLAW
Weezy's Route 66 Bar & Grill ★ MAKES 4 SERVINGS

HAMEL

½ cup (100 g) granulated sugar
¼ cup (60 ml) olive oil
¼ cup (60 ml) distilled white vinegar
1 teaspoon fine salt
½ teaspoon ground black pepper
¼ teaspoon celery seeds
4 cups (280 g) shredded green cabbage
1 cup (70 g) shredded purple cabbage
1 cup (110 g) shredded carrots
Dried cranberries (optional)

During the height of the Depression, automobile dealer George Cassens and his sons, Arnold and Albert, entered the trucking business to make ends meet. They hauled milk, corn, apples, and potatoes and soon realized they could also use their trucks to save money by hauling new cars from Detroit back to their dealership in Hamel. Their commercial trucking business boomed and grew to become Cassens Transport.

In 1937, George opened the Tourist Haven Restaurant and Hotel next to his terminal to host Cassens drivers and Route 66 travelers. His wife, Louise, managed the restaurant, and in the decades since, the classic brick roadhouse has been sold and operated under several names, including the Village Inn, Earnie's Restaurant, and Scotty's Bar & Grill.

Karen Wiesemeyer took over in 2009 and rebranded as Weezy's—a nod to her name as well as her life and business partner, Coleman Weissman. The walls inside are lined with remnants from the past, including Mother Road memorabilia and vintage signs from each of the former restaurants. Despite its different identities over the past ninety years, one thing hasn't changed here: The building continues to be a home away from home for Route 66 travelers and the Hamel community.

INSTRUCTIONS

In a large bowl, stir together the sugar, olive oil, vinegar, salt, pepper, and celery seeds until well blended. Add the green and purple cabbage, carrots, and dried cranberries (if using). Toss to combine and coat the vegetables evenly with the dressing. Cover and refrigerate for at least 1 hour before serving.

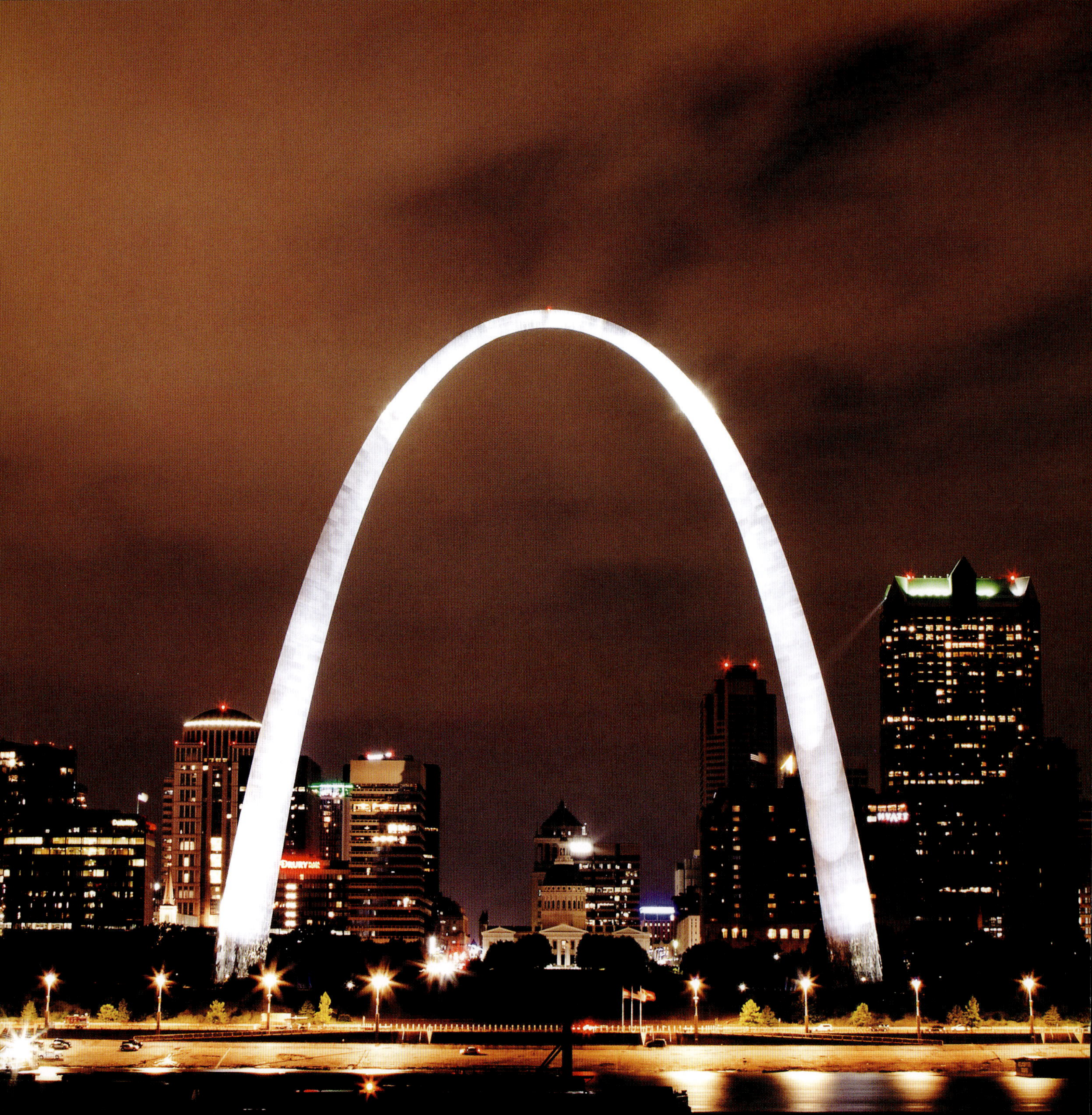
DRURY

Two
MISSOURI

THE NEXT THREE HUNDRED MILES (483 km) through the birthplace of Route 66 start in St. Louis and end just west of Joplin. It was in Missouri where the famed highway was officially named via telegram in 1926, and it helped connect urban and rural communities across the Midwest. Along this stretch of highway, local specialties have helped put a smattering of small towns on the map for food-loving (and wine-loving) travelers. You won't find a curly hot dog just anywhere, and you might be surprised that one of the country's top award-winning wineries is right here in the "Forest City of the Ozarks," built on the traditions of the Italian immigrants who settled in Missouri in the late nineteenth century.

ST. LOUIS

HEAVENLY HASH

Crown Candy Kitchen ✶ MAKES 21 SERVINGS

---

1 pound (455 g) dark baking chocolate, finely chopped

21 jumbo marshmallows

¾ cup (83 g) chopped pecans

Tips for Successful Tempering

- If you don't have a double boiler, set a heatproof mixing bowl over a saucepan of gently simmering water. Make sure the bowl is completely dry, or the chocolate will seize and turn lumpy!

- The working temperature of the chocolate should be 87°F to 91°F (31°C to 33°C). If it drops below that range, retemper the chocolate by heating it in the double boiler again.

- No patience for tempering? You can melt the chocolate in a microwave in 30-second intervals, stirring between each. Your heavenly hash will need to stay refrigerated to maintain a hard chocolate coating.

As St. Louis's oldest soda fountain, Crown Candy (the kitchen came later) opened in 1913, just a block from where City US 66 would eventually enter downtown in the 1940s. Greek immigrant Harry Karandzieff and his best friend Pete Jugaloff started the confectionery together, but within a year, Harry became the sole owner of the two-story brick building. He ran the shop until 1951, when his son George took the reins and spent the next four decades building the business into a cultural icon.

The second-generation owner was known for living and breathing the candy business—he lived above the shop for twenty years and there's a family anecdote that when George was on his deathbed, he refused to pass until the shop had made it through Easter, its busiest week. His sons (and third-generation owners) Mike, Andy, and Tommy bought the business from their father in 1991. Following Mike's death and Tommy's retirement, Andy (with his wife, Sherri) has carried on the family's legacy.

The shop still makes all of its chocolate candy by hand with the same metal molds that Harry and George had used. Their signature candy is this heavenly hash. If you think you don't like marshmallows, this recipe might make you change your mind about that.

INSTRUCTIONS

Line a small baking dish with parchment paper and set aside.

Begin by tempering the chocolate. Place two-thirds of the chocolate in the top pot of a double boiler on the stove. Heat over very hot (but not boiling) water, stirring constantly, until the chocolate is fully melted and registers 110°F to 114°F (43°C to 46°C) on a candy thermometer. Transfer the top pot to a towel and cool the chocolate to 95°F to 100°F (35°C to 38°C). Stir in the remaining unmelted chocolate until it is liquid and smooth.

One by one, roll the marshmallow in the tempered chocolate until coated on all sides. Use a toothpick to stir them around and transfer to the prepared baking dish. Arrange the coated marshmallows 7 across and 3 deep in a single layer with their sides touching.

Toss the pecans in the chocolate. Spread the coated pecans on top of the marshmallows with a spatula. Let the "brick" harden at a cool room temperature out of direct sunlight.

CROWN
CANDY
CROWN
CANDY
CROWN CANDY
LUNCH
ICE CREAM
ICE CREAM

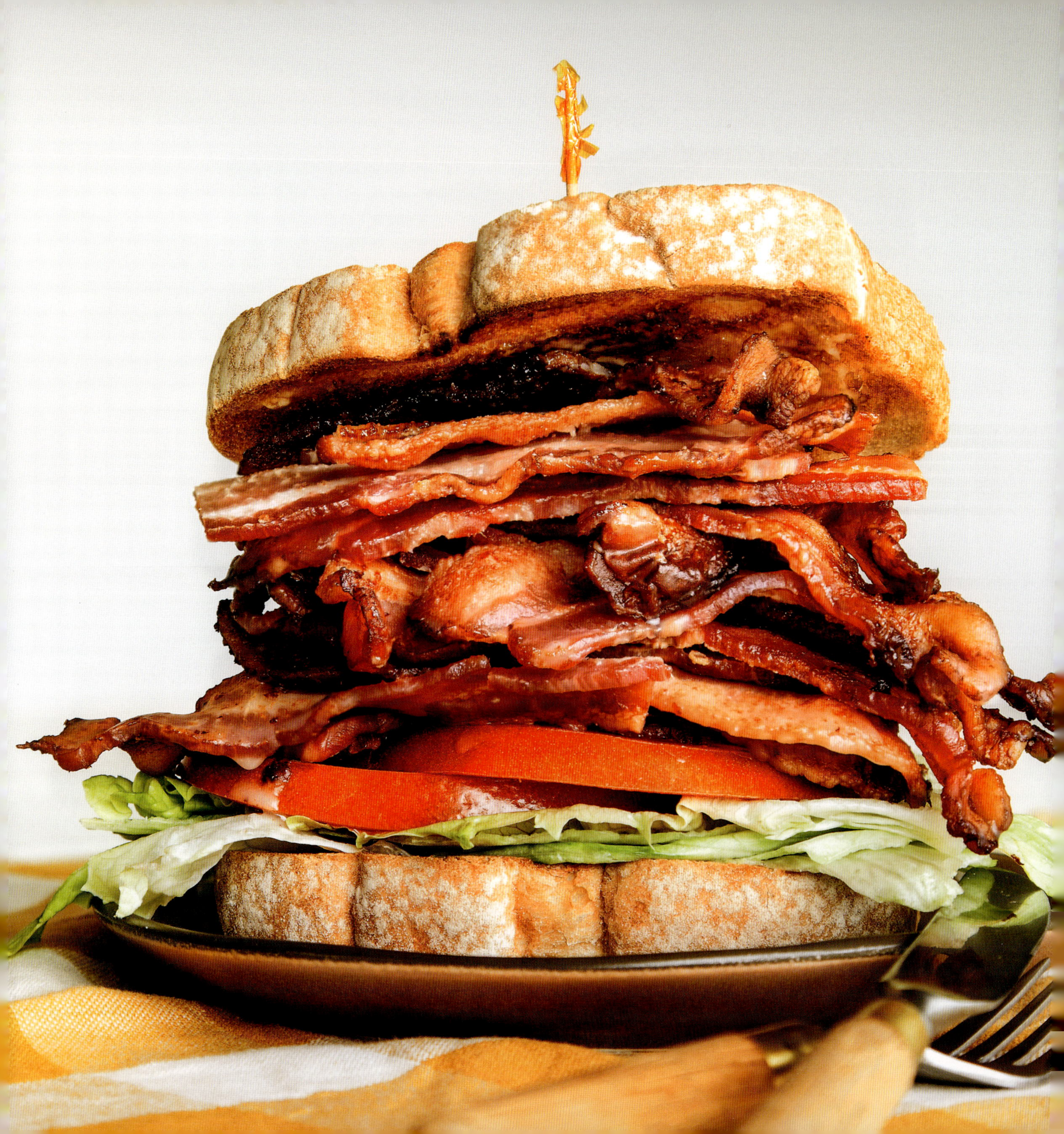

ST. LOUIS

HEART-STOPPING BLT
Crown Candy Kitchen ★ **MAKES 1 TO 2 SERVINGS**

- 2 tablespoons (28 g) Miracle Whip
- 2 slices Texas toast, toasted
- 2 to 3 leaves iceberg lettuce
- 2 slices tomato
- 1 pound (455 g) bacon, cooked and cut in half (see sidebar)

The famous—and aptly named—heart-stopping BLT wasn't always this big. In fact, it started out fairly normal until employees kept adding more and more bacon to the sandwich, turning it into the kitchen's best-selling menu item and earning it a spot on the Travel Channel show *Adam Richman's Best Sandwich in America*. Crown Candy cooks 10-pound (4.6 kg) batches of bacon at a time in a big kettle bubbling with vegetable oil, then piles about fourteen crispy slices on top of Texas toast. The whole sandwich is more than your mouth can handle, but this is the stuff of legend.

INSTRUCTIONS

Spread 1 tablespoon (14 g) Miracle Whip on each slice of toast. Assemble the sandwich by layering the lettuce, tomato, and bacon on one slice of bread, then top with the second slice of bread, Miracle Whip–side down. Cut the sandwich in half on a diagonal and secure each half with a toothpick before serving.

Splatter-Free Bacon in the Oven

While you *could* fry bacon on the stove, this monstrous BLT calls for a lot of bacon (for just one sandwich!). Save yourself the greasy cleanup by cooking the full pound (455 g) of bacon in the oven, splatter-free. This method works for both regular and thick-cut bacon.

1. Arrange the bacon in a single layer on a parchment paper–lined sheet pan.
2. Cook for 10 to 20 minutes in a preheated 400°F (200°C, or gas mark 8) oven (rotating the sheet pan halfway through), until crispy to your liking.
3. Transfer the bacon to a paper towel–lined plate to drain.

MISSOURI | 51

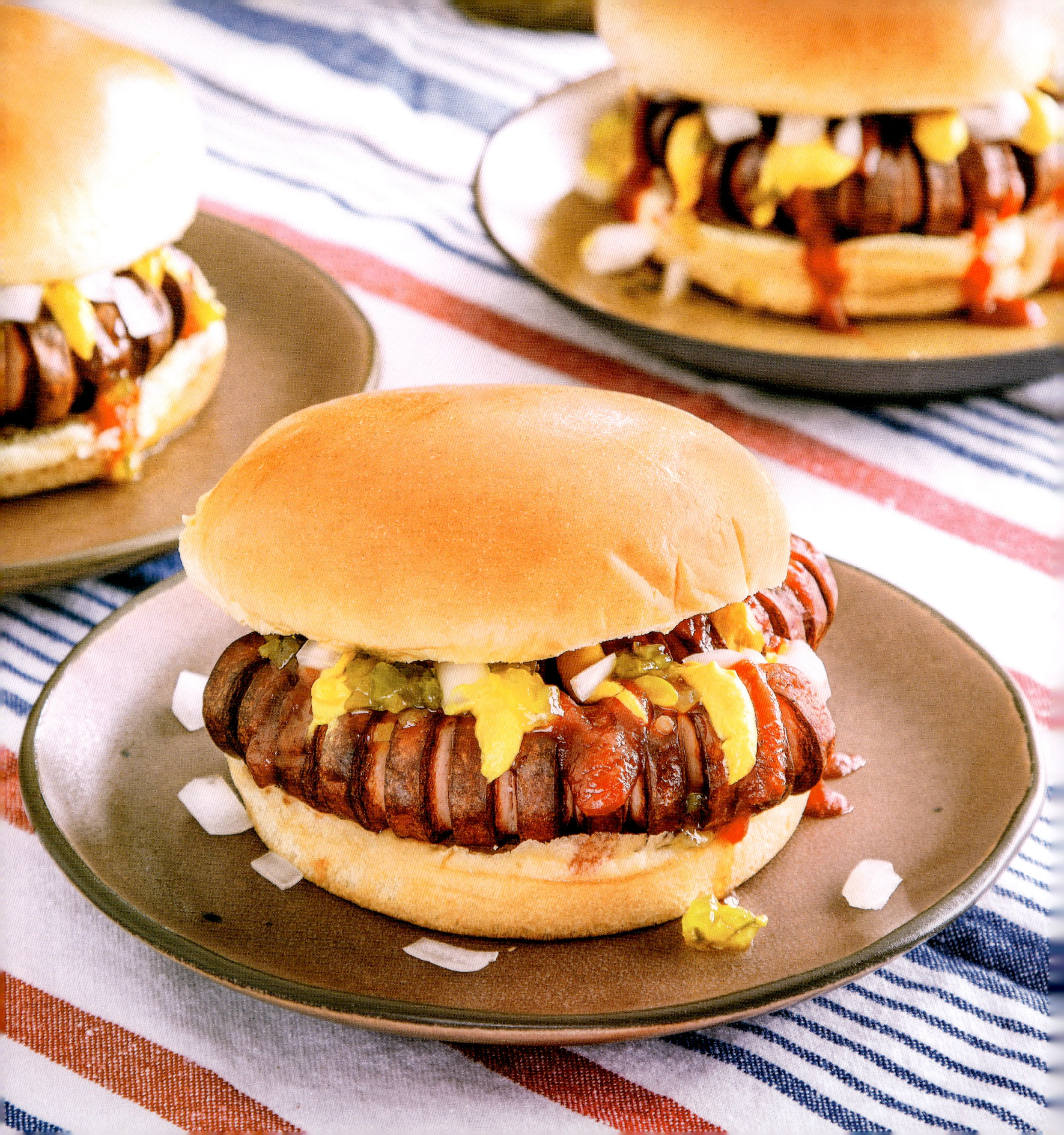

BRENTWOOD

CURLY-Q DOG
Carl's Drive-In ★ MAKES 1 SERVING

HOT DOG
1 Nathan's Famous® Jumbo Foot Long Beef Frank
Neutral oil, for frying
1 Ball Park® Hamburger Bun, steamed

TOPPINGS
Yellow mustard
Sweet pickle relish
Diced white onions
Ketchup

The original Carl's Drive-In building on Manchester Road predates Route 66 by nearly a decade. It was built in 1918 as a Lubrite Service Station before becoming a Walter Schuermann filling station and M. Nezol Gas Company (1930s), Foot Long Hot Dog Company (1940s), and Breeden's Good Food Drive-In (1950s). Smashburgers didn't hit the griddle until 1959, when Carl Meyer bought the restaurant and renamed it Carl's Drive-In, complete with carhop service and a walk-up window. (Word has it that Carl was a bookie and ran a book in the back of the restaurant . . . which is why he probably needed to sell a lot of burgers.)

The trademark counter seating with sixteen swivel stools—eight on opposite sides of the open kitchen—were added in 1962. Another signature menu item was added in 1975 when Carl acquired the original formula for IBC Root Beer, which the restaurant still makes fresh in their root beer barrel every week.

Carl eventually sold the business to Frank Cunetto in 1987, who shaped Carl's Drive-In into what it is today. The restaurant changed hands in 2015 and again in 2021. Longtime customer and current owner, David Kraemer, has kept tradition going with the same menu and same staff (sisters Kelly and Pam—both Steak 'n Shake alumni—have worked at Carl's Drive-In since the late 1990s).

David doesn't see much need for change, except for maybe accepting credit cards one day. People still line up for a coveted seat at the counter and a frosty mug of root beer. If they aren't getting a smashburger, they're getting a Curly-Q, which *does* come standard with ketchup ('cause this isn't Chicago).

INSTRUCTIONS

Using a sharp knife, score the hot dog every ½ inch (13 mm) along its entire length by making a slit halfway through the meat.

Heat 1 to 2 inches (2.5 to 5 cm) of oil in a deep, heavy saucepan to 360°F (182°C). Fry the hot dog for about 1 minute, gently stirring it around so it browns on all sides. The hot dog will start to curl up. Transfer the hot dog to the bottom bun and arrange it into a circular shape to fit. Add mustard, relish, onions, and ketchup and top with the remaining bun.

MISSOURI | 53

WILDWOOD

FRENCH ONION SOUP
Historic Big Chief Roadhouse ★ MAKES 6 SERVINGS

- 8 yellow onions, sliced ¼-inch (6 mm) thick
- ¼ cup (55 g) butter
- 1 tablespoon (3 g) dried thyme
- 1 tablespoon (6 g) ground black pepper
- ½ tablespoon fine salt
- 2 bay leaves
- 2½ cups (595 ml) chardonnay wine
- 5 quarts (4.7 L) water
- ¼ cup (96 g) beef base

Originally called the Big Chief Hotel under its owner William Clay Pierce, the complex was built in 1929 to serve transcontinental travelers on Route 66. The hotel was unique in its time as it was one of the first and largest tourist cabin courts in Missouri (with sixty-two cabins and a Conoco gas station in front) and it offered elegant, full-service dining. Pavement was key to the Big Chief's success; the section of Route 66 through Pond (now called Wildwood) was one of the earlier parts of the highway to be paved, and it was paved all the way to St. Louis by 1924. This brought a steady stream of travelers looking for an elaborate meal, a place to sleep, and some groceries to take on the road.

After Route 66 was realigned off Manchester Road (which was a part of the highway from 1926 to 1932), the Big Chief lost most of its visitors and eventually closed. In 1946, the restaurant became Mike Aceto's Cafe 66. The false bell tower was taken down in 1959, and the cabins were demolished in the 1970s. The building (now listed in the National Register of Historic Places) was later revived as a resale shop and a landscaping company before returning to its roots as a restaurant in 1995.

After several restorations, the Big Chief looks and operates much as it did in its heyday when Route 66 passed by its door. The Spanish Mission Revival styling and porte cochere remain intact, and it is one of the few surviving full-service restaurants on Missouri 66.

INSTRUCTIONS
In a stockpot over medium-low heat, add the onions and butter. Cook until the onions start to soften, stirring occasionally. Add the thyme, pepper, salt, and bay leaves and continue to cook, stirring and scraping the bottom of the pot periodically to incorporate all the brown bits. Once the onions are dark and caramelized (1 to 2 hours), deglaze the pot with the chardonnay. When the chardonnay has reduced by half, add the water and beef base and stir until the beef base is well blended. Increase the heat to medium-high and simmer for 10 minutes.

HISTORIC
"BIG CHIEF"
ROADHOUSE
The Original
66
Established 1929
17352
"BIG CHIEF"
Established
1929
MISSOURI
US
66

WEIR ON 66
Kabobs 66 Salads 66 Burgers
FRESH FOOD & DRINKS
102
P
Budweiser
OPEN
KABOBS
66
BIG SCREEN

CUBA

CREAM OF CHICKEN AND WILD RICE SOUP
Weir on 66 ★ MAKES 4 SERVINGS

- 6 tablespoons (85 g) butter
- 4 green onions, sliced
- ½ cup (60 g) all-purpose flour
- ½ teaspoon ground white pepper
- 4 cups (946 ml) chicken broth
- 2 carrots, shredded
- 1 cup (160 g) uncooked long-grain wild rice
- 2 cups (475 ml) half-and-half
- 2 chicken breasts, cooked and shredded

Before it was a restaurant, the charming building at "the four way," as locals call the intersection, was a filling station. Paul T. Carr built the Type B brick service station in 1932 and provided the first jobs for many young people in Cuba. He operated Carr Service Station under the Phillips 66 and Standard Oil brands for three decades and ran a Pontiac auto dealership on-site until his death in 1964.

When Bill and Lynn Wallis bought the station in 1968, it became their first Mobil station and an office for the fledgling Wallis Oil Company. They outgrew their space by 1985 and moved across the street, converting the building into the Washington Street Bakery to supply fresh-baked doughnuts for their convenience stores. The building sat empty after the bakery closed, but the Wallis family embarked on a restoration project in 2005 to preserve the building's history and honor both Bill's legacy and Paul's vision. New murals adorned the old garage bays, in line with Cuba's designation as the Route 66 Mural City.

In 2016, the little corner station began a new chapter as The FourWay restaurant under proprietor Joanie Weir. Five years later, the restaurant changed hands and was rebranded as Weir on 66 by Joanie's brother, Patrick Weir. While the interior has evolved over the years, the restored exterior has remained true to the 1930s cottage style, complete with a "P" on the chimney to signify the original Phillips 66 station.

INSTRUCTIONS

In a large saucepan over medium heat, melt the butter. Add the onions and cook for 2 to 3 minutes, until soft. Whisk in the flour and white pepper and cook on low for 2 minutes, until the onions are fully coated. Slowly pour in the broth, whisking constantly. Bring to a boil, then reduce the heat to a simmer. Stir in the carrots and wild rice and simmer for about 45 minutes, or until the rice is cooked. Add the half-and-half and chicken and cook until the meat is warmed up. Serve immediately. If the soup thickens too much while it sits, thin it out with a little more broth and half-and-half.

MISSOURI | 57

CUBA

CUCUMBER AND ONIONS
Missouri Hick Bar-B-Que ★ MAKES 8 SERVINGS

¼ cup (50 g) granulated sugar

¼ cup (60 ml) hot water

3 tablespoons (45 ml) red wine vinegar

3 tablespoons (45 ml) distilled white vinegar

2 English cucumbers, thinly sliced

1 red onion, thinly sliced into half moons

Though MO Hick, as it's known by the locals, has been in business since 2002, the building was originally an expansion of the Wagon Wheel Cabins, cafe, and gas station owned by Robert and Margaret Martin. Seeking to add a second café and station next door, Robert built Chester's Cafe and Cooke Service Station in 1944. The add-on became known simply as the Wagon Wheel Annex, and in 1946, new owners Paul and Barbara Killeen shortened the name to just The Annex. The business suffered once Interstate 44 was built, so in 1966, Barbara opened a beauty shop on the property. She continued to run the shop until the mid-1970s, after which the building was turned into storage.

When Dennis Meiser came to look at the building in 2001, The Annex had been vacant for many years. He saw potential in the space and set out to differentiate his new barbecue joint from the competition. Using his woodworking skills, he handcrafted the restaurant's wooden tables, chairs, and stairs and erected a new cedar log exterior to emulate an Old West saloon.

Missouri Hick Bar-B-Que was born, and today it's known for its fun and quirk, Kansas City-style barbecue, and fifteen side dishes. Second-generation owner Ryan Meiser continues his late father's legacy and shares this popular MO Hick side, which was one of his grandmother's recipes.

INSTRUCTIONS

In a large bowl, dissolve the sugar in the hot water. Add both of the vinegars and stir to combine. Add the cucumbers and onion and toss until evenly coated. Refrigerate and let the mixture sit for 12 hours before serving.

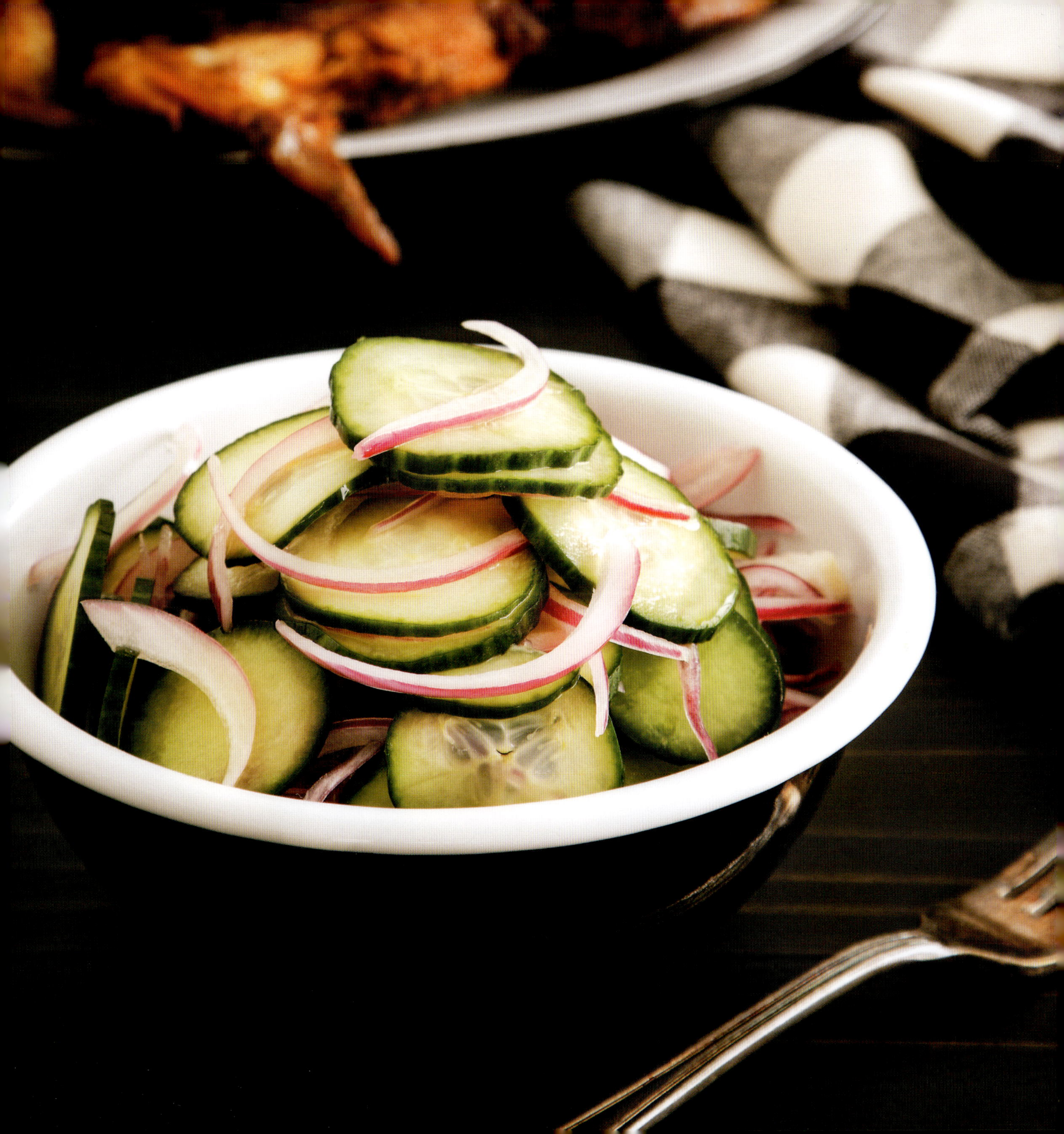

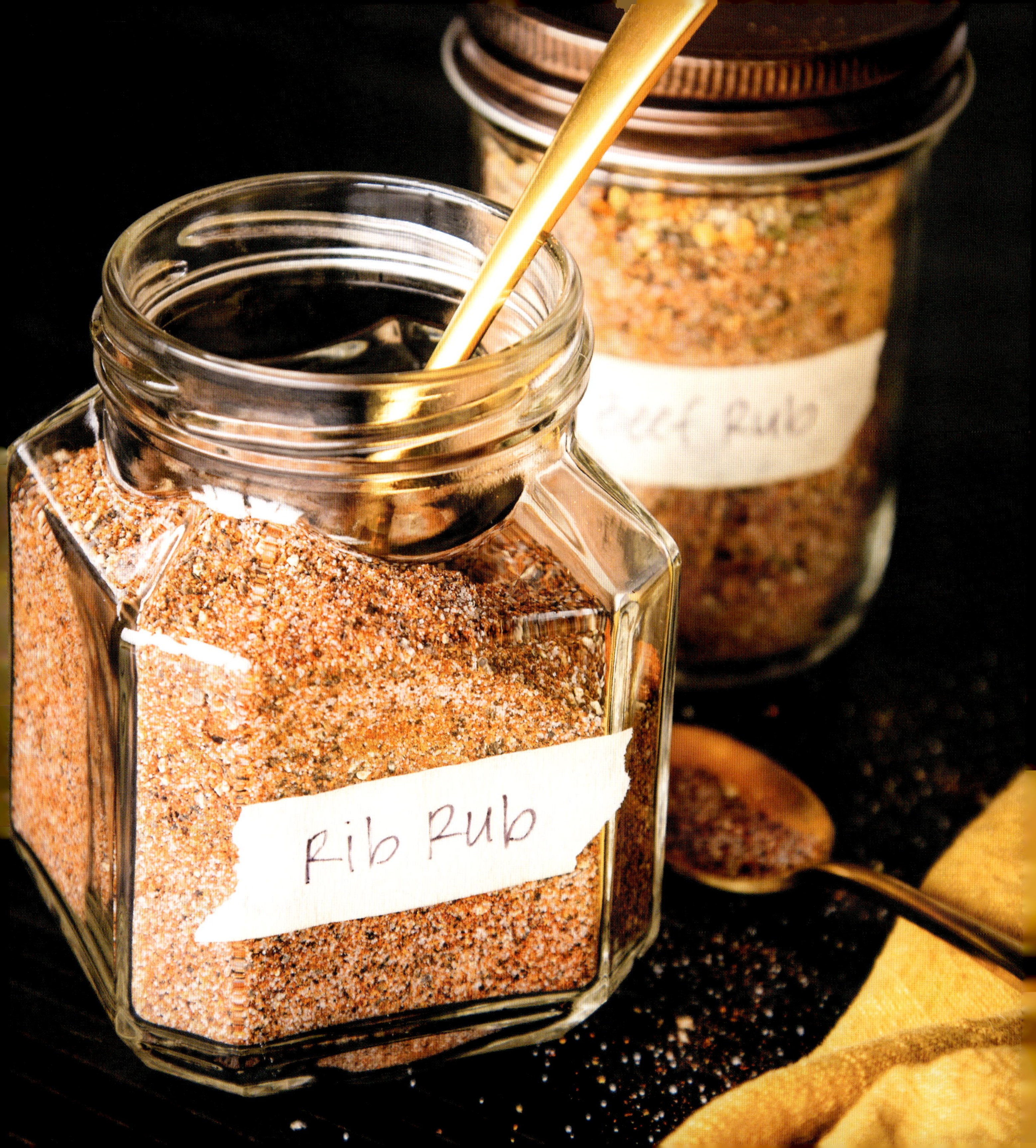
Rib Rub

CUBA

BEEF RUB AND RIB RUB
Missouri Hick Bar-B-Que ✶ **MAKES ABOUT 1 CUP (235 ML) EACH**

BEEF RUB
¼ cup (72 g) fine salt
2 tablespoons (17 g) paprika
2 tablespoons (12 g) ground black pepper
2 tablespoons (8 g) crushed red pepper flakes
2 tablespoons (24 g) lemon pepper
2 tablespoons (14 g) ground cumin
1½ tablespoons (1.5 g) dried parsley

RIB RUB
¼ cup (28 g) paprika
3 tablespoons (39 g) granulated sugar
2 tablespoons (14 g) ground cumin
2 tablespoons (12 g) ground black pepper
2 tablespoons (16 g) chili powder
2 tablespoons (36 g) fine salt

Every type of meat at MO Hick has its own specialty rub, and these spice mixes are the same ones used on the restaurant's cherry wood–smoked brisket and ribs.

INSTRUCTIONS
For each rub, combine all the ingredients in a small bowl. Use immediately to season your meat and store any remaining mixture in a small jar. Rubs can be stored indefinitely, but will start to lose flavor and potency after 6 months.

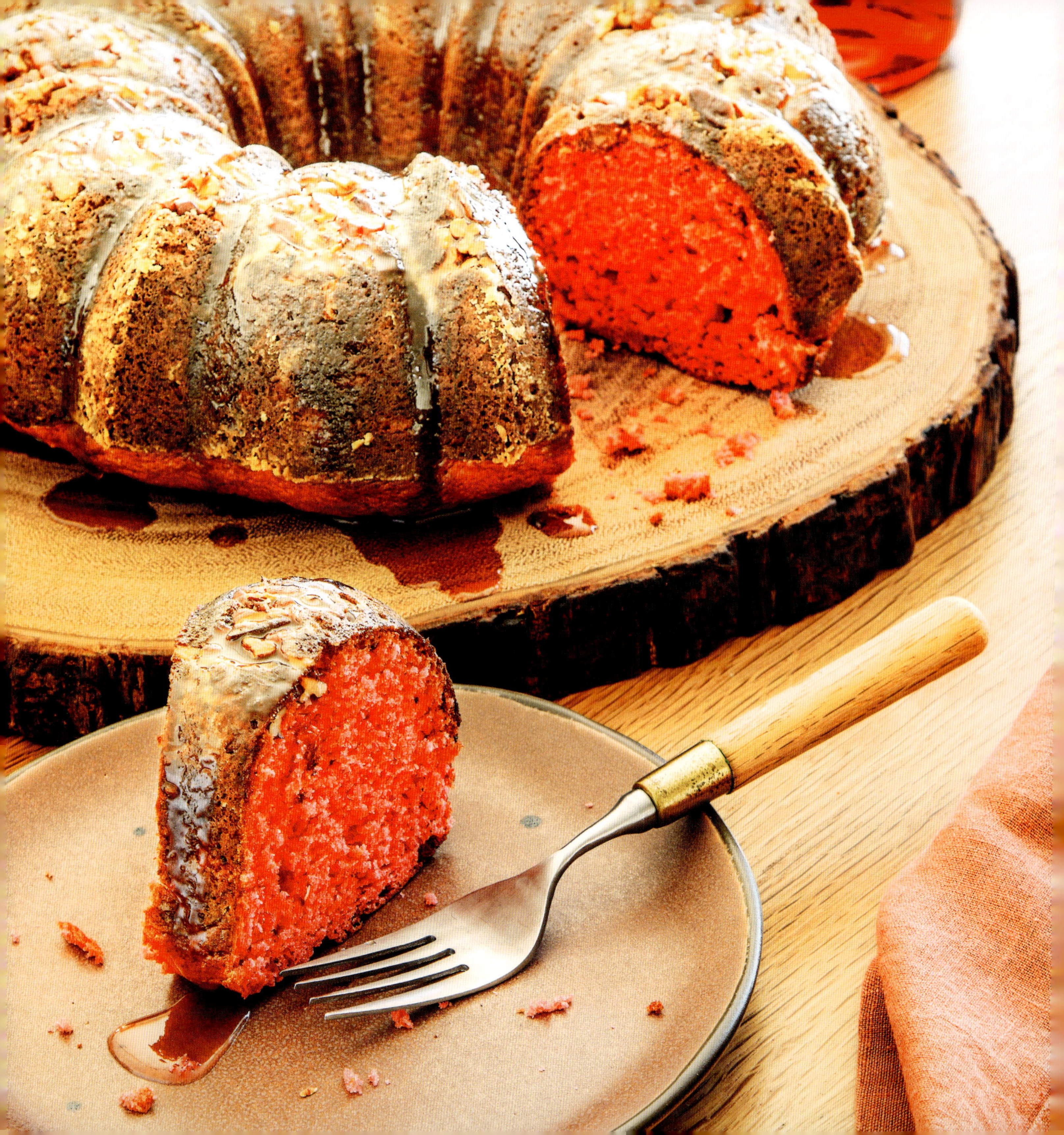

ST. JAMES

BLACKBERRY WINE CAKE
St. James Winery ★ MAKES 12 SERVINGS

CAKE
Butter, for greasing

All-purpose flour, for dusting

½ cup (55 g) chopped pecans

1 box (18.25 ounces, or 511 g) white cake mix

1 box (3 ounces, or 85 g) berry-flavored gelatin

4 eggs

½ cup (120 ml) neutral oil

1 cup (235 ml) St. James Winery Blackberry Wine

GLAZE
1 cup (120 g) powdered sugar

½ cup (120 ml) St. James Winery Blackberry Wine

½ cup (112 g) butter

High-Altitude Tip
When I made this cake at 4,000 feet (1,219 m) elevation, I had the best results adding 2 tablespoons (16 g) all-purpose flour to the cake mix and baking at 350°F (180°C, or gas mark 4) for 33 to 35 minutes.

In the late 1800s, Italian immigrants settled in the St. James area of the Meramec Highlands and started planting Concord grapes for juice and jelly production. By 1922, the community grew to over two hundred wineries with more than a thousand acres of vineyards. These Italian families helped make Missouri the second-largest wine-producing state in the United States—that is, until Prohibition forced the closure of all their wineries. Though they could no longer sell wine, the Italians continued to grow grapes and set up fruit stands along Route 66 and Interstate 44 to sell their fruit to locals and travelers.

When Missouri wines began to make a comeback in the 1960s, Jim and Pat Hofherr decided to resurrect the region's Italian wine-making heritage. They opened St. James Winery in 1970 and, in their first year, produced about 8,000 gallons (30,283 L) of wine. They also grew blackberries and started producing blackberry wine—the first of many fruit wines to come—all made with real fruit.

Their award-winning fruit wine lineup now includes cherry, peach, strawberry, blueberry, and the original blackberry wine—and any of them can be used to make this cake! Simply match the gelatin and fruit wine flavors to create your own.

INSTRUCTIONS
Preheat the oven to 375°F (190°C, or gas mark 5). Grease and flour a Bundt pan and sprinkle pecans around the bottom.

Make the cake: In a large bowl, combine the cake mix and gelatin. Whisk in the eggs, oil, and wine until well blended. Pour the batter into the prepared Bundt pan and bake for 50 to 60 minutes, until a toothpick inserted into the cake comes out clean. Remove from the oven and turn the cake out onto a cooling rack.

Make the glaze: In a small saucepan over medium-low heat, stir together the powdered sugar, wine, and butter until blended. Bring to a simmer and then remove from heat. Drizzle half the glaze over the warm cake and let it set for 30 minutes. Pour the remaining thickened glaze over the cake.

MISSOURI | 63

WAYNESVILLE

BANG BANG BURGER
Hoppers Pub ★ MAKES 4 SERVINGS

BANG BANG SAUCE
1 cup (225 g) mayonnaise
¼ cup (56 g) sweet Thai chili sauce
2 teaspoons ground cayenne

BURGER
Garlic butter
4 brioche buns, halved
8 slices bacon
1½ pounds (680 g) ground beef
Salt and ground black pepper
4 slices pepper jack cheese

TOPPINGS
Lettuce
Sliced tomato
Sliced red onion
Jar of sliced jalapeños
4 fried onion rings (optional)

✳ Hop Over to Rolla

If you decide that you *do* want to try frog legs after all, head a bit further north to Hoppers Pub in Downtown Rolla, where the Lebiodas have a second location on Route 66 (on North Pine Street).

During the 1980s cultural shift to shopping in the suburbs, downtown Waynesville was largely abandoned. A community effort to revitalize the downtown area began in the early 2000s, and two of the early investors were Jake and Ursula Lebioda. They wanted to create a place where people could park their car, eat, shop, and explore, and one of their first projects was Hoppers Pub, which opened on the square in 2010.

The restaurant's name is a spin-off of the hops in beer as well as the town's official mascot, a frog sculpture on a steep hill that overlooks Route 66. Known as W. H. Croaker (Waynesville Hill Croaker) or Frog Rock, the rock formation was exposed during a highway widening project and it's been a local landmark since the mid-1990s.

Frog legs do make an appearance on the menu at Hoppers Pub (because, when in Rome . . .), but if you aren't feeling that adventurous, rest assured that this place is actually known for their burgers and the sixty-six kinds of beer they have on tap.

INSTRUCTIONS

Make the bang bang sauce: In a small bowl, combine all the sauce ingredients and set aside.

Make the burger: Spread the garlic butter on each cut side of the buns. Toast, buttered-sides down, in a large skillet over medium-high heat for about 1 minute, or until golden brown, and set aside.

In the same skillet over medium-high heat, cook the bacon to desired doneness and transfer to a plate lined with paper towels to drain. Reserve 2 tablespoons (28 ml) of bacon grease in the pan.

Form the beef into 4 patties. Season both sides with salt and pepper. Reheat the bacon grease over medium-high heat and cook the patties for about 4 minutes, or until the bottom is caramelized. Flip the patties, top each with a slice of cheese, and cook until the patty reaches the desired temperature (130°F to 135°F [54°C to 57°C], or 3 minutes more for medium-rare).

Assemble each burger by placing the patty, lettuce, tomato, and red onion on the bottom bun. Top with 2 slices of bacon, a spoonful of sliced jalapeños, and an onion ring (if using); drizzle the bang bang sauce and finish with a top bun.

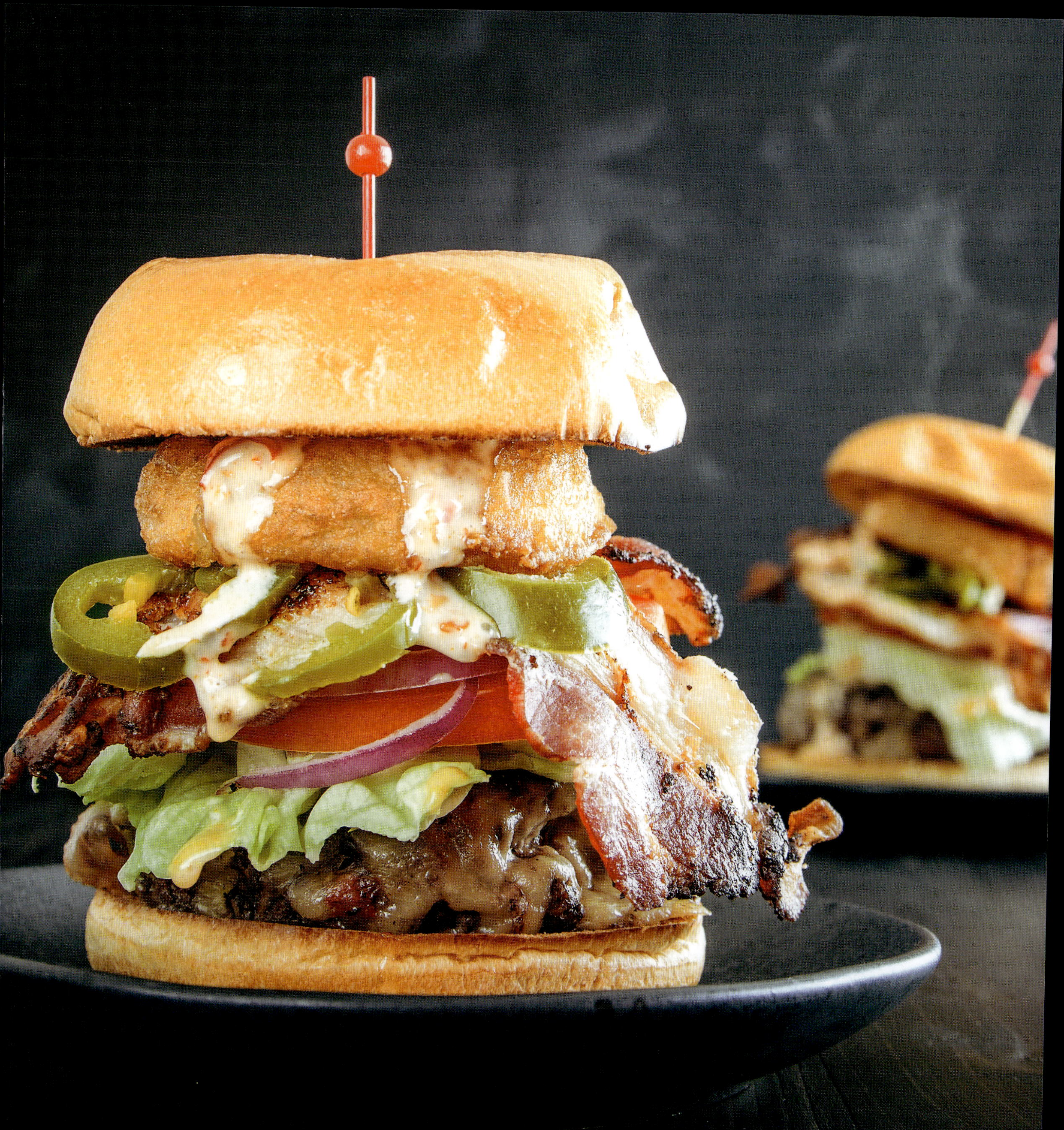

College Street
CAFE
Coca-Cola
College Street
CAFE
Coca-Cola
COLLEGE STREET
CAFE
College Street
Café
College Street
Ca
HOURS
MISSOURI
US 66
ROUTE
66

SPRINGFIELD

THE VERNON—THE ULTIMATE ROUTE 66 BURGER

College Street Cafe ★ **MAKES 1 SERVING**

---

6 ounces (170 g) ground beef

Salt and ground black pepper

1 slice American cheese

2 slices Texas toast, grilled

1 heaping cup (248 g) cooked crispy French fries

1 cup (248 g) nacho cheese sauce, warmed

Bacon bits, for garnishing

Sliced jalapeños, for garnishing

The little white building with cheerful red trim on College Street—what used to be Route 66—began as Pat's Cafe around 1953. An early photo of the restaurant reveals there used to be a sign out front that advertised "man-size hamburgers" for just 25 cents. Since then, it's gone by many names, before becoming College Street Cafe, which Marylou Meierotto purchased in 2016.

She used to work there before she bought the business, and a visit to the restaurant shows just how tight she is with all her customers. She knows (or remembers) almost all of them, and it's the type of friendly, familiar hole-in-the-wall where locals often come in every day for at least one meal (if not two).

One of these locals is Vernon, who's been a regular for nearly forty years—way back before Marylou bought it. Vernon is there so much that he even has a burger named after him. The original burger came from Ginny Lee's Restaurant just down the street (now the Rockwood Motor Court, a Route 66 landmark that returned to its original name), where Vernon used to eat. After Ginny Lee's closed down, Vernon brought the recipe to Marylou and asked her to make it for him. It's reminiscent of a horseshoe, a signature sandwich from that *other* Springfield (in Illinois), but Vernon and Marylou have given it their own flair. (Tip: Vernon likes his with grilled onions, though it normally comes without.)

INSTRUCTIONS

Form the beef into a patty and season both sides with a few pinches of salt and pepper. Heat a small skillet over medium-high heat. When hot, add the patty and cook until the meat has browned halfway up the side. Flip the patty and cook for about 4 minutes, or until a thermometer reads 150°F to 155°F (66°C to 68°C) for medium-well. Remove from heat, top the patty with the slice of cheese, and cover with a lid to allow the residual heat to melt the cheese.

Assemble the burger by placing one slice of toast on a plate. Add the patty with melted cheese and top with the second slice of toast. Pile the French fries over the burger, smother with cheese sauce, and sprinkle with a handful of bacon bits and jalapeños.

MISSOURI

2pk Cinn. Rolls
$7.50

MOM'S YEAST ROLLS
Rise & Grind Coffee Station ★ MAKES 18 ROLLS

YEAST
1 cup (235 ml) warm water
3 tablespoons (36 g) active dry yeast
1 tablespoon (13 g) granulated sugar

DOUGH
Nonstick cooking spray
1 cup (235 ml) warm water or scalded milk
1 cup (225 g) butter, melted and cooled
2 eggs
⅔ cup (133 g) granulated sugar
2 teaspoons fine salt
6 to 7 cups (720 to 840 g) all-purpose flour, plus more for dusting

FILLING
½ cup (112 g) butter, extra softened
1 cup (225 g) packed brown sugar
2 tablespoons (14 g) ground cinnamon

GLAZE
2 cups (240 g) powdered sugar
¼ cup (60 ml) milk
2 tablespoons (28 g) butter, melted
2 teaspoons vanilla extract

The story of how I stumbled on this little coffee shop in Southwestern Missouri is a delightful example of "don't judge a book by its cover." While driving along a stretch of farmland one day in our motor home, with the propane meter reading low, my husband spotted a sign on the highway for propane and quickly pulled off at a nondescript white shack surrounded by cornfields. When he came back a few minutes later, he asked if I wanted some cinnamon rolls that the two cute ladies in the shack were selling. I followed him inside, expecting a basic mini mart with generic pastries, but as soon as I walked through the door, it was like I'd entered a secret portal that led into a hip urban coffeehouse.

Yes, it looks like an abandoned 1950s filling station on the outside, but Rise & Grind sells neither propane nor gasoline (though it does lease the property from a local propane company, hence the sign). Shanna Garner and her family (including her sister Dana Clayton and their daughters, who all help in the coffee shop) opened the coffeehouse for business in 2024 after a gut remodel. The interior was transformed *nearly* top to bottom, as the family preserved the building's wood plank pavilion ceiling, an original detail that beautifully complements their cozy and newly modern space.

The coffee station had been open for only a few months when I visited in the summer, but it was already a staple in the community. Locals drop in for their morning coffee, homemade pastries, charcuterie boxes, sandwiches, and hot meals to go, and occasionally, a lucky traveler may find them by happy accident. We devoured the cinnamon glazed yeast rolls, a recipe from Shanna and Dana's mother, and they were exactly the kind of belly-warming, soft and fluffy treat we needed to get on our way.

MOM'S YEAST ROLLS
CONTINUED

INSTRUCTIONS

Activate the yeast: Pour the warm water into a small bowl and sprinkle the yeast on top of the water. Stir in the sugar. When the mixture is completely foamy on top, the yeast is activated. (Depending on the temperature of the water and your home, this may take anywhere from 5 to 15 minutes.)

Make the dough: Lightly mist a large bowl with cooking spray and set aside.

In the bowl of a stand mixer, combine the warm water, butter, eggs, sugar, and salt. Add the activated yeast, then slowly add in the flour and mix with a wooden spoon until a soft dough forms. Attach a dough hook to your mixer and mix for 5 minutes on medium speed. The dough should be tacky but not sticky; start with 6 cups (720 g) of flour and add more as needed to reach a tacky consistency.

Gather the dough into a smooth ball, place it in the prepared bowl, and cover with plastic wrap. Allow the dough to rise in a relatively warm environment for 60 to 90 minutes, until doubled in size.

Make the rolls: Lightly mist two 9 x 13-inch (23 x 33 cm) baking dishes with cooking spray and set aside.

After the dough has doubled in size, turn it out onto a lightly floured surface and roll into a 12 x 36-inch (30 x 90 cm) rectangle. Spread the softened butter over the dough and sprinkle evenly with brown sugar and cinnamon. Roll the long way into a tight log and cut the dough into 18 equal rolls, each about 1½ to 2-inches (4 to 5 cm) wide. Place the rolls cut-side down and evenly spaced in the prepared baking dishes. Loosely cover the dishes and let rise a second time for about 1 hour, or until doubled in size.

While the rolls are rising, preheat the oven to 375°F (190°C, or gas mark 5). Uncover the baking dishes and bake for 20 to 25 minutes, until golden brown. Place the buns on a wire rack to cool.

Make the glaze: Whisk all the glaze ingredients in a medium bowl until the mixture is smooth. Drizzle the glaze over the warm buns.

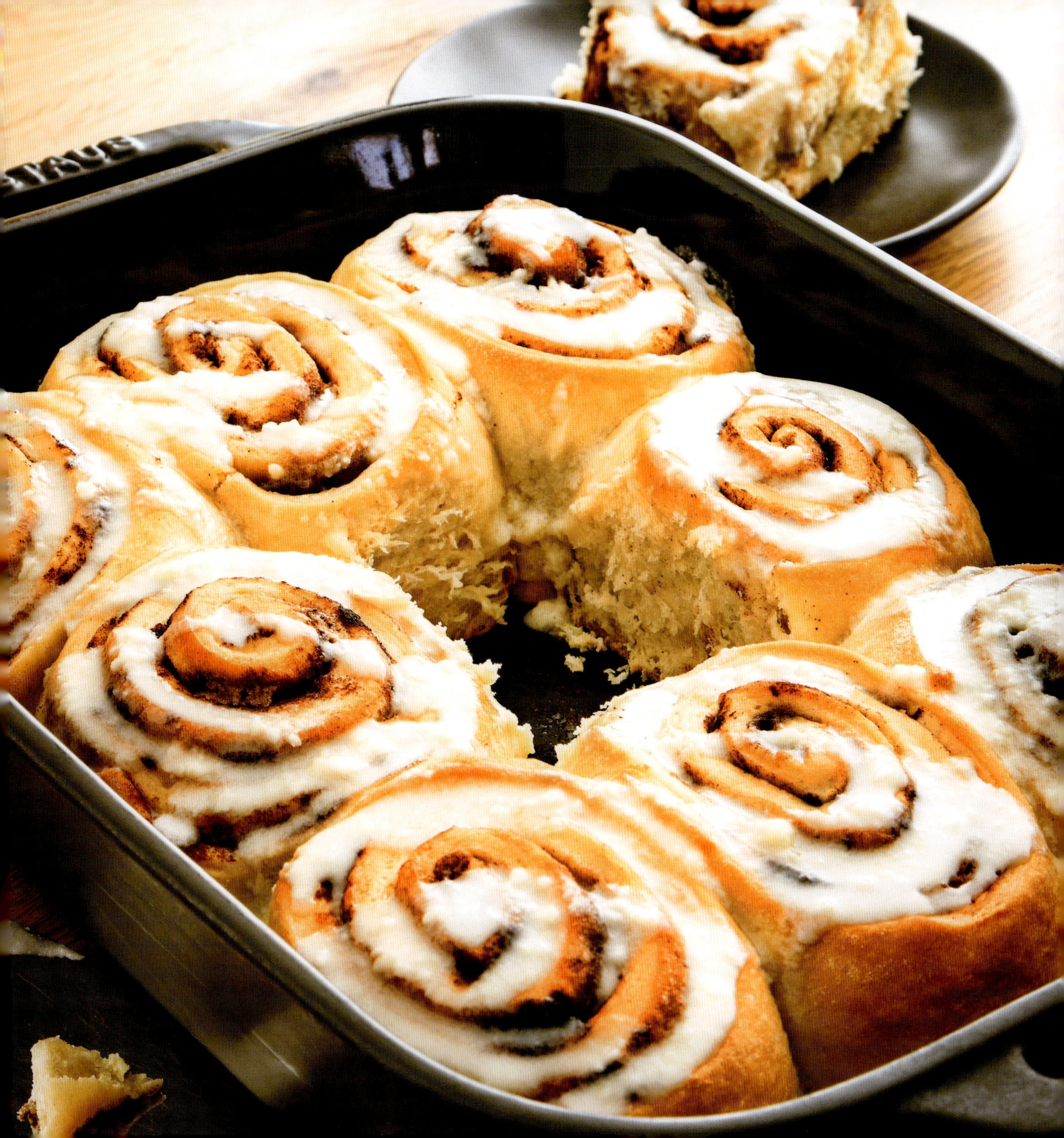

CARTHAGE

BEANS AND CORN BREAD
The Carthage Deli ★ MAKES 6 SERVINGS

BEANS
½ pound (225 g) dried navy beans
½ pound (225 g) dried pinto beans
1 cup (150 g) diced ham
1 onion, chopped
2 cloves garlic, minced
1 teaspoon celery salt
1 teaspoon fine salt
½ teaspoon ground black pepper
¼ teaspoon crushed red pepper flakes
¼ teaspoon dried thyme
6 cups (1.4 L) chicken broth

CORN BREAD
Butter or nonstick cooking spray
1½ cups (207 g) self-rising cornmeal
½ cup (60 g) all-purpose flour
¼ cup (50 g) granulated sugar
½ teaspoon fine salt
1 cup (235 ml) buttermilk
1 egg
¼ cup (55 g) butter, melted

Gustavius Adolphus Cassil, who helped incorporate Carthage as a city, established the Bank of Carthage in 1868 on what would later become the northwest corner of Carthage Square. The two-story brick building that stands today was built in 1884. When the bank moved out in the 1950s, Gray-Seaver Drug Store moved in.

In 1979, Tom and Corrine Candela took over the space and opened The Carthage Deli. Vintage remnants from the old bank days were kept intact, including the marble wainscotting around the center column.

Eventually, in 1998, Chris and Mary Brown bought the business. Mary had worked at the deli as a teenager, and the Browns' three children (Amanda, Brandon, and Nathan) have all worked in the family business through the years. Nathan even met his wife, Christina, on the job when she worked summers at the deli, and the couple now manage the day-to-day operations. The family used to sell beans and corn bread seasonally, a favorite that customers would ask for each year, and if you're one of these customers who wished they would bring it back, you're in luck—the Browns are sharing their recipe here.

INSTRUCTIONS
Make the beans: Rinse the beans and soak in water overnight. Drain and rinse them again. In a large pot, combine the beans with the remaining ingredients and bring to a boil. Reduce the heat and simmer for 2 to 3 hours, until the beans are tender. Stir occasionally and add a little water if the liquid is evaporating too much.

Make the corn bread: Preheat the oven to 425°F (220°C, or gas mark 7). Grease a 9-inch (23 cm) pie plate or 8 x 8-inch (20 x 20 cm) baking dish and set aside.

In a large bowl, combine the cornmeal, flour, sugar, and salt. In a separate small bowl, whisk together the buttermilk, egg, and melted butter. Pour the wet ingredients into the dry ingredients and stir until just combined. Do not overmix.

Pour the batter into the prepared baking dish and bake for 20 to 25 minutes, until golden brown. Serve the corn bread alongside the cooked beans.

BRUTON
BRUTON
BRUTON
CARTHAGE
HISTORIC DRIVE
BIKE ROUTE
Garde Manger
Keeper of the Pantry
Charcuterie and more!
COME SEE US
Diverse wine selection & specialty grocery from small batch kitchens around the world.
OPEN
301

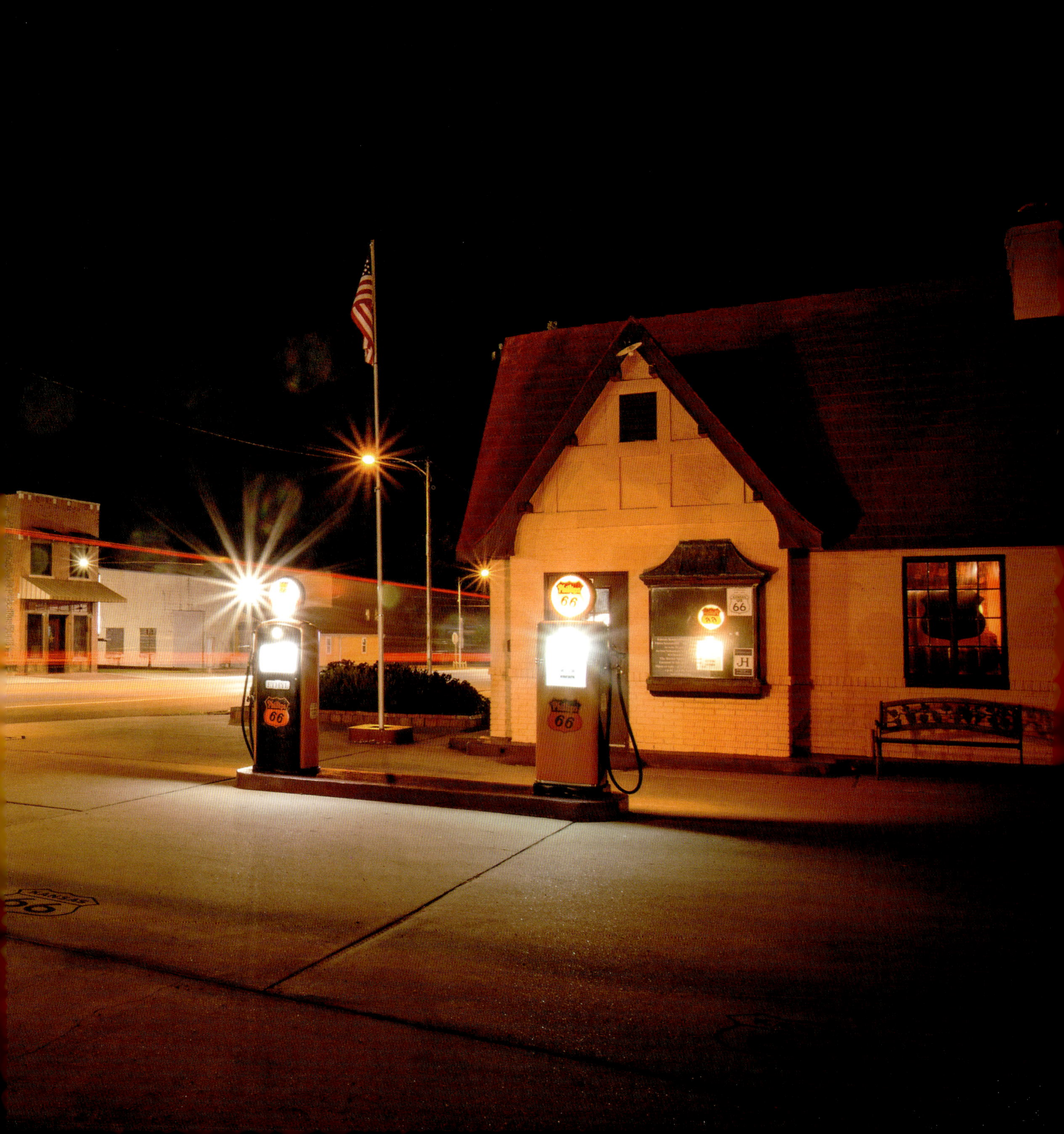
Phillips 66
Phillips 66

Three
KANSAS

THE MOTHER ROAD SPANS just three communities and thirteen miles (21 km) in Kansas, slicing through Galena, Riverton, and Baxter Springs on the southeast edge of the state. In 1929, the Kansas section of Route 66 became the first in the country to be entirely hard surfaced. Okay, maybe it's easier when it's only thirteen miles (21 km) rather than hundreds of miles, but Kansas also paid for this honor in 1961, when it became the only state to be entirely bypassed by the new interstate. Pick up a sweet treat or quick meal on your jaunt through the Sunflower State—but be sure not to blink, or you'll be saying (as Dorothy did in *The Wizard of Oz*), "We're not in Kansas anymore."

GALENA

GOULASH

Streetcar Station Coffee Shop ★ MAKES 10 SERVINGS

- 24 ounces (680 g) large elbow pasta
- 2 tablespoons (28 ml) olive oil
- 2 pounds (910 g) ground beef
- ½ cup (64 g) mild chili seasoning
- ¼ cup (32 g) regular chili seasoning
- 1 can (15 ounces, or 425 g) crushed tomatoes
- 1 can (10 ounces, or 280 g) RO-TEL® diced tomatoes and green chilies
- 1 can (14.5 ounces, or 410 g) stewed Mexican-style tomatoes

At one time, Galena had been tagged by the U.S. Geological Survey as the most polluted city in the state. The former mining town boomed in 1877 when lead was discovered in the area, leading it to become the wealthiest city per capita in the world. But by the time the mines were exhausted in the 1970s, Galena's population had dwindled to a tenth of its peak and it was rife with environmental problems. Its 800 recorded mine shafts and 3,000 mine features were a scar on (and under) the landscape, and business along Main Street (where Route 66 had been established in 1926) struggled for decades.

In the early 2000s, extensive efforts to clean up the downtown and fill the mines that ran under an estimated 60 percent of the city began to breathe new life into Galena. A downtown streetscape project followed, and that's when Kathleen and Danny Anderson decided to open a coffee and sandwich shop as their retirement project. Streetcar Station Coffee Shop opened in 2012 during the resurgence of downtown, but don't let the "coffee shop" in the name fool you. Sure, it's got the usual coffee and sweet treats, but it also serves a full breakfast and lunch menu, and this goulash is a customer favorite.

INSTRUCTIONS

Cook the pasta according to the package directions, drain, and set aside.

In a large pot over medium-high heat, drizzle the oil and add the ground beef. Break the meat into smaller chunks with a wooden spoon and cook until browned. Sprinkle the mild and regular chili seasonings over the meat and stir until evenly coated. Add all the canned tomatoes, stir to combine, and bring to a simmer. Fold in the cooked pasta and heat through before serving.

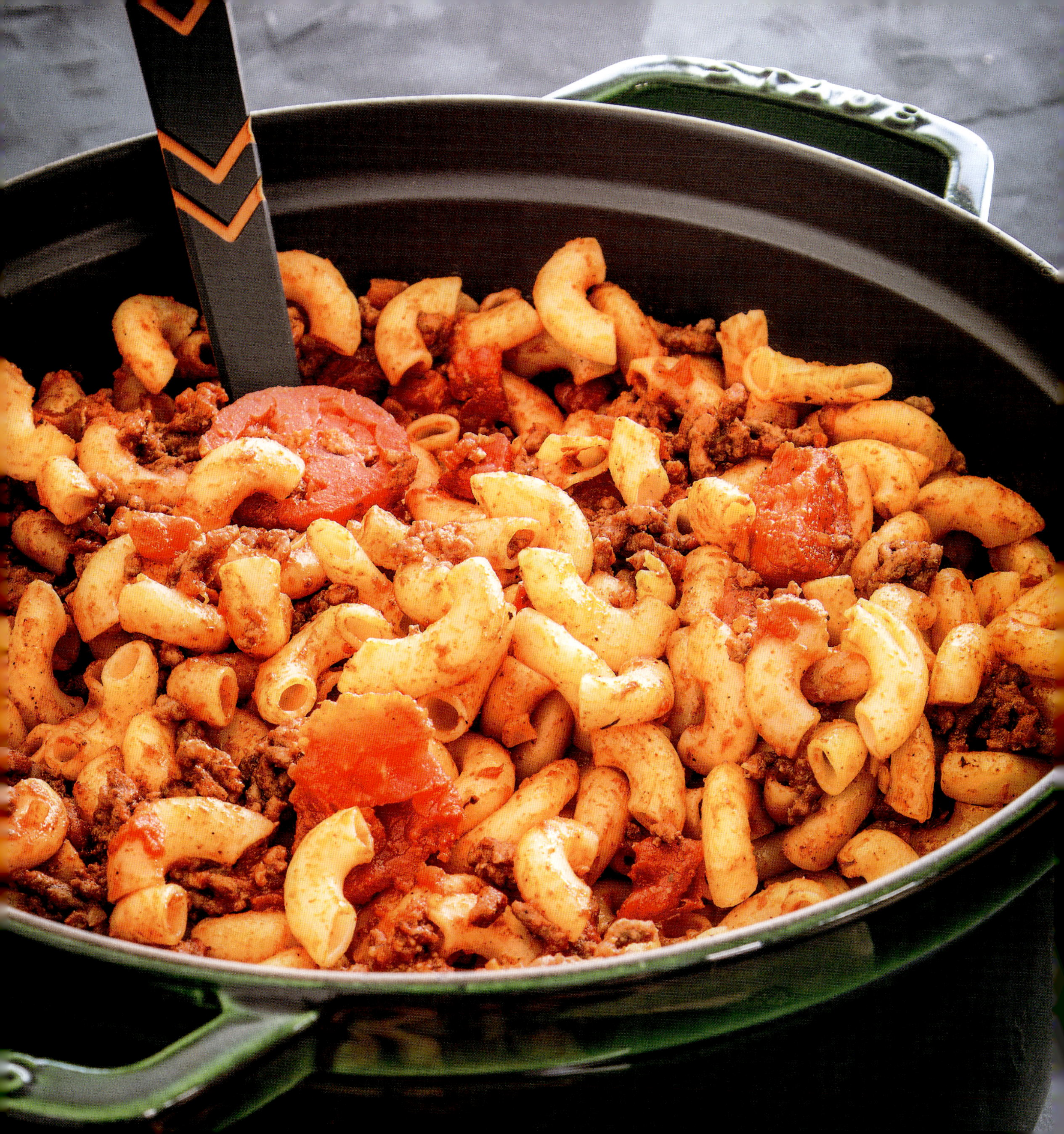

FOOD
Nelson's Old Riverton Store
MARKET
ROUTE 66
FOOD
MARKET
ROUTE U.S. 66
7109
ICE
Home City Ice

ROAST BEEF SANDWICH
Nelson's Old Riverton Store ★ MAKES 1 SERVING

---

2 slices wheat bread, buttered on one side
Thinly sliced roast beef
Thinly sliced cheddar cheese
Thinly sliced tomato
Lettuce leaves, torn to fit sandwich
Sweet sandwich pickles

In 1925, Leo and Lora Williams built a grocery and general store on the road that would soon become Route 66. Half the building was an apartment (where they lived with their daughter), and the other half was known as the Williams' Store. It was a staple among locals but later became a major stop for motorists, who dropped by for directions, coffee, Lora's special chili, or Leo's famous barbecue sandwiches. The family later bought a roller rink in Galena, and after twenty years in the grocery business, they leased the store to Lloyd Paxon. After Leo's death and the end of Lloyd's lease, Lora returned to the store and operated as Lora Williams AG Food Market until she retired in 1970. The property passed on to her daughter and then to her daughter's mother-in-law.

In 1973, Joe and Isabell Eisler purchased the building and renamed it Eisler Bros. Old Riverton Store. They erected a greenhouse but preserved most of the red brick building's historical charm, including the glass-enclosed front porch, pressed metal ceiling, and deli counter in the back. The Eislers' nephew, Scott Nelson, started managing the store in the 1980s and eventually bought it from the Eisler estate in 2011.

The building—now known as Nelson's Old Riverton Store—is listed in the National Register of Historic Places and continues to operate as a grocery and deli. Little has changed in the last hundred years since it was built, though the Williamses' old living room has since been turned into a souvenir shop. This roast beef is Scott's personal favorite, and their roast is made in-house.

INSTRUCTIONS
On a slice of bread with the buttered-side up, layer the roast beef, cheddar, tomato, lettuce, and pickles. Top with the remaining slice of bread, buttered-side down, and serve.

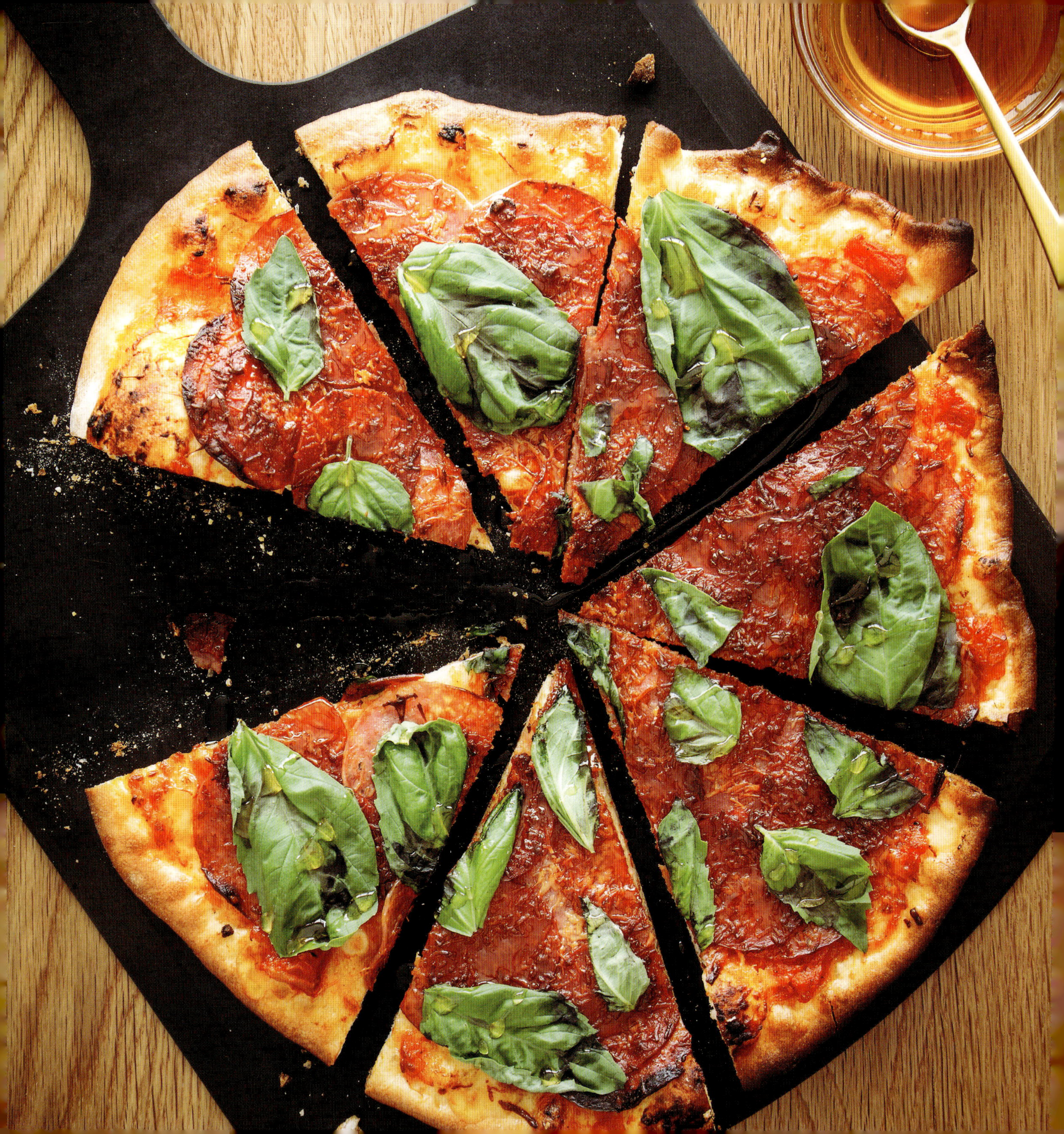

BAXTER SPRINGS

THE VOODOO CHILD PIZZA
Bricks & Brews Woodfire Grill & Pub ★ MAKES ONE 12-INCH (30 CM) PIZZA

Cornmeal, for dusting
1 ball (9 ounces, or 255 g) pizza dough
⅓ cup (80 ml) marinara sauce
4 ounces (115 g) salami
1½ ounces (42 g) pepperoni
¼ cup (25 g) grated Parmesan cheese
Fresh basil leaves
Hot honey (see sidebar)

In 2014, a tornado blew through town and took off the roof of a stout, two-story building on Military Avenue (and obliterated many other buildings on the street) but—fortunately and quite literally—it was built like a pile of bricks and survived. The former automotive shop has been standing since 1908, when it was originally built for a school (but never used as a school). Over the years it housed the Baxter Stove Co. (1921), Hale Bros. Garage (1925), and Breeding Transport Company (1930s). Breeding Transport leased half the building to Bob Page Auto Supply in 1954, and in 1974, Bob Page bought the building, expanded his auto parts business, and operated in that location until 2016.

Baxter Springs resident Doug Puckett actually worked for Bob Page when he was in high school and college. When an opportunity came to purchase the building, Doug fulfilled his dream of owning a restaurant and opened Bricks & Brews in 2021. You could say he came full circle: The pizza joint and brewpub's automotive theme is a nod to its history as an auto parts store and its glory days as a trucking company.

INSTRUCTIONS
Place a pizza stone on the middle rack of the oven and preheat to 500°F (250°C, or gas mark 10). Lightly dust a pizza peel with cornmeal.

Roll or stretch out the dough to form a 12-inch (30 cm) circle and place it on the prepared pizza peel. Spread the marinara evenly over the dough, leaving a ½-inch (13 mm) border all the way around. Arrange the salami and pepperoni in a single layer and sprinkle with Parmesan. Transfer the pizza to the preheated pizza stone and bake for 10 to 12 minutes, until the crust is browned. Remove from the oven, arrange a handful of basil evenly over the pizza, and drizzle with hot honey.

Hot Honey at Home
You can usually find hot honey in the grocery store, but it's also very easy to make at home. Combine ½ cup (170 g) honey and 1 teaspoon crushed red pepper flakes in a small saucepan. Bring to a light simmer over medium heat, then remove from heat. Cool to room temperature before transferring to a jar for storage. Homemade hot honey can keep for about 6 months in a cupboard.

KANSAS | 81

Monarch Pharmacy
Soda
Welcome to Baxter Springs, KS
FLOATS & SUNDAES
ANDERSON'S ICE CREAM

BAXTER SPRINGS

EGG CREAM
Monarch Pharmacy and Soda Fountain ✱ **MAKES 1 SERVING**

3 ounces (85 g) whole milk
1 ounce (28 ml) Ghirardelli chocolate syrup
Cold soda water
Vanilla ice cream (optional)

After a tornado leveled several buildings in downtown Baxter Springs in 2014, the property at 1601 Military Avenue became a vacant lot. When it came time to rebuild, pharmacist Kelly McAllister knew she wanted to provide something a little more to appeal to travelers on Route 66. Many of the other convenience-type stores in town carried general merchandise or snacks; she envisioned bringing in a different element that celebrated the spirit of 66.

Working with the owner of the property, Kelly designed an old-timey brick building with a traditional wood and marble soda fountain, walnut-paneled walls, and vintage ceiling tiles. She hired an artist out of Joplin to create retro-style Coca-Cola murals on the sides of the building, beckoning travelers who come from either direction on Historic Route 66.

In 2017, Kelly opened Monarch Pharmacy and Soda Fountain with a nostalgic menu that includes hand-dipped ice cream, shakes and malts, and sodas and phosphates. It's a community staple where people come to fill their prescriptions, but just like the old days, many more come just for the delight of a soda jerk serving a cold treat on a hot day.

INSTRUCTIONS

Pour the milk and chocolate syrup into a glass and stir well to mix. Add soda water to fill the glass to the top and stir again.

If desired, pour the whole concoction over a scoop or two of ice cream and enjoy!

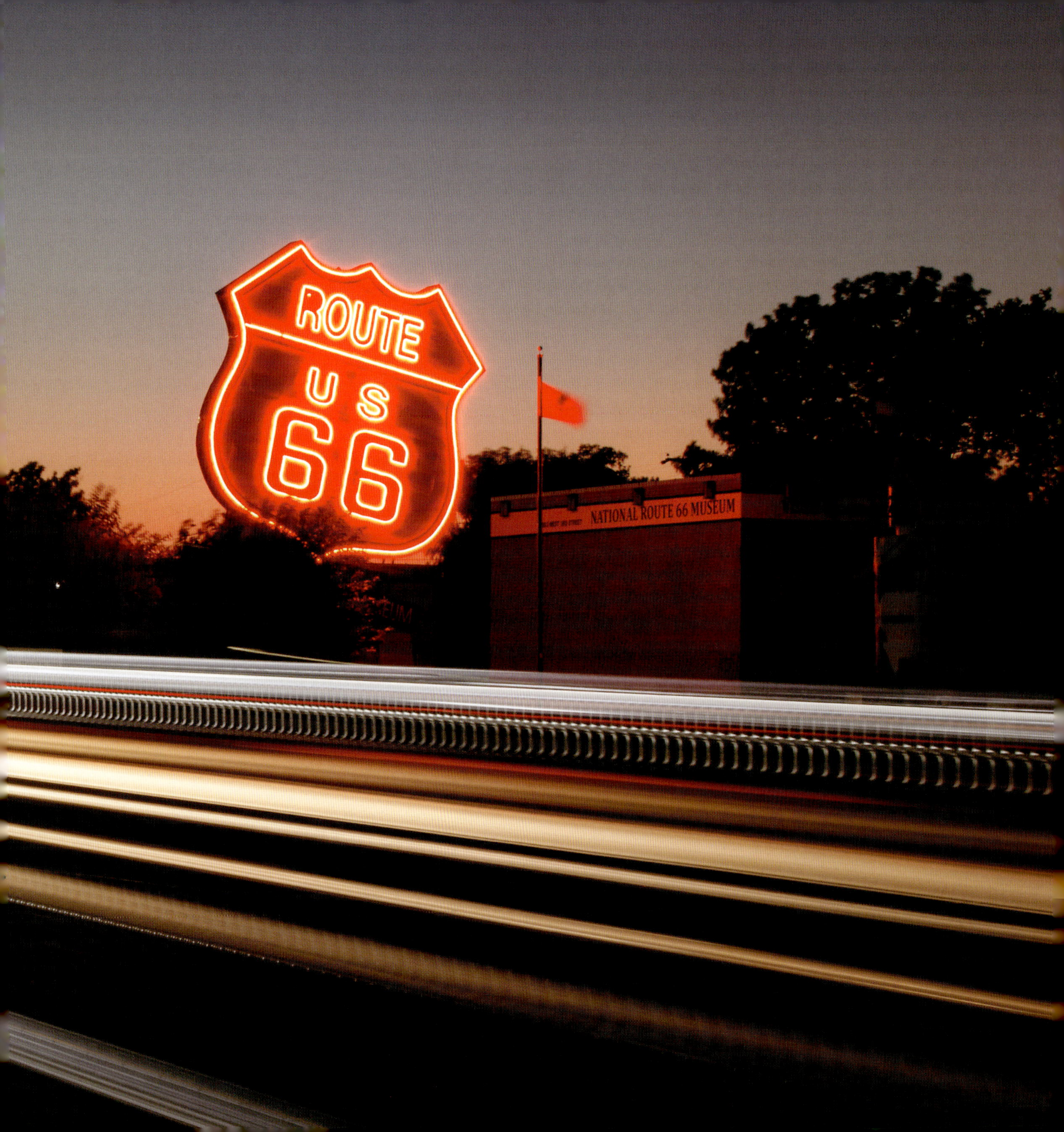
ROUTE
US
66
NATIONAL ROUTE 66 MUSEUM

Four
OKLAHOMA

FROM QUAPAW TO TEXOLA, the mid-section of the Mother Road offers the kind of stick-to-your-ribs sustenance that your no-nonsense grandmother insists you eat more of—and also take home. But it's more than just meat and potatoes along these four hundred miles. Influences from east and west feature heavily in Oklahoman cuisine, and you're just as likely to find a greasy smashburger or a hearty bowl of Southwestern stew as you are to sit down to an authentic Brazilian or German-inspired meal. The Sooner State is a place where the food reflects the people's love of the land and the food that's grown and raised on it.

EAT
Clantons
HISTORIC
OKLAHOMA
66
ROUTE
CLOSED
VINITA
OK
66

VINITA

CALF FRIES
Clanton's Cafe ★ MAKES 4 SERVINGS

DIPPING SAUCE
2 cups (475 ml) blue cheese dressing

2 tablespoons (28 ml) Arizona Gunslinger Smokin' Hot Jalapeño Pepper Sauce (or your preferred hot sauce)

Pinch of ground cumin

CALF FRIES
1¼ cups (295 ml) buttermilk

1 egg

2 cups (550 g) cornmeal

1 cup (120 g) all-purpose flour

1 tablespoon (5 g) ground cayenne pepper

1 pound (455 g) calf fries, membrane removed, fries cut into bite-size pieces

Neutral oil, for frying

✻ The Original Sack Lunch

Depending on the location, veal testicles may go under different (and rather colorful) names, including bull fries or calf fries, bull's eggs, huevos de toro, cowboy caviar, swinging beef, dusted nuts, prairie oysters, Rocky Mountain oysters, and Montana tendergroins.

The original Clanton's Cafe opened in 1930, but didn't move to its present-day location on East Illinois Avenue until 1947. A long line of Clantons have run the restaurant since: Ma and Cleve Clanton in the 1940s and '50s, Tom and Argene in the late 1950s and '60s, Aunt "Leftie" in the 1970s, and Tom and Linda in the late 1970s. In 1997, Melissa (Clanton) and Dennis Patrick became the fourth-generation owners, making Clanton's Cafe the oldest family-owned restaurant on Route 66 in Oklahoma. Their son Shaun, who manages the restaurant, is the fifth generation of this Mother Road icon, known for its neon red "EAT" sign out front and classic American comfort food—with some recipes going back more than eighty years.

But you can't leave Vinita without trying the local delicacy for which it's best known: calf fries. In fact, the small town is considered the "Calf Fry Capital of the World" and hosts an annual cook-off featuring thousands of pounds of the famous cowboy cuisine—a testicle festival, if you will.

Calf fries are a clever euphemism for veal testicles, an organ meat that's surprisingly tender and flavorful. I know it's kind of a cliche, but it tastes a lot like chicken. (And for the uninitiated, it never gets old serving them a plate of battered and fried calf fries and not telling them what it is. Ha!) Clanton's serves theirs with what they call Guy's Sauce, a dipping sauce originally created by Guy Fieri when he visited the restaurant during an episode of Food Network's *Diners, Drive-Ins and Dives*.

INSTRUCTIONS

Make the dipping sauce by combining the ingredients in a small bowl. Set aside.

In a bowl, beat the buttermilk and egg until combined. In a separate bowl, stir together the cornmeal, flour, and cayenne.

Dip each calf fry into the buttermilk mixture, then roll in the flour mixture until coated on all sides.

Line a plate with paper towels. Heat 1 to 2 inches (2.5 to 5 cm) of oil in a deep, heavy saucepan to 360°F (182°C). Fry the calf fries for about 3 minutes, or until crisp and golden brown. Use a slotted spoon to transfer the finished calf fries to the prepared plate to drain. Serve with the dipping sauce.

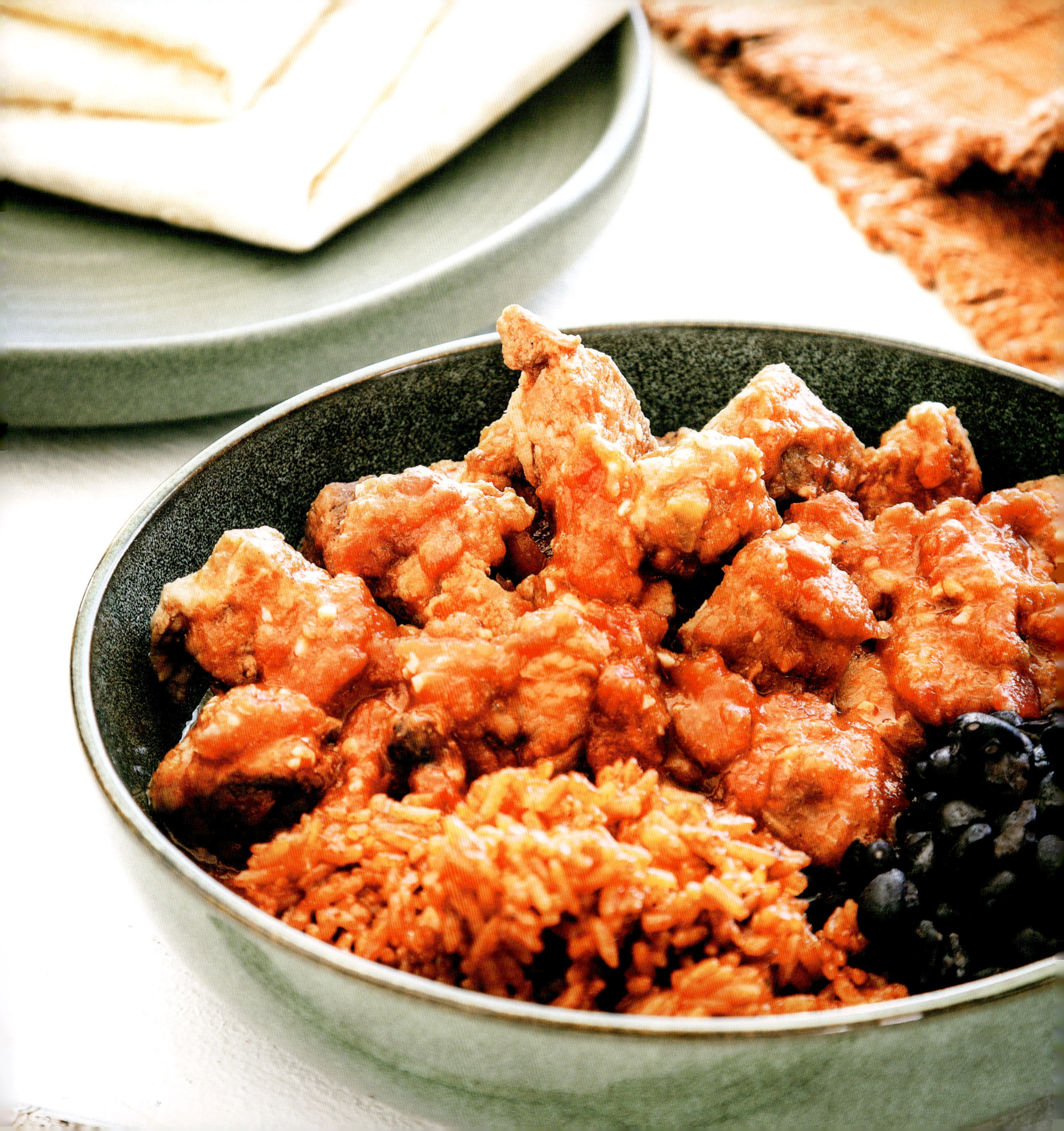

TULSA

CHILE COLORADO
El Rancho Grande Mexican Food ★ MAKES 6 TO 8 SERVINGS

- 4 to 5 jalapeños (6 ounces)
- 2 ribs celery
- ½ onion
- ½ green bell pepper
- ¼ cup (60 ml) neutral oil
- 4 pounds (1.8 kg) pork butt, trimmed and cut into 1-inch (2.5 cm) cubes
- ⅔ cup (80 g) all-purpose flour
- 2 tablespoons (36 g) fine salt
- 3 tablespoons (30 g) granulated garlic
- 1½ tablespoons (11 g) ground white pepper
- 1 tablespoon (7 g) ground cumin
- 2 cans (28 ounces, or 795 g each) crushed tomatoes
- 2 cups (475 ml) water
- Rice and beans, for serving
- Corn or flour tortillas, for serving

In 1953, Ruby Rodriguez moved El Rancho Grande and its iconic neon marquee from its original downtown location to a two-story brick building on Route 66. (The business had been open since 1950, however, making it the oldest Mexican restaurant in Tulsa.) Her new location, the historic Leyh Building, was built in 1921 by John J. Leyh. El Rancho Grande occupied the west side of the building when it first moved in, but expanded its dining room in the 1960s to occupy the entire first floor.

The building—but not the restaurant—changed hands in 1974 when Jeff Walden Sr. bought the property as an investment. Ruby's daughters, Martha and Judy, were running El Rancho Grande at the time, but went out of business in 1982. The Walden family bought the restaurant and reopened it in 1984. They rehired many of the former employees, including Inez "Larry" Lara, who would ultimately work at the restaurant for more than fifty years and teach the family how to make many of the original recipes from Ruby's days.

The elder Jeff's sons, Jeff Jr. and John, took over the restaurant in 2005. They converted the upstairs apartments to a cantina in 2017 and brightened up the interior, but have never touched the Tex-Mex menu. (The regulars would know!) John has cooked this recipe for the past forty years and believes it has been an El Rancho Grande staple since 1953.

INSTRUCTIONS

Chop the jalapeños, celery, onion, and bell pepper into large chunks and place them in the bowl of a food processor. Pulse all the ingredients until pureed and set aside.

Heat the oil in a large pot over medium-high heat. Add the pork and brown on all sides. Add the flour, salt, garlic, white pepper, and cumin and stir to coat. Add the crushed tomatoes and pureed vegetables. Pour in the water and bring to a simmer, then reduce the heat and simmer for 30 to 45 minutes, until the sauce is thickened and the pork is tender and cooked through.

Serve with rice and beans and warm tortillas, if desired.

OKLAHOMA | 89

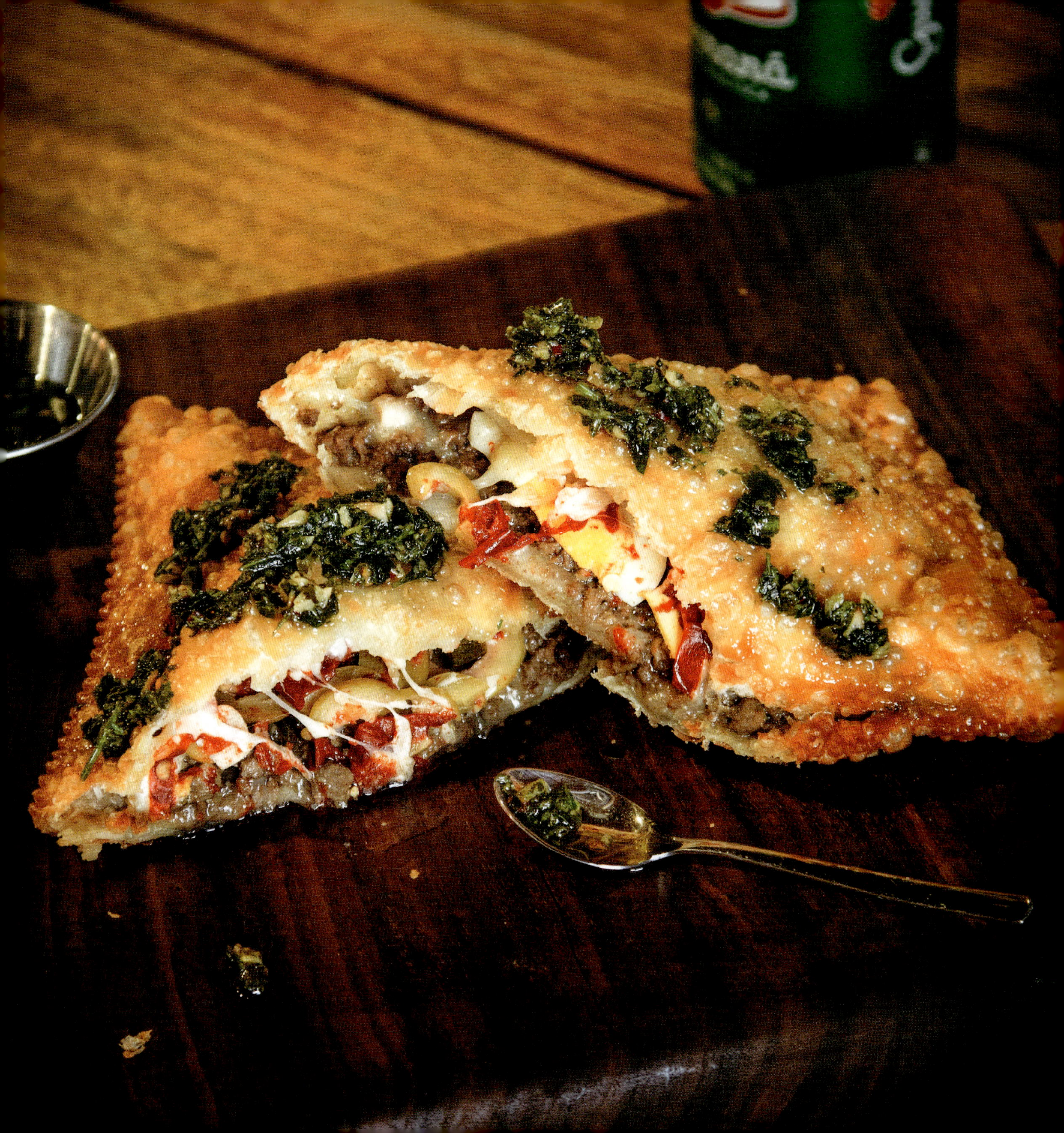

TULSA

CHEF'S SPECIAL PASTEL
Doctor Kustom Bistro ★ MAKES 8 PASTÉIS

FRESH HERB SAUCE
1 bunch parsley, finely chopped
1 bunch cilantro, finely chopped
1 bunch green onions, finely chopped
5 cloves garlic, minced
2 tablespoons (8 g) crushed red pepper flakes
1 cup (235 ml) olive oil
¼ cup (60 ml) distilled white vinegar
Salt and ground black pepper to taste

DOUGH
9 cups (1.1 kg) all-purpose flour, plus more for dusting
3 tablespoons (54 g) fine salt
½ cup (120 ml) olive oil
3 tablespoons (45 ml) cachaça (see sidebar)
3 cups (700 ml) warm water, divided, plus more as needed

FILLING
1 tablespoon (15 ml) olive oil
1 onion, diced
3 cloves garlic, minced
1 pound (455 g) lean ground beef
Salt
1 pound (455 g) shredded mozzarella cheese
20 green olives, thinly sliced
1 jalapeño, thinly sliced
4 hard-boiled eggs, chopped

Neutral oil, for frying

One might think that a place on Route 66 called Doctor Kustom Bistro has something to do with cars, but it's a restaurant—and the very first Brazilian restaurant on the Mother Road. Before he was a chef, Alex Figueira worked in information technology and found a hobby in building motorcycles. After moving to Tulsa in 2016 (and a stint as a chef at another restaurant), Alex realized that he could cook *and* he could build motorcycles, so . . . he could build a food truck! That food truck (named after his motorcycle accessory business) evolved into a food stall at Mother Road Market in 2020 and eventually to a stand-alone space on Route 66 in 2025.

The restaurant is a family affair with his wife, Gi, working alongside as co-chef. Their menu changes each day, but one constant is a collection of pastéis (the plural form of pastel), a popular Brazilian street food. The fillings for the fried hand pies are always different, but this combination—dubbed the Chef's Special—is Alex's personal favorite.

OKLAHOMA | 91

CHEF'S SPECIAL PASTEL
CONTINUED

INSTRUCTIONS

Make the fresh herb sauce: In a large bowl, combine the parsley, cilantro, green onions, garlic, red pepper flakes, oil, and vinegar. Taste and season with salt and pepper to your liking. (This recipe makes more sauce than you need for serving. You can refrigerate any remaining sauce for up to 3 weeks for another use.)

Make the dough: In a large bowl, combine the flour and salt. Make a hole in the center and add the oil, cachaça, and a bit of water. Mix the liquid with the flour little by little with a wooden spoon, each time incorporating more flour from the edge of the hole. If the dough becomes too firm, add a few spoonfuls of water to soften it. If the dough feels too wet or sticky, add a little more flour. Once the dough begins to take shape, transfer to a floured work surface and knead until the dough is smooth, elastic, and no longer sticking to your hands. Let the dough rest for 20 minutes while you prepare the filling.

Make the filling: In a large skillet over medium-high heat, drizzle the oil and add the onion and garlic. Cook for about 5 minutes, or until the onion is soft and translucent, stirring occasionally. Add the ground beef and break it into smaller pieces with a wooden spoon. Cook until all the beef is browned, then season with a few pinches of salt and remove from heat.

Make the pastéis: On a floured work surface, roll out the dough into a long rectangle about 1/16 inch (2 mm) thick. (You should be able to see your hands through the dough. If it isn't thin enough, it won't be crispy after frying.) Cut the dough into 8 rectangles, each about 8 x 7½ inches (20 x 19 cm).

Assemble each pastel by spooning the filling onto one side of each rectangle: a layer of cheese, followed by the beef, olives, jalapeño, hard-boiled eggs, and another layer of cheese on top. Moisten the edges of the dough with a little water and fold the other side over to seal the filling. Press the edges closed. Using a fork, pinch the edges together all the way around. Each pastel should be about 4 x 7½ inches (10 x 19 cm).

Line a plate or platter with paper towels. Heat 2 to 3 inches (5 to 7.5 mm) of oil in a deep, heavy saucepan to 360°F (182°C). Fry the pastéis in batches until the crust is bubbly, crisp, and golden brown. Use a slotted spoon to transfer the finished pastéis to paper towels to drain. Serve with a bowl of fresh herb sauce alongside.

At-Home Tip

Don't skip the cachaça in your dough! The Brazilian spirit (made from sugarcane juice) is the secret ingredient that makes the crust so light and bubbly. If it isn't available, substitute any grain alcohol (such as vodka or rum).

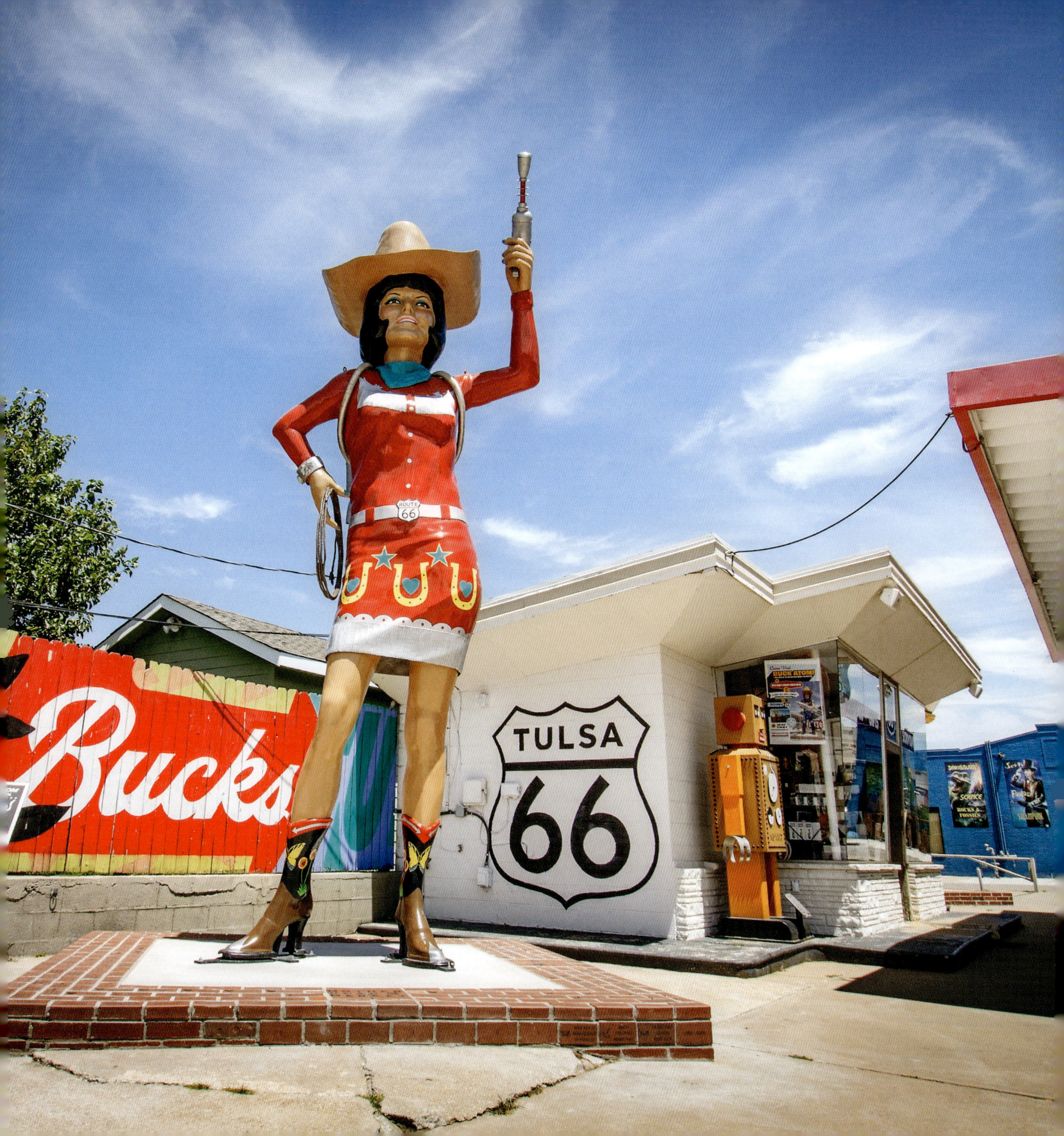
Bucks
TULSA
66

STROUD

POOR MAN'S PECAN PIE, A.K.A. OATMEAL PIE

Rock Cafe ★ MAKES 8 SERVINGS

3 eggs
1 cup (200 g) granulated sugar
¼ cup (55 g) butter, melted
1 cup (80 g) quick oats
1 cup (235 ml) pancake syrup
1 prepared deep-dish 9-inch (23 cm) pie crust
Vanilla ice cream, for serving (optional)

✳ At-Home Tip

The café uses quick oats since they always have those on hand, but you can also use rolled oats or steel cut oats. Any type of syrup will also work, including pure maple syrup if you want a richer flavor. Longtime manager Beverly Thomas recommends placing the pie on an aluminum foil–lined sheet pan to bake, just in case the pie bubbles over a bit. (It makes for easier cleanup!)

Many Route 66 enthusiasts know the Rock Cafe and its owner, Dawn Welch, from the animated movie *Cars*. When the Pixar crew came to Stroud in 2000 to research the fabled highway, they met Dawn and based the movie's main character, Sally Carrera, on the spunky owner—from her color (blue, which was Dawn's daughter's favorite at the time) to her broken neon sign to the "tramp stamp" that was inspired by one of Dawn's stories. But before Dawn's character made the café famous around the globe, it started out as a little truck stop and local gathering spot under a string of other operators.

The Rock Cafe takes its name from the Kellyville sandstone used on the now-iconic building exterior. The stone was left over from a construction project on Route 66, and as legend has it, Roy Rives bought it all for $5 and spent three years building on the land.

The Rock opened in 1939, but Roy never actually ran the business—he left that up to his tenants, including Thelma Holloway, Allene and Ed Riffe, and Ed Smalley. The café flourished during World War II, in part because it doubled as a Greyhound bus stop serving thousands of travelers and service technicians. In 1959, Ed Smalley's aunt, Mamie Mayfield, acquired the lease and operated the café 24/7 until her retirement in 1983. Ed then purchased the building from Roy and spent the next decade renovating it.

Unsure of the café's ultimate fate, Ed held off on selling until serendipity led him to Dawn Welch in 1993. Then 24 years old, with plans to run off to Costa Rica and open a restaurant, Dawn thought she would only stay for six months to learn how to run a business and, you know, cook. She ended up falling in love with Stroud and the simple life, took over the Rock that year, and the rest is history.

This poor man's pecan pie started off as a special at the café. It's a truly foolproof pie, and most people are skeptical that the oats can mimic the texture and flavor of pecans—but you'll have to try it to believe it.

INSTRUCTIONS

Preheat the oven to 325°F (170°C, or gas mark 3). In a medium bowl, combine the eggs, sugar, and butter. Stir in the oats and pancake syrup until all the ingredients are well blended. Pour the mixture into the pie crust and bake for 1 hour. Let cool before slicing and serving. Try it with a scoop of ice cream on top!

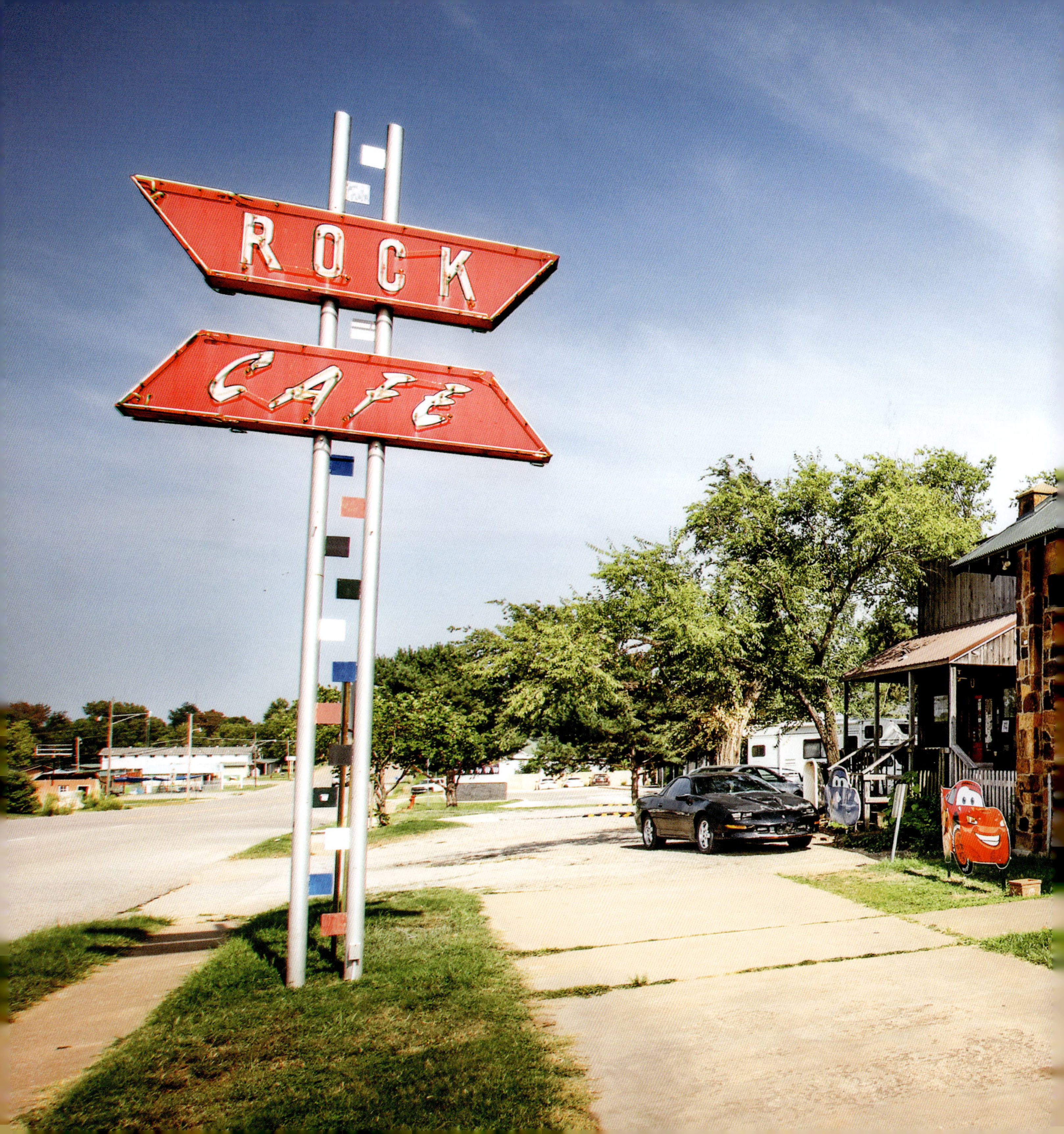
ROCK
CAFE

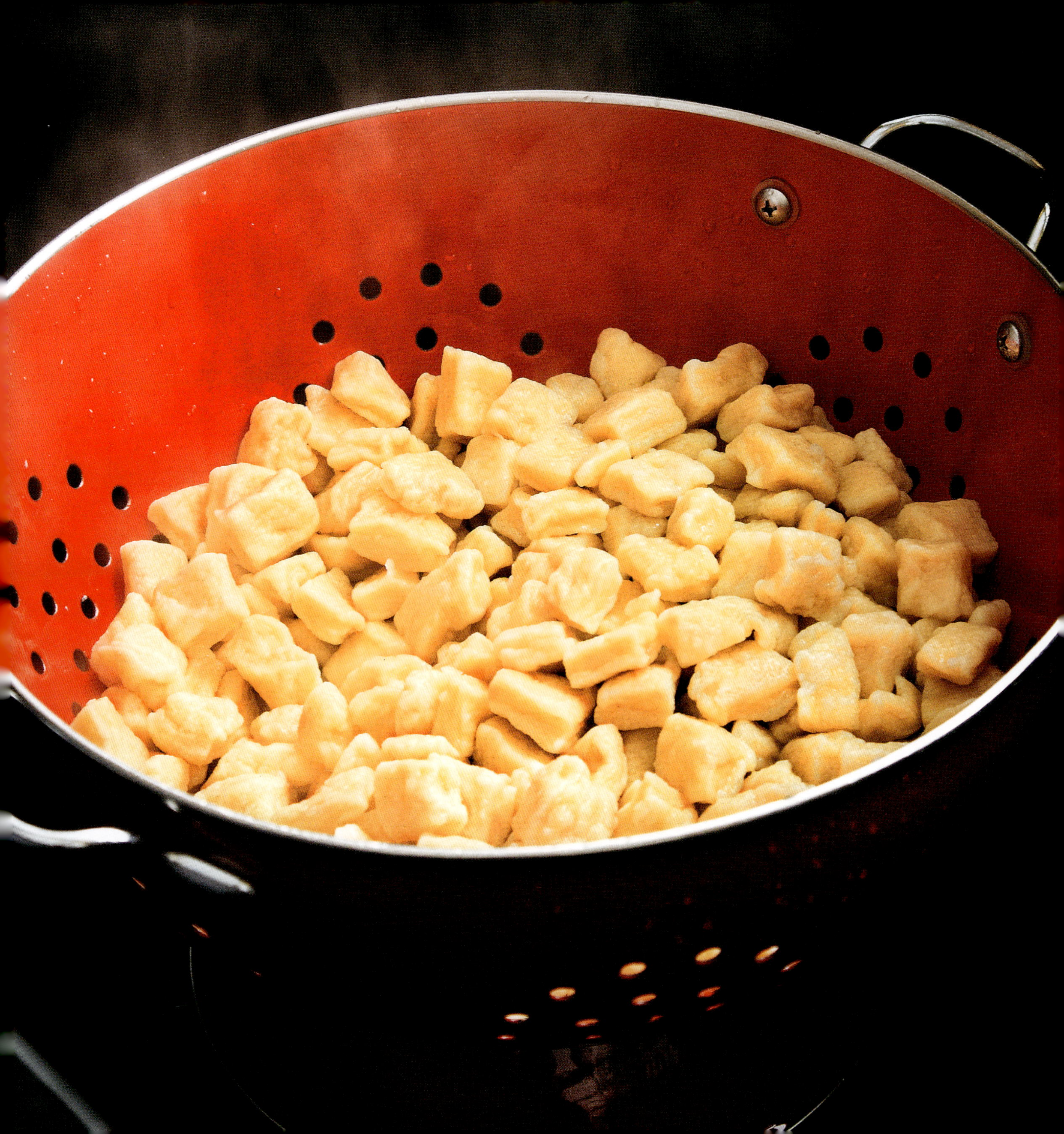

STROUD

SPÄETZLE

Rock Cafe ★ **MAKES 8 SERVINGS**

4 cups (480 g) all-purpose flour, plus more for dusting
3 eggs
1 cup (235 ml) milk
Melted butter, for serving

Späetzle appears several times on the Rock Cafe menu—you'll see it served as a side dish to jagerschnitzel and smothered in gravy; topped with melted cheese for a unique take on mac and cheese; or mixed with onions, bell peppers, and tomatoes. The German-style noodles have a chewy bite, kind of like gnocchi, and came to the Rock via Dawn's first husband's mother (thanks, Gertrude Herr!) from Thun, Switzerland.

INSTRUCTIONS

In a large bowl, add the flour, eggs, and milk. Mix with a rubber spatula until a shaggy dough forms. As the dough comes together, knead it lightly with your hands and gather it into a ball. Transfer the dough to a generously floured surface. Cut off a 1-inch (2.5 cm) section and flatten it into a ¼-inch (13 mm)-thick round with your hands, coating both sides with flour to prevent sticking. Cut the round into ½-inch (13 mm)-wide strips, then rotate all the strips 90 degrees and cut into ½-inch (13 mm)-wide strips again to create squares. (The squares don't have to be perfect or even.) Transfer to a large colander.

Cut off another 1-inch (2.5 cm) section from the dough ball and repeat the flattening and cutting process until there is no dough remaining. Run your hands through the dough squares to loosen them up and shake off excess flour.

Bring a large pot of water to a boil. Add the dough squares and boil for about 15 minutes, or until they float to the top, stirring occasionally. Strain the späetzle and rinse with cold water to remove excess starch. Drain the späetzle, toss with melted butter, and serve warm.

✳

Beverly's Quick Tip

If you don't have the patience to cut the dough into squares with a knife, manager Beverly Thomas recommends using a pizza cutter to speed the process.

OKLAHOMA | 97

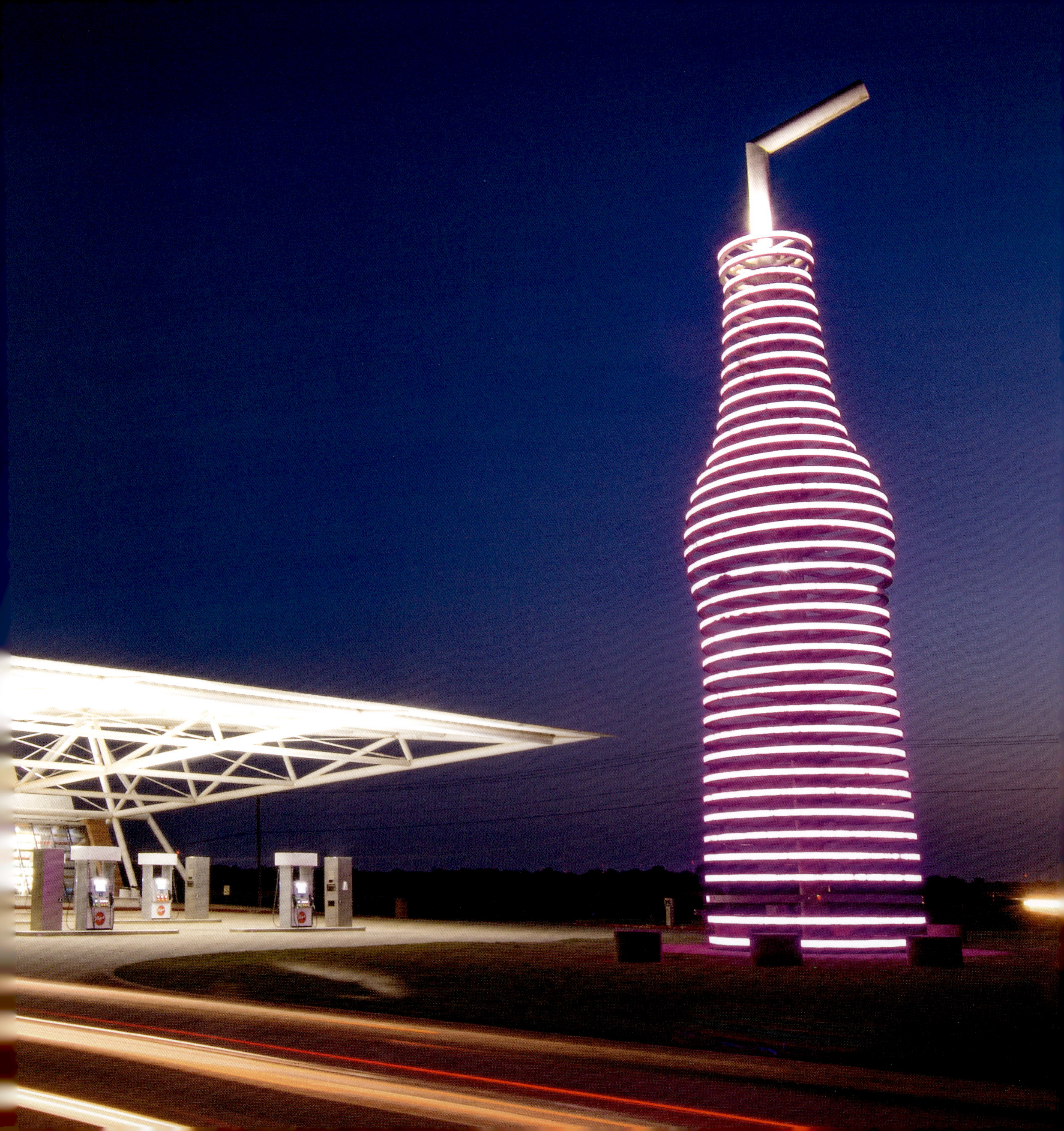

ROOT BEER BREAD PUDDING
Pops 66 ★ MAKES 12 SERVINGS

Nonstick cooking spray

BREAD PUDDING
3 cups (700 ml) heavy cream
4 eggs
⅓ cup (80 ml) root beer syrup (concentrate)
1 tablespoon (15 ml) vanilla extract
½ cup (100 g) granulated sugar
¾ cup (110 g) raisins
1 loaf Texas toast, cut into 1½-inch (4 cm) cubes
¾ cup (170 g) brown sugar

GLAZE
1½ cups (355 ml) heavy cream
2 tablespoons (28 ml) root beer syrup
2 tablespoons (28 g) butter, melted
3 tablespoons (45 g) brown sugar

Purveyor of food, fuel, and fizz, Pops 66 is relatively new as far as Route 66 landmarks go. It was built in 2007 by the late oil and gas magnate Aubrey McClendon, and the iconic 66-foot (20-m) soda bottle sculpture—a stunning spectacle lit by rings of multicolored lights at night—can be seen from miles away in any direction. (Fun fact: The sculpture stands exactly 66 feet [20 m] away from the historic highway.)

True to Route 66 culture, the roadside stop serves travelers as a convenience store, gas station, and restaurant—but most people know it as a soda mecca. The store carries more than 700 types of sodas, ranging from everyday flavors like orange and cola to oddities like ranch dressing–flavored soda and even something called "pimple pop."

Despite the impressive (and at times, totally weird) selection, good old-fashioned root beer is the store's top-selling flavor. At one point, it even produced a proprietary house blend called Round Barn Root Beer (named after the equally iconic attraction just down the road in Arcadia). Root beer is also the star in this signature dessert.

While one might assume that Pops 66 was so-called because it sold, well, lots of soda pops, Pops was actually Aubrey's affectionate nickname for his father. After Aubrey's death in 2016, his estate sold the property and Pops 66 quietly changed hands in 2021.

INSTRUCTIONS
Preheat the oven to 350°F (180°C, or gas mark 4). Lightly coat a 9 x 13-inch (23 x 33 cm) baking dish with cooking spray and set aside.

In a large bowl, whisk the heavy cream, eggs, root beer syrup, vanilla, granulated sugar, and raisins until combined. Add the Texas toast and stir to saturate the bread in the batter. Spread the mixture across the prepared baking dish and sprinkle with brown sugar. Bake for 35 minutes, or until puffed and golden brown and the bread pulls away from the edges of the dish. Let cool for 5 minutes before serving.

Meanwhile, make the glaze by stirring all the glaze ingredients together in a small bowl. Slice and serve the bread pudding with a drizzle of glaze on top.

OKLAHOMA CITY

GREEN CHILE GRIT CAKES
Classen Grill ★ **MAKES 12 GRIT CAKES**

Butter, for greasing
3 cups (700 ml) milk
3 cups (700 ml) chicken or vegetable broth
2 cups (376 g) stone-ground grits
1 tablespoon (18 g) fine salt
5 tablespoons (70 g) butter, plus more for reheating
1 cup (240 g) chopped green chiles
2 cups (450 g) shredded cheddar cheese

In the late 1970s, Tupper and Linda Patnode—members of the local art and theater community—opened the Classen Grill to fund and showcase their work, provide a place for artists to meet, and employ their fellow thespians and writers. The restaurant wasn't breakfast-exclusive back then; dinner was an upscale experience with a full bar, steaks, and chops. The venue was named for its location on Classen Circle, which sat at the intersection of Route 66 and Classen Boulevard.

Today's Classen Circle is—curiously—far from circular or even arcing. It's a straight line. That's because by the mid-1970s, Classen Circle was reconstructed during a Route 66 bypass realignment and the roundabout (for which the road was named) was removed.

By the 1990s, dinner was dropped and the Classen Grill became known for its line-out-the-door weekend breakfast and fresh-squeezed orange juice machine. It survived a planned (and heavily protested) demolition in 2018 before undergoing extensive renovations and reopening in 2024. The new owners, Happy Plate Concepts, expanded the menu *and* brought back the bar and the famous OJ.

INSTRUCTIONS
Grease the bottom of a 9 x 13-inch (23 x 33 cm) sheet pan with butter and set aside.

In a medium saucepan, stir together the milk, broth, grits, and salt. Bring to a boil over medium-high heat, stirring constantly. Cover, reduce the heat to a gentle simmer, and cook for 20 to 25 minutes, until the grits are very thick. Remove from heat and stir in the butter, chiles, and cheese until the cheese is melted. Evenly spread the mixture across the bottom of the prepared sheet pan and let cool to room temperature. Refrigerate for 3 to 4 hours.

Once the grits are fully cooled and very firm, cut them into 12 equal pieces. To serve, reheat the grit cakes in a buttered skillet over medium-high heat for 3 to 4 minutes per side until warm, golden, and crisp.

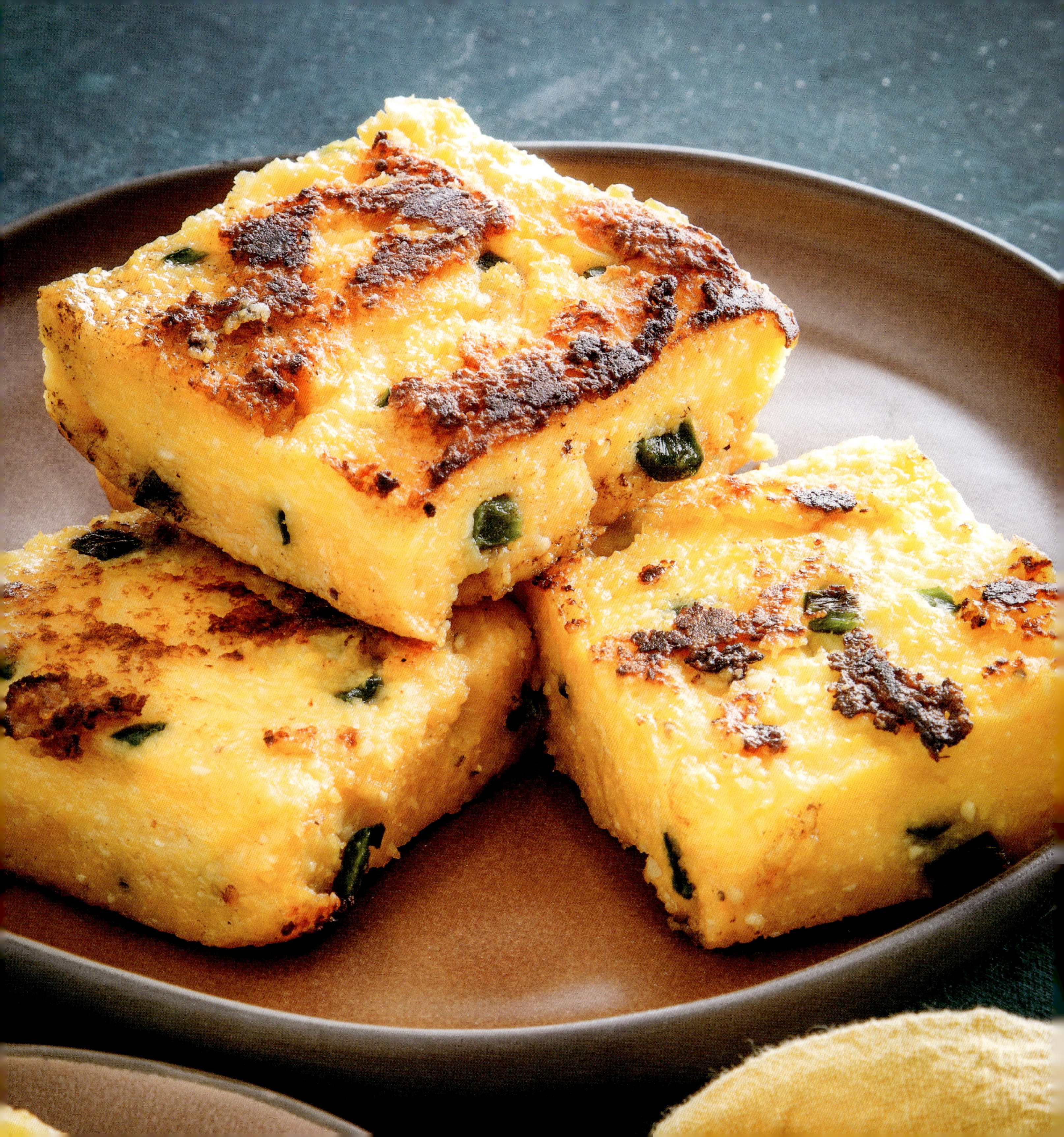

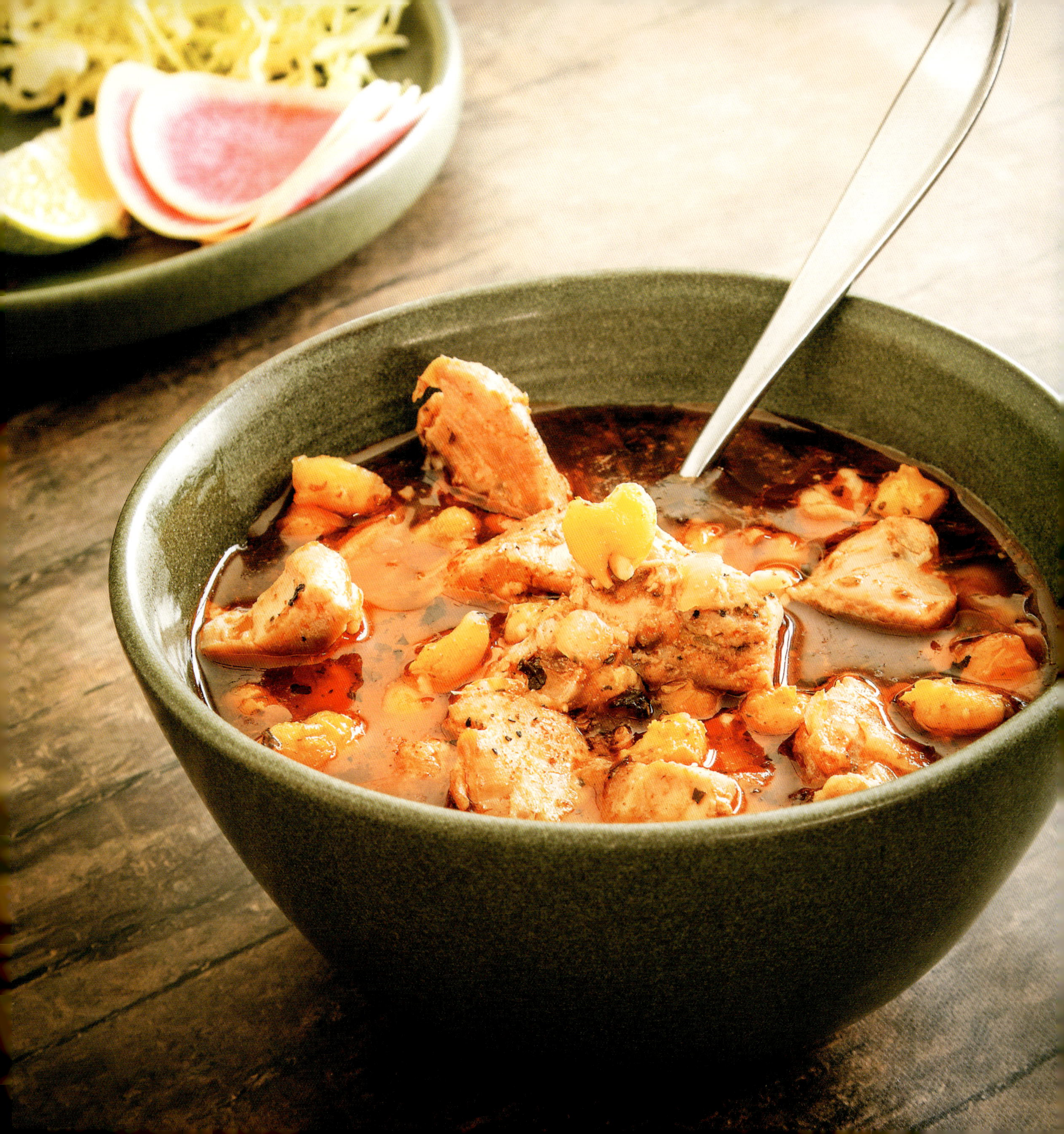

YUKON

POSOLE
Green Chile Kitchen ★ MAKES 4 SERVINGS

MARINADE
2 pounds (910 g) boneless chicken thighs
2 tablespoons (28 ml) olive oil, divided
1 tablespoon (9 g) garlic powder
¼ teaspoon minced garlic
¼ teaspoon fine salt
¼ teaspoon ground black pepper

POSOLE
2 tablespoons (28 ml) neutral oil
½ cup (80 g) chopped onion
½ teaspoon minced garlic
1 tablespoon tomato sauce
1 tablespoon (16 g) BUENO® New Mexican Style Red Chile Sauce
2 teaspoons chicken base
4 cups (946 ml) water

1 teaspoon fine salt
1 teaspoon dried oregano
1 teaspoon Los Chileros® Posole Spice Blend (see sidebar)
1 teaspoon BUENO® Red Chile Powder
½ teaspoon ground cumin
1 bay leaf
1 can (16 ounces, or 455 g) hominy, rinsed and drained

During his college years in Santa Fe, Trevor Logan fell in love with the flavors and food of New Mexico and decided to open the original Green Chile Kitchen in his adopted hometown of San Francisco. His first restaurant spawned two spin-off locations, and he wanted to bring a fourth to Oklahoma, where he grew up and where his family still lived. The Yukon location on Historic Route 66 was no accident: Trevor was trying to decide between two buildings (one in Downtown Yukon and one near Interstate 35) when a visit with a cousin on the Santa Monica Pier led him to the famous "End of the Trail" sign on Route 66.

Together with his siblings, Tara Peters and Trent Logan, Trevor opened Green Chile Kitchen in 2012, becoming the first (and now the oldest) New Mexican restaurant in Oklahoma. It remains a family-run business with Tara managing the restaurant and the kids pitching in.

Staying true to New Mexican cuisine, they use BUENO® Foods chile (another long-standing family-owned and -operated business) in all their recipes, including their traditional posole, a house favorite. You can eat the stew as is, or serve it the way the restaurant does, garnished with chopped cilantro, onion, shredded cabbage, and a side of corn tortillas.

OKLAHOMA | 103

POSOLE
CONTINUED

INSTRUCTIONS

Make the marinade: Place the chicken in a large bowl. Drizzle 1 tablespoon (15 ml) of the olive oil over the chicken and sprinkle the garlic powder, minced garlic, salt, and pepper. Toss to coat the chicken on all sides. Cover with plastic wrap and marinate overnight in the refrigerator.

Make the posole: Cut the marinated chicken into 1-inch (2.5 cm) cubes. Heat the remaining 1 tablespoon (15 ml) olive oil in a large skillet over medium-high heat and add the chicken. Cook until the chicken is browned on all sides, stirring occasionally. Remove from heat and set aside.

In a large saucepan over medium heat, drizzle the neutral oil and add the onion. Cook for about 5 minutes, stirring occasionally, until the onion is translucent. Add the garlic and cook for 1 minute. Add the tomato sauce, red chile sauce, and chicken base and stir to blend. Add the water, salt, oregano, posole spice blend, red chile powder, cumin, and bay leaf and bring to a boil. Stir in the cooked chicken and the hominy, reduce the heat, and simmer uncovered for about 25 minutes to meld all the flavors together.

Discard the bay leaf before serving.

Make Your Own Posole Spice Blend

If you can't source the spice blend from Los Chileros®, you can make a similar blend at home using equal amounts of crushed chile caribe (or crushed red pepper flakes), dried minced onion, dried minced garlic, dried oregano, and salt.

GREEN CHILE APPLE PIE

Green Chile Kitchen ★ MAKES 8 SERVINGS

WALNUT STREUSEL TOPPING

- ¾ cup (88 g) chopped walnuts
- ¾ cup (90 g) all-purpose flour
- ¼ cup (60 g) plus 2 tablespoons (30 g) brown sugar
- ½ cup (112 g) plus 2 tablespoons (28 g) butter, melted

FILLING

- 6 green apples, peeled, cored, and coarsely chopped
- ½ cup (115 g) BUENO® Mild Chopped Green Chile
- ½ cup (64 g) cornstarch
- ½ cup (100 g) granulated sugar
- ¼ cup (60 g) brown sugar
- ½ teaspoon ground cinnamon
- ¼ teaspoon ground nutmeg
- ¼ teaspoon ground allspice
- 1 tablespoon (15 ml) lemon juice
- 1 prepared 9-inch (23 cm) pie crust

When the Logan siblings were growing up, their Grandma Eloise Rose (affectionately referred to as Weezie) always baked the best pies. She passed in 2012, but not before sharing her homemade pie crust recipe—made with half shortening, half butter—which the restaurant still uses today. The scratch-made pies are a house specialty at Green Chile Kitchen, and they're a tribute to Weezie, who lived to be 91 years old.

INSTRUCTIONS

Preheat the oven to 350°F (180°C, or gas mark 4).

Make the walnut streusel topping: In a medium bowl, mix the walnuts, flour, and brown sugar by hand until combined. Add the melted butter and mix again by hand until the mixture is crumbly. Set aside.

Make the filling: In a large bowl, combine the apples, green chile, cornstarch, all the sugars and spices, and the lemon juice.

Mound the filling into the pie crust and sprinkle the walnut streusel topping evenly over the filling. Bake for 20 minutes, then cover the pie with a sheet of aluminum foil and bake for another 45 to 50 minutes, until the juices have set up and are no longer runny.

EL RENO

ONION FRIED BURGER

Sid's Diner ★ MAKES 4 SERVINGS

---

1 pound (455 g) ground Angus beef (70/30)
1 Spanish yellow onion, thinly sliced
Salt and ground black pepper
4 hamburger buns
12 slices dill pickles
Red Boy Brand® prepared mustard

✶ Adam's Tips

- Use a good cast-iron skillet seasoned with salt pork.
- Beef should be on the fattier side (no less than 30% fat).
- Spanish yellow onions are preferred for their smoky sweet flavor (white onions are too hot).
- Use a mandolin to get paper-thin onion slices.

What's now known as a smashburger was originally called a Depression burger, as it was created in the late 1920s when hamburger meat was expensive and scarce, but onions were cheap and plentiful. By smashing onions into a patty, a cook could stretch the meat and feed more railroad workers and motorists for less. The idea was born at a now-defunct Hamburger Inn on Route 66 in El Reno and soon spread to other restaurants.

The burgers are a regional favorite that visitors from all over the world come for at Sid's Diner. Marty Hall built the restaurant in 1989 and named it after his dad, Sid. His son (and second-generation owner) Adam has been working at Sid's Diner for the last thirty years, continuing the Hall family tradition of smashing burgers using a modified masonry trowel that the diner makes (and sells) themselves.

True to Oklahoma style, they keep it simple with Red Boy Brand® mustard (which they say has a little more depth than yellow mustard) and crinkle-cut dill pickles—otherwise, says Adam, the flavor of the burger gets lost in all the other condiments and toppings.

INSTRUCTIONS

To prepare the meat, divide the beef into 4 equal portions and roll each portion into a ball.

Heat a medium cast-iron skillet over medium-high heat. Place a ball of meat in the pan and smash it halfway down with a spatula so it resembles a hockey puck. Pile one-quarter of the sliced onions onto the meat patty and smash the onions down into the patty. Season with a pinch of salt and pepper. Sear for 1 to 1½ minutes, then flip and sear the other side for 1 to 1½ minutes. Use the onions as a visual cue; you want a little bit of char on the edges and good caramelization before you take the patty off.

While the second side is cooking, place a top bun on the patty to warm it and toast the bottom bun in the skillet. Once the patty is almost done cooking, swap the buns by placing the bottom bun on the patty and toasting the top bun in the pan.

Flip the patty and bottom bun into your hand (or a small plate) and remove the top bun from heat. Arrange the pickles on the patty, squeeze some mustard over them, and top with a bun.

Repeat the process with the remaining beef, onion, and buns.

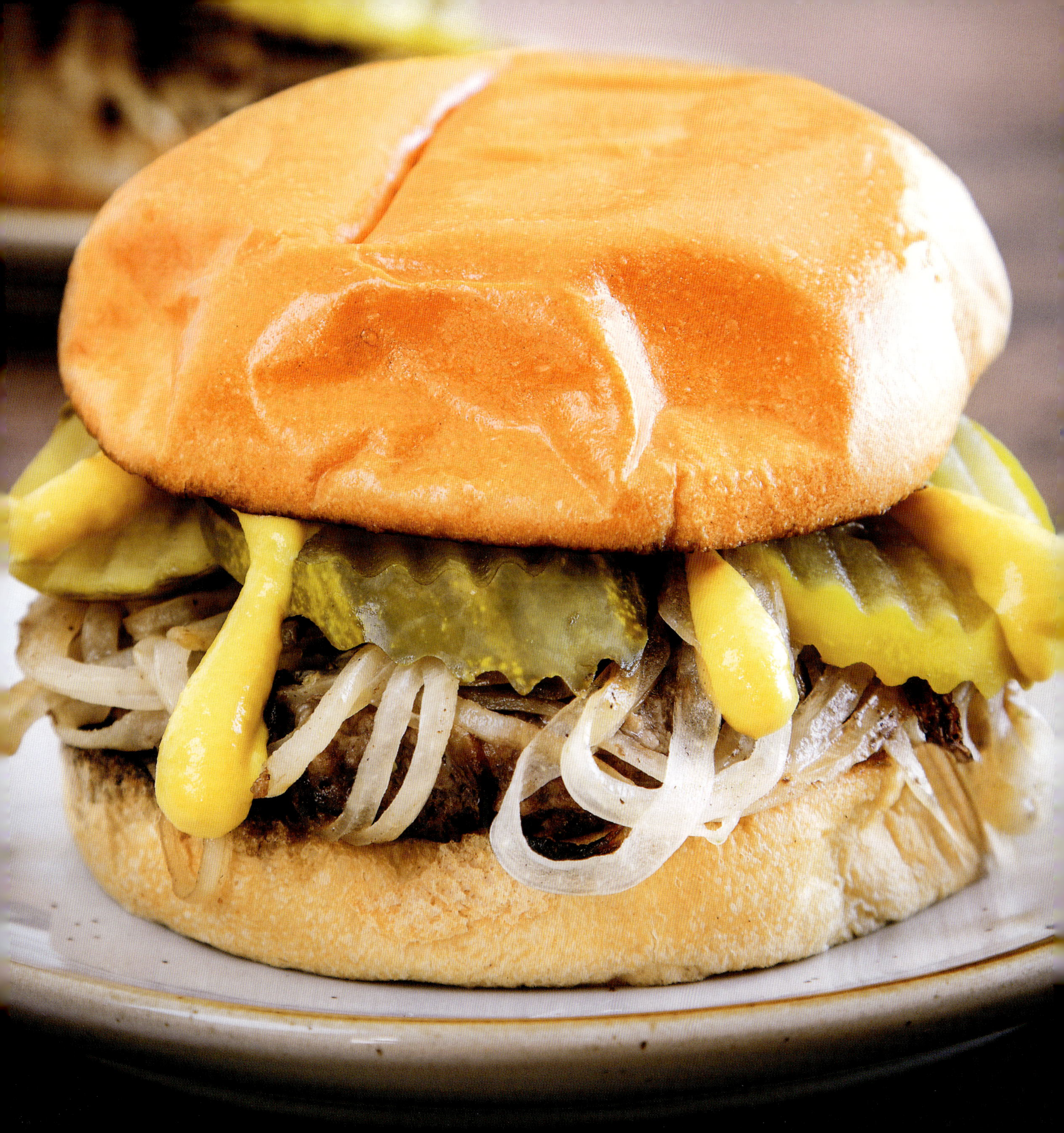

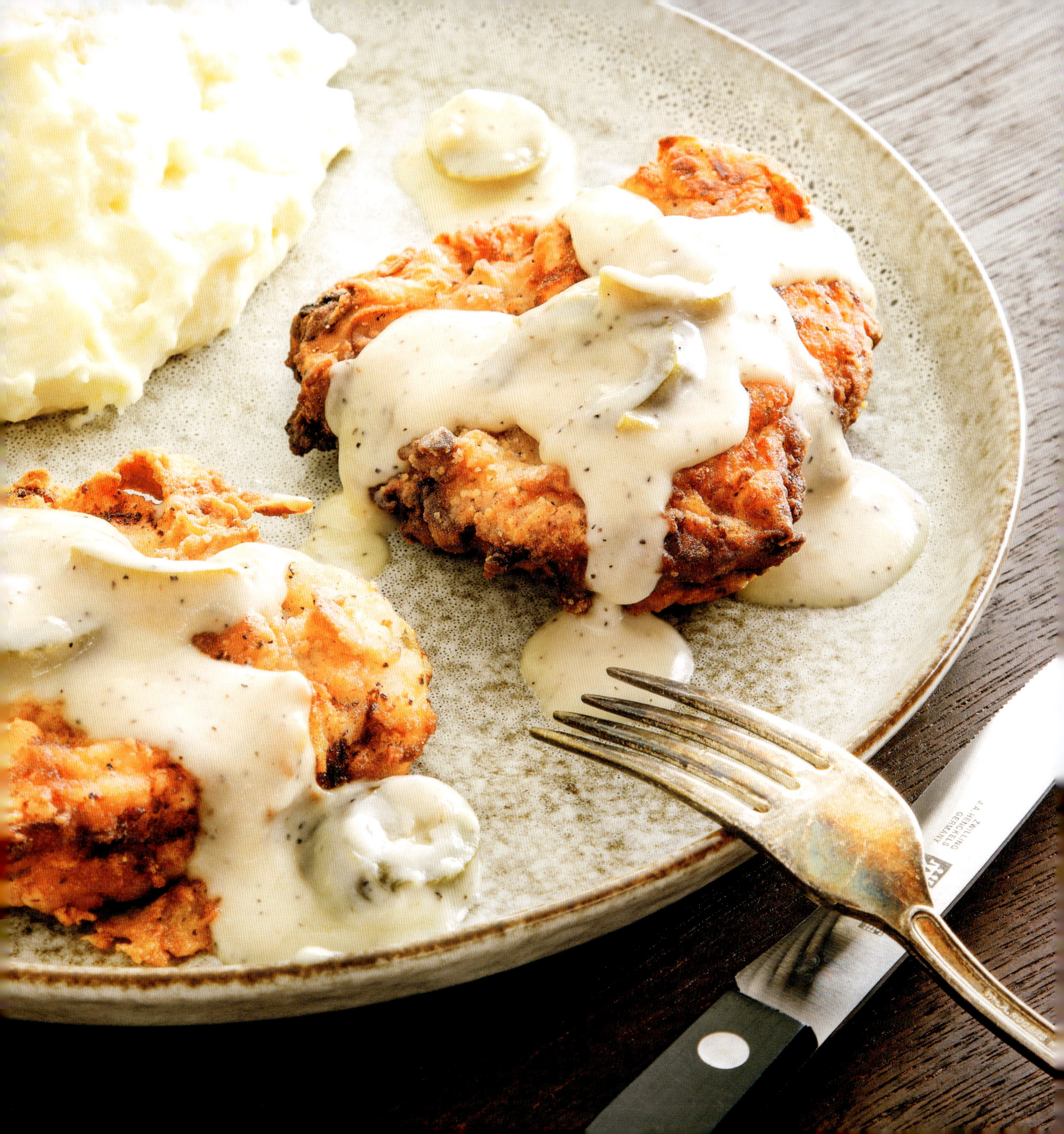
ZWILLING
J.A. HENCKELS
GERMANY

WEATHERFORD

LUCILLE'S JALAPEÑO FRIED PORK CHOPS

Lucille's Roadhouse ★ MAKES 4 TO 6 SERVINGS

JALAPEÑO GRAVY
- ¼ cup (55 g) butter
- ¼ cup (30 g) all-purpose flour
- 1½ teaspoons ground black pepper
- ½ teaspoon fine salt
- ¼ teaspoon garlic powder
- 2 cups (475 ml) milk
- ½ cup (120 ml) jalapeño juice (from canned jalapeños)
- ¼ cup (60 g) canned jalapeños

PORK CHOPS
- 3 to 5 cups (360 to 600 g) all-purpose flour
- 1 teaspoon granulated garlic
- 1 teaspoon ground black pepper
- 1 teaspoon seasoning salt
- ½ teaspoon dried parsley
- 2 pounds (910 g) pork loin, cut into 3-ounce (85 g) portions
- 2 cups (455 ml) buttermilk
- Neutral oil, for frying

Lucille's Roadhouse, the 1950s-themed restaurant on Historic Route 66, was modeled after the original Lucille's just a few miles up the road in Hydro—and that's where the real history lies.

In 1929, Carl Ditmore opened Provine Service Station as a two-story filling station with living quarters upstairs. When Lucille and Carl Hamons took over in 1941, the couple lived in the residence above the pumps with their three children. To make ends meet during World War II, Carl started working as a trucker, leaving Lucille to largely run the business on her own. She pumped gas and fed hungry travelers for the next 59 years.

When Interstate 40 officially bypassed the little station in 1971, Lucille kept the fuel pumps open, welcoming travelers from near and far. Her hospitality was legendary on the road, earning her the nickname of "Mother of the Mother Road," and the station would eventually become known as Lucille's Place. It was listed on the National Register of Historic Places in 1997. After Lucille's death in 2000, a Route 66 enthusiast purchased the station and restored it to preserve her legacy. Her story inspired a replica roadhouse in Weatherford, which opened in 2006 serving scratch-made American classics.

INSTRUCTIONS

Make the jalapeño gravy: Melt the butter in a medium saucepan over medium heat. Whisk in the flour, pepper, salt, and garlic powder until the mixture has a smooth and uniform consistency. Remove from heat and let rest for 10 minutes.

Return the pan to the stove over medium heat. Slowly pour in the milk while whisking continuously. Cook for about 5 minutes, or until the gravy has thickened, stirring occasionally. Whisk in the jalapeño juice until smooth, then add the jalapeños. Keep warm.

Make the pork chops: In a large bowl, combine the flour, garlic, pepper, salt, and parsley to make a breading mix. Pour the buttermilk into a shallow dish. Dip the pork loin, one at a time, into the buttermilk, then coat both sides with the breading mix.

Line a plate with paper towels. Heat 1 to 2 inches (2.5 to 5 cm) of oil in a deep, heavy saucepan to 340°F (171°C). Fry each pork loin for 5 minutes, gently turning halfway through, until golden brown and crisp. Transfer to the prepared plate to drain. Serve with a drizzle of jalapeño gravy on top.

ELK CITY

FRENCH SILK PIE
Country Dove Gift & Tea Room ✶ MAKES 8 SERVINGS

PIE CRUST
1 cup (120 g) all-purpose flour
1 cup (110 g) finely chopped pecans
½ cup (112 g) butter, softened

FILLING
1⅓ cups (267 g) granulated sugar
¾ cup (165 g) butter, softened
2 squares (1 ounce [28 g] each) unsweetened baking chocolate, melted and cooled
2 teaspoons vanilla extract
3 jumbo eggs

WHIPPED CREAM TOPPING
1 cup (235 ml) heavy cream
¼ cup (50 g) granulated sugar
1 teaspoon vanilla extract
Sweetened German chocolate shavings, for sprinkling

Recipe Note
If you're concerned about the safety of consuming raw eggs, use pasteurized eggs for the filling.

Driving down West Third Street—Elk City's Historic Route 66—you might be surprised to find a quaint little tearoom amidst all the chain restaurants and retailers. The Victorian farmhouse, built in 1924, has been home to the Country Dove for over forty years. As soon as you step through the doors, it feels like you're visiting your grandmother in her cozy living room (and honestly, you kind of are). Gifts and home decor line the walls on both floors of the farmhouse, but people really come here for the tea and the simple menu.

Friends and business partners Glenna Hollis and Kay Farmer originally envisioned the Country Dove as a small gift shop. They opened their space in 1983, never imagining they'd go into the restaurant business. A fortuitous encounter with a pair of customers (who owned a restaurant themselves) convinced Glenna and Kay to give it a go in 1986.

Fast-forward to today, and Kay is often cooking in the kitchen while Glenna hosts visitors from far and wide. Their guest books are filled with messages from four generations of customers, many of whom come for a taste of their famous French silk pie.

INSTRUCTIONS

Make the crust: Preheat the oven to 350°F (180°C, or gas mark 4). In a medium bowl, mix all the ingredients until a dough forms. Form the dough into a ball, then press it into the bottom and up the sides of a 10-inch (25 cm) pie pan, creating a thin crust. Bake for 20 minutes. About 9 minutes into baking, check the crust and gently pat down any bubbles with the back of a spoon. Continue baking until golden brown. Remove the crust from the oven and let it cool.

Make the filling: Using a stand mixer fitted with a paddle attachment, cream together the sugar and butter for about 5 minutes, or until thoroughly blended. Beat in the chocolate and vanilla. Add the eggs one at a time, beating for 5 minutes on high speed after each addition. Pour the mixture into the prepared crust and refrigerate for several hours (or overnight).

Make the topping: Using an electric hand mixer, beat the cream, sugar, and vanilla until stiff peaks form. Spread the filling over the pie, then sprinkle chocolate shavings on top.

610
WELCOME
Country Dove
GIFTS
CHRISTIAN BOOKS
ACCESSORIES
OPEN
LUNCH 11-2
GIFT SHOP 9-5

CONOCO
CONOCO
STOP
AUTO LAUNDRY LUBRICATION
OPEN
VISITOR INFORMATION CENTER
SHAMROCK TEXAS
GIFT SHOP

Five
TEXAS

AS THE SECOND SHORTEST STRETCH of Historic 66 in the country, the old highway courses across the Texas Panhandle for less than two hundred miles (322 km) between the tiny towns of Shamrock and Adrian. Most everything else, however, is big: the tumbleweeds, the belt buckles, the food portions, and the flavors. Lone Star cuisine is cowboy comfort food with bold influences from immigrant communities across the state and its New Mexican and Louisiana Creole neighbors. In between roadside oddities and Route 66 relics, you can feast like a rancher on local favorites like barbecue, chili, and Tex-Mex.

AMARILLO

MASHED POTATOES
The Big Texan Steak Ranch ★ MAKES 10 SERVINGS

- 5 pounds (3.6 kg) russet potatoes, peeled and cut into large chunks
- ¾ pound (340 g) sour cream
- ¾ pound (340 g) cream cheese, softened
- 1½ cups (337 g) butter, softened
- 1 tablespoon (18 g) fine salt

As soon as you pull up to The Big Texan Steak Ranch, you'll realize it's very aptly named. Everything here is big: the towering neon cowboy sign, the boot-wearing dinosaur in the parking lot, the famous cow that beckons visitors, and even the compound itself. Besides the banquet hall, beer garden, gift shop, and arcade, there's a center stage for intrepid contestants willing to take on the restaurant's notorious 72-ounce (2 kg) steak challenge. (Yes, you have to eat the baked potato *and* the bread roll with it.)

The steak challenge has been around since 1960 when R. J. Lee opened The Big Texan on Route 66. The restaurant took over the former Underwood's Bar-B-Q location on an older alignment (what is now East Amarillo Boulevard) inside city limits, where liquor sales were prohibited on weekends. Wanting to expand his business, R. J. purchased a tract of land several miles east of town so he could build a weekend tavern.

As luck would have it, this land was situated on what would eventually become I-40—and The Big Texan is perhaps one of the few Route 66–era restaurants that actually flourished *because* of the interstate. R. J. and his family rebuilt The Big Texan on the new land in 1969, then rebuilt even bigger in 1978 after a fire destroyed the restaurant. When R. J. passed away in 1990, his sons Bobby and Danny took over, and The Big Texan remains in the family, continuing to grow each decade. Everything in the restaurant is made from scratch, and the mashed potatoes are one of their most popular side dishes.

INSTRUCTIONS

Place the potatoes in a stockpot and add enough water to cover the potatoes by about 1 inch (2.5 cm). Bring to a gentle boil, then reduce the heat to a simmer and cook for about 20 minutes, or until you can easily pierce the potatoes with a fork. Drain the water. In the same warm pot, lightly mash the potatoes to break them apart. Add the sour cream, cream cheese, butter, and salt and mash all the ingredients together with a potato masher until smooth and fluffy. Do not overmix or the mashed potatoes will become gluey.

✴

At-Home Tip

This recipe is slightly adapted from The Big Texan's original version, which calls for almost 2½ cups (562 g) of butter! If you dare to use that much, try it!

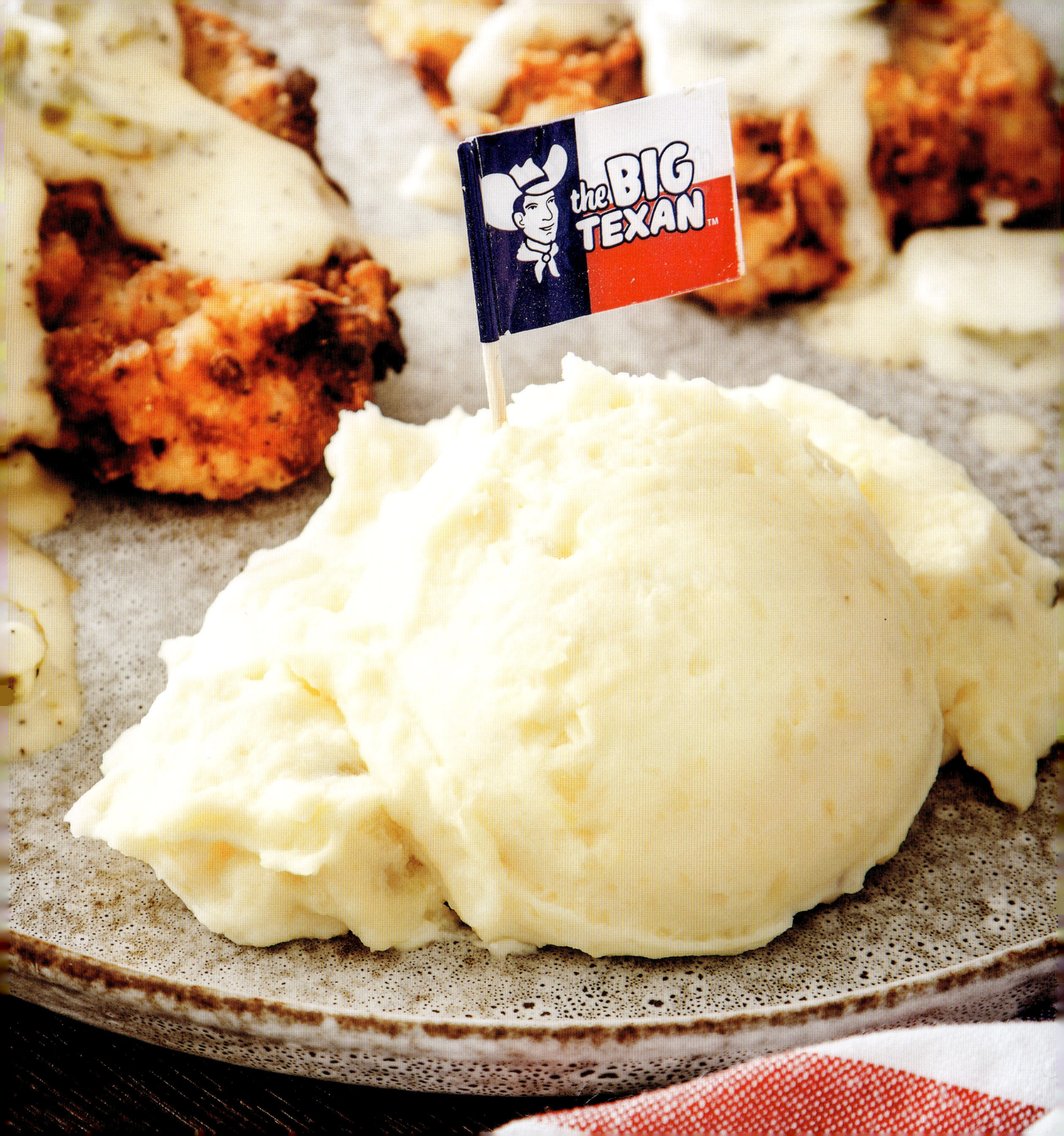
the BIG TEXAN™

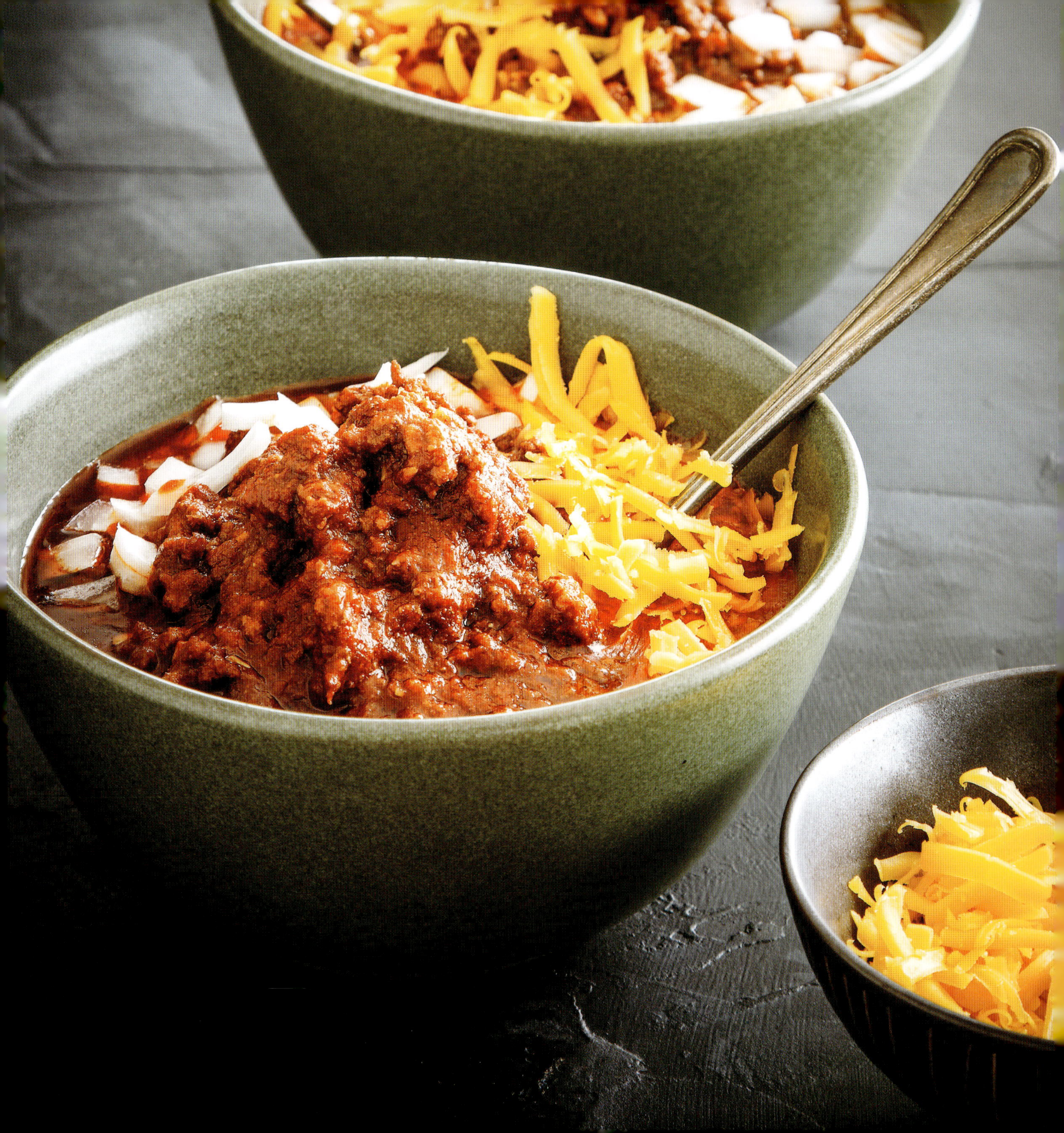

AMARILLO

GOLDENLIGHT CAFE CHILI
The GoldenLight Cafe & Cantina ✶ MAKES 8 SERVINGS

¼ cup (60 ml) olive oil

2½ pounds (1.1 kg) 80/20 ground beef

2 cans (15 ounces [425 g] each) crushed tomatoes

2 cups (475 ml) water

½ cup (64 g) chili powder

¼ cup (40 g) minced garlic

1 tablespoon (7 g) ground cumin

1 teaspoon granulated sugar

Salt and ground black pepper to taste

Diced onions, for garnishing

Shredded cheddar cheese, for garnishing

As you make your way across Route 66, you'll notice the most enduring establishments laying claim to a number of different "oldest" titles, whether it's the oldest restaurant in town, oldest on a particular stretch of the highway, or oldest continuously operating. Well, The GoldenLight Cafe & Cantina has some play in this game: Not only is it the oldest restaurant in Amarillo, but it also claims to be one of the oldest continuously operating restaurants *in the same building* anywhere on Route 66.

Chester "Pop" Ray and his wife, Louise, opened The GoldenLight in 1947 in the very location it's in today. He served burgers until 1957, when he sold to Dorothy Gaulden. Dorothy ran the restaurant until 1979, then passed the torch to Bill and Pat Alexander, who continued to serve the same great burgers as those before them. The fourth owner, Marc Reed, added the Cantina in 1996, and the fifth owner, Angela Corpening, took over in 2001.

With each ownership change, the house chili recipe has also changed. Pop's original recipe was lost, Dorothy wouldn't let anyone have hers, Bill and Pat's recipe was too hard to cook consistently, and Angela could never get Marc's chili quite right. So, she came up with her own recipe, which is her version of a good ol' Texas Red.

INSTRUCTIONS

In a large pot over medium-high heat, drizzle the oil and add the ground beef. Brown the beef until fully cooked, stirring occasionally and breaking up the meat into smaller chunks with a wooden spoon. Add the crushed tomatoes, water, chili powder, garlic, cumin, and sugar and stir to combine. Bring to a boil, then reduce the heat to a simmer and cook for 15 minutes, stirring occasionally. Taste the chili and add salt and pepper to your liking. Serve each bowl with a heaping of diced onions and shredded cheese on top.

WELCOME
ADRIAN, TEXAS
ROUTE
US
66
MIDPOINT
LOS ANGELES
1139 MILES
CHICAGO
1139 MILES

When You're Here,
YOU'RE ALMOST THERE

Cruising west out of Amarillo, the city quickly melts into the flat Texas landscape. Every so often, a grain elevator or two-blink town punctuates the dusty horizon. Don't drive too fast or you'll miss it: a white stripe on the road, marked "Midpoint" and flanked by US 66 shields painted on the asphalt.

Welcome to Adrian, Texas, recognized by (most) authorities as the halfway point between Chicago and Los Angeles. As they like to say—when you're here, you're almost there.

Adrian isn't shy about its designation as the midpoint of Route 66. It says so on a water tower as you come into town; the famous Midpoint Cafe attracts thousands of visitors every year; and across the historic highway, there's even a selfie stand that invites you to take a picture in front of a large sign. With arrows pointing west and east—1,139 miles (1,833 km) to Los Angeles and 1,139 miles (1,833 km) to Chicago—the sign is a (literal) milestone for roadside travelers who've come this far.

You'll often read that Adrian (and specifically, Midpoint Cafe) is the "exact geo-mathematical center of Route 66."

But it's curious that the sign references Los Angeles and not Santa Monica (the official end of the old highway). When you think about it, with all the bypasses and realignments over the years, the midway point was an ever-shifting location.

In the earliest years of Route 66 (when the roads were dusty and the history a little hazy), Adrian was close to being—but was not exactly—the midpoint. (Rough calculations using historical highway data suggest it was somewhere between Adrian and Glenrio.) But by 1937, the midpoint was, mathematically, quite a ways east (due to the New Mexico section of the highway being shortened by more than a hundred miles [161 km]).

There was no "Midpoint Cafe" until 1995, when—as the story goes—the founder of the US Route 66 Association convinced then-owner Fran Houser to rename her restaurant to capitalize on its location. (The painted stripe and sign were installed by subsequent owners Dennis and Donna Purschwitz in 2012.)

But for Route 66 travelers drawn to the romance and lore of the Mother Road, none of this really matters. The fortuitous little café—which likely owes its survival to the well-publicized designation—is considered the longest continuously operating restaurant on US 66 between Amarillo, Texas, and Tucumcari, New Mexico, and the "ugly crust pies" for which it's known (page 122) are a worthy stop in Adrian.

VEGA

BOBBY'S EGG CUSTARD PIE
Mama Jo's Pies & Sweets ★ MAKES 8 SERVINGS

---

3 cups (700 ml) milk
4 eggs
1 cup (200 g) granulated sugar
1 prepared 9-inch (23 cm) pie crust
Grated nutmeg

Who Is Bobby?

This recipe comes from Joann's time at Midpoint Cafe, when Bobby Speed was one of their regulars and became a good friend. His grandparents were among the first settlers in Oldham County, and Grandpa Speed was a Texas Ranger. Bobby, an avid collector of vintage planes, was so fascinated with airplanes and flying that he eventually became one of the best crop dusters in the area. This egg custard pie was one of his all-time favorite comfort foods.

If you're a fan of the famous pies at Midpoint Cafe (like the Elvis Ugly Crust Pie, page 122), you should know it all started with Joann Harwell. In the 1990s, the newly single mom took on a second job at Fran Houser's café as a waitress. She had a collection of her Grandma Glenn's recipes, so after Fran's baker quit, Joann volunteered to make the pies . . . after all, how hard could it be? As she found out, her crusts didn't turn out quite as perfectly as her grandma's—hence the joke of calling them "ugly crust pies"—but they tasted just as good and apparently, everyone else thought so, too.

When Midpoint Cafe was sold to a new owner, Joann moved on with other jobs and interests, but continued to bake for family and friends. After she retired, she decided that she wasn't quite ready to hang up her apron—so she purchased a historic building on Main Street (the original Route 66 alignment) and opened her own bakery in 2022. The pies are still made with the same hand-formed buttery crusts, and Joann believes that every pie made is a pie that comes forth through love.

INSTRUCTIONS

Preheat the oven to 325°F (170°C, or gas mark 3).

Pour the milk into a small saucepan and place over medium heat. Heat the milk, stirring frequently, until bubbles form around the edges and the milk starts to give off steam. (Do not let it boil.) Remove from heat and let cool completely.

In a medium bowl, whisk the eggs and sugar until foamy. Add the milk and whisk until blended. Pour the mixture into the prepared pie crust and sprinkle lightly with nutmeg. Bake for 50 to 60 minutes, until the custard is set.

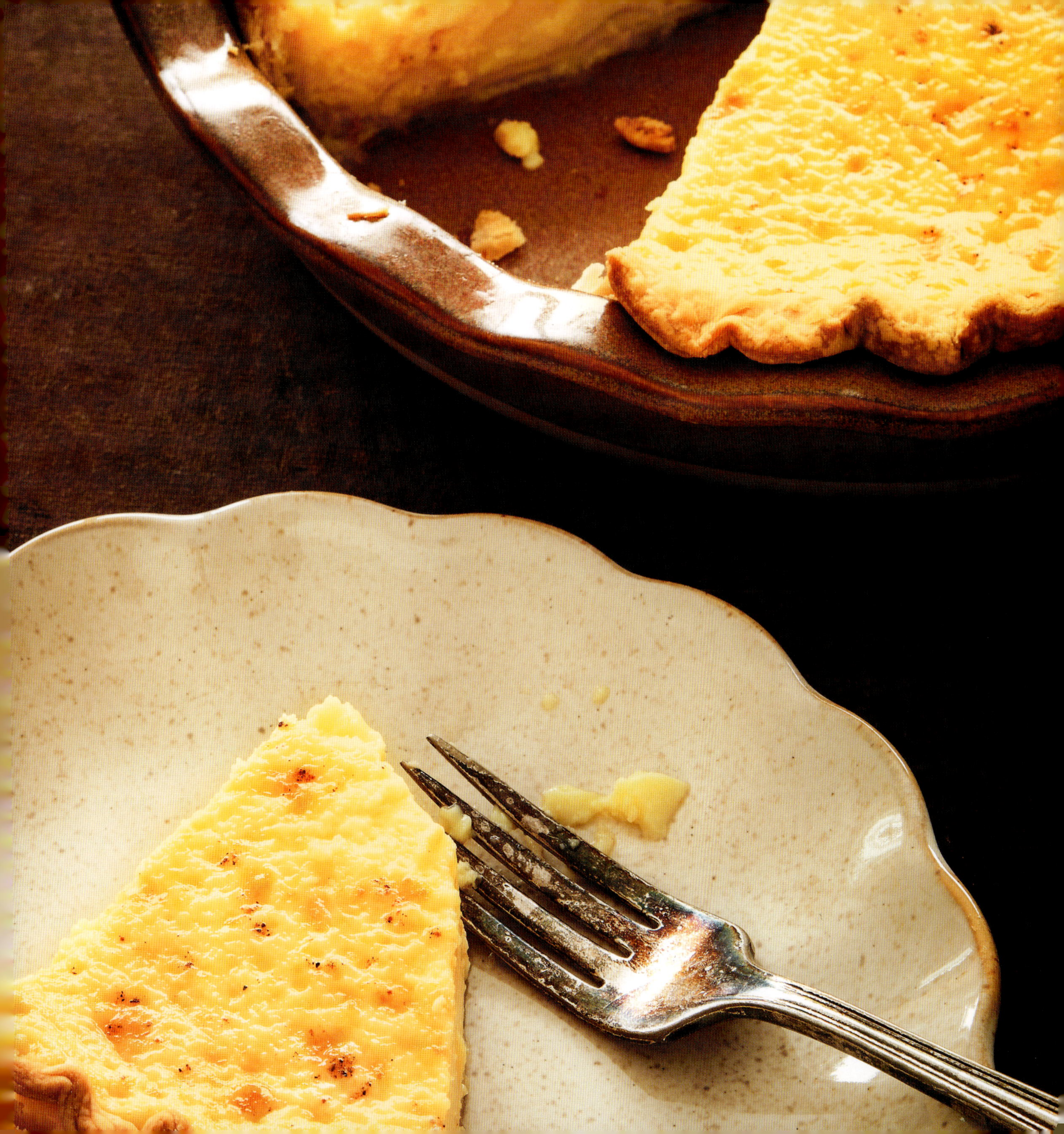

ADRIAN

THE ELVIS UGLY CRUST PIE
Midpoint Cafe ★ MAKES 8 SERVINGS

FILLING
3 cups (700 ml) milk
⅓ cup (109 g) light corn syrup
2 tablespoons (28 g) butter
1½ teaspoons vanilla extract
3 egg yolks
⅔ cup (133 g) granulated sugar
3 tablespoons (24 g) cornstarch
3 tablespoons (21 g) cocoa powder
2 tablespoons (16 g) all-purpose flour
½ teaspoon fine salt

PEANUT BUTTER CRUMBLES
1 cup (250 g) peanut butter
1 cup (120 g) powdered sugar, plus more as needed

TOPPING
1 prepared 9-inch (23 cm) pie crust
2 bananas, sliced
Whipped cream
Grated chocolate
Hershey's chocolate syrup

As the oldest continuously operating Route 66 restaurant between Tucumcari and Amarillo, the building that now houses Midpoint Cafe was originally built in 1928. It underwent several ownership and name changes until Fran Houser bought the business in 1990, calling it Adrian Cafe at first before renaming it Midpoint Cafe. (Get the real scoop behind the name change on page 119.) Fans of the Pixar movie *Cars* might recognize Fran and Midpoint Cafe as the inspiration for the character Flo and Flo's V8 Cafe.

But this wasn't the only reason more people started flocking to the landmark. During this period, one of their waitresses, Joann Harwell (see page 120), started baking pies using her grandmother's recipe—what would become their most famous menu item, the "ugly crust pie." The house-made pies endured even after Brenda Hammit-Bradley took ownership in 2018. Though the recipes have changed (with Brenda's mother taking over as the pastry chef for a spell) and the crusts are far from ugly, the pies are still a highlight of any visit and induce plenty of plate licking.

INSTRUCTIONS

Make the filling: In a medium saucepan over low to medium heat, combine the milk, corn syrup, butter, vanilla extract, and egg yolks. Whisk until the butter is melted and the mixture is smooth. Keep warm. In a medium bowl, combine the sugar, cornstarch, cocoa powder, flour, and salt. Slowly whisk the dry ingredients into the wet ingredients in the saucepan. Bring to a simmer over medium heat, whisking constantly until the mixture begins to thicken. Reduce the heat and whisk for 2 more minutes, then remove from heat.

Make the peanut butter crumbles: Add the peanut butter to a medium bowl. Using a pastry blender, cut the powdered sugar into the peanut butter until a coarse and crumbly texture forms. Add a little more powdered sugar as needed to reach this consistency.

Make the pie: In the prepared pie crust, scatter the peanut butter crumbles across the bottom (save some for garnish). Layer the bananas over the crumbles, then pour the filling on top and let cool. Cover the pie with a layer of whipped cream, then sprinkle with grated chocolate and the remaining peanut butter crumbles. Finish with a generous drizzle of chocolate syrup.

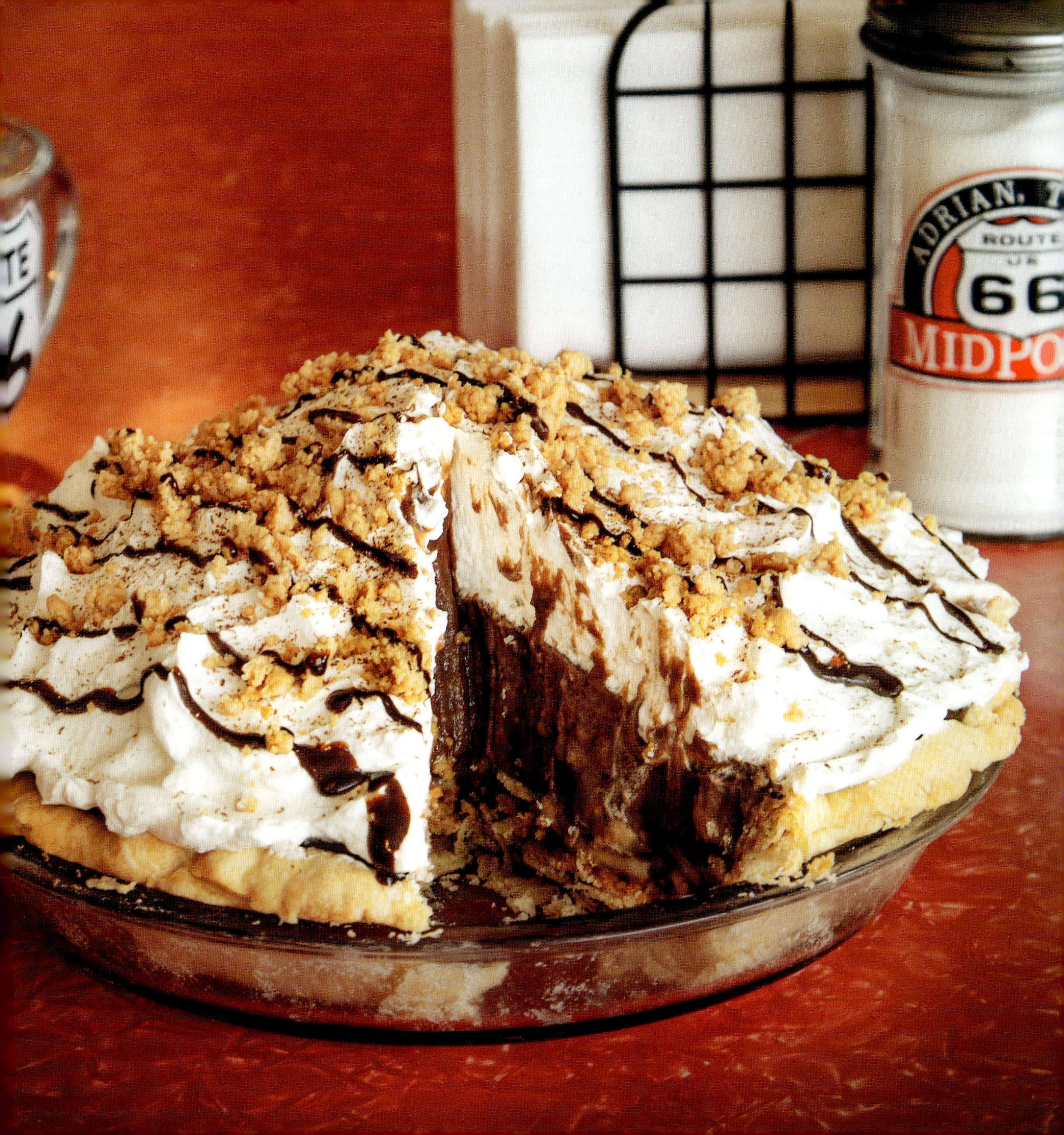
ADRIAN,
ROUTE
US
66

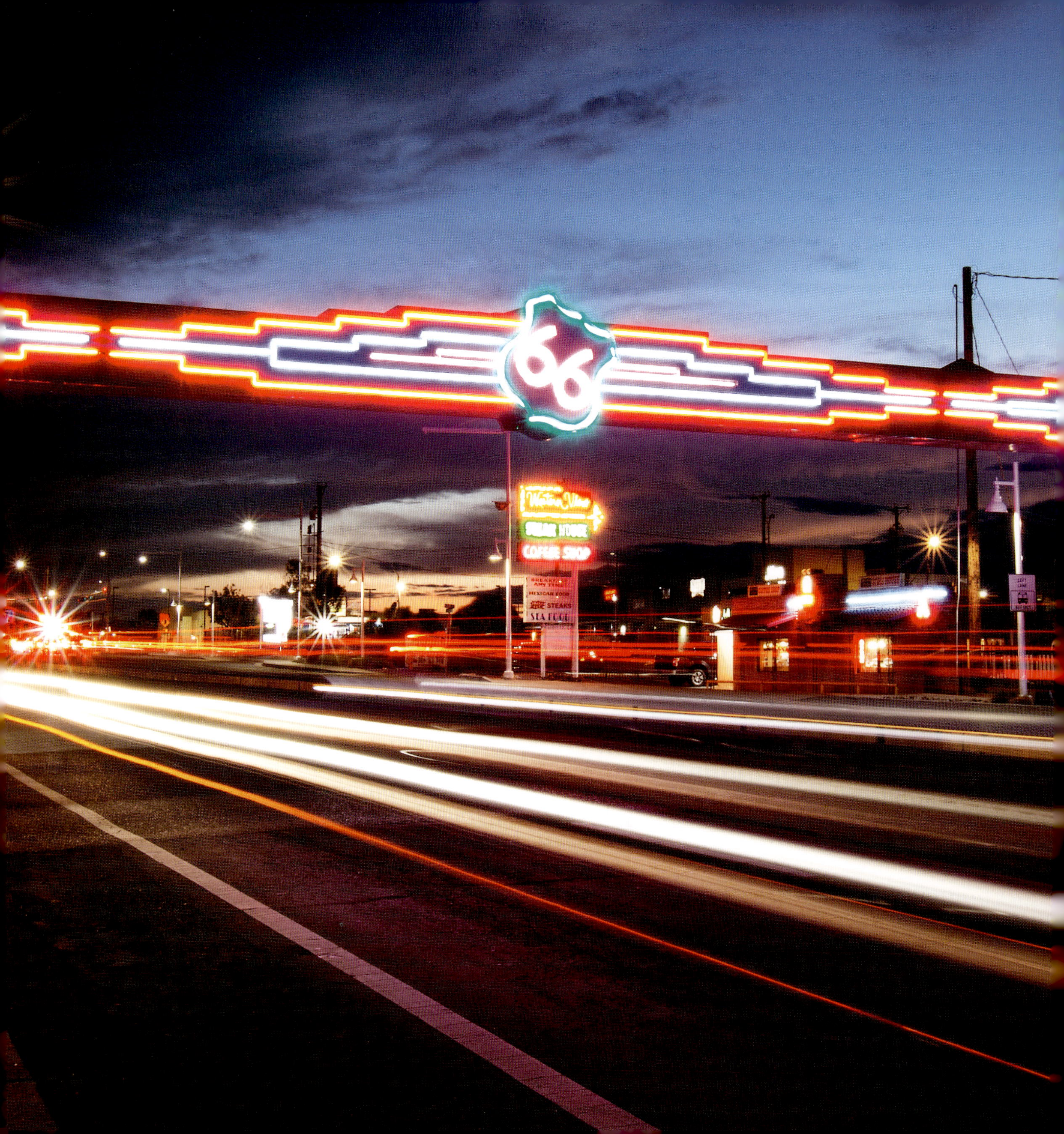
66
COFFEE SHOP
STEAKS
SEA FOOD

Six
NEW MEXICO

MORE THAN FIVE HUNDRED MILES (805 km) of Historic Route 66 wind through New Mexico from the ghost town of Glenrio to the historic village of Manuelito. This segment is a vibrant swath of cultures, weaving together tribal, Spanish, Mexican, and American history in its landscapes, traditions, and food. New Mexican cuisine is bold and fiery, creatively seasoned, and deeply rooted in the region's cultural heritage. This is the land of chiles (which, along with pinto beans, are the official state vegetables), and almost everything you can order is cooked with red or green chiles. Can't decide? Then order your plate "Christmas style" to deck your dish in both sauces.

TUCUMCARI

DEL'S RELLENOS
Del's Restaurant ★ MAKES 6 SERVINGS

6 New Mexico Hatch green chile peppers
½ cup (50 g) panko breadcrumbs
½ cup (60 g) all-purpose flour
½ teaspoon fine salt
3 eggs
3 tablespoons (45 ml) water
8 ounces (225 g) cheddar cheese, cut into long strips about ½-inch (13 mm) wide
Neutral oil, for frying

✴
Chase's No-Fail Tip
Chase recommends frying the chile rellenos while they're frozen; otherwise, they will fall apart in the oil.

Del Akin built his namesake restaurant in 1955, complete with its trademark Hereford bull sitting on top of the towering neon-lit sign. He and his wife, Wilma, owned and operated the business until 1978, when they sold it to Jessica Braziel, Del's former secretary. Jessica ran the restaurant until 1995, at which point her daughters, Yvonne Braziel and Yvette Peacock, took over the family business for another twenty-six years.

During the sisters' time, a fifteen-year-old boy named Chase Waters started working as a host. He eventually graduated and left Tucumcari for a few years to manage restaurants in Texas, all the while keeping in touch with his former bosses. Yvonne and Yvette periodically texted him, asking when he'd come back to buy them out, and in 2021, he finally did. Chase took ownership of the historic restaurant where he'd started as a teen, proud to bring back the neon and be a part of the revitalization of his hometown.

INSTRUCTIONS
Roast the peppers: Line a sheet pan with aluminum foil and arrange the chile peppers in a single layer. Set an oven rack directly underneath the broiler and turn the broiler on. Broil the peppers for about 5 minutes, or until the skins are blackened and blistered. Carefully turn the peppers over and broil for an additional 5 minutes. Remove from the oven and loosely cover the sheet pan with aluminum foil to steam the peppers. Once they're cool enough to handle, peel the skins off completely with your hands.

Prepare the batter: Spread the panko across a wide shallow bowl. In a second shallow bowl, combine the flour and salt. In a third shallow bowl, whisk the eggs with the water.

Make the chile rellenos: Cut a small slit about ½ inch (13 mm) across the top of each pepper near the stem. Stuff a piece of cheese inside each pepper through the slit.

Dip a pepper in the egg wash, roll it in the flour mixture, dip it again in the egg wash, and roll it in the panko until evenly coated on both sides. Return the pepper to the sheet pan. Repeat the process with the remaining peppers, then put them in the freezer until firm.

Line a plate with paper towels. Heat 2 inches (5 cm) of oil in a deep, heavy saucepan to 360°F (182°C). Fry the frozen peppers in batches until golden brown. Transfer to the prepared plate to drain. Serve immediately with salsa, queso, or other sauce choice smothered on top.

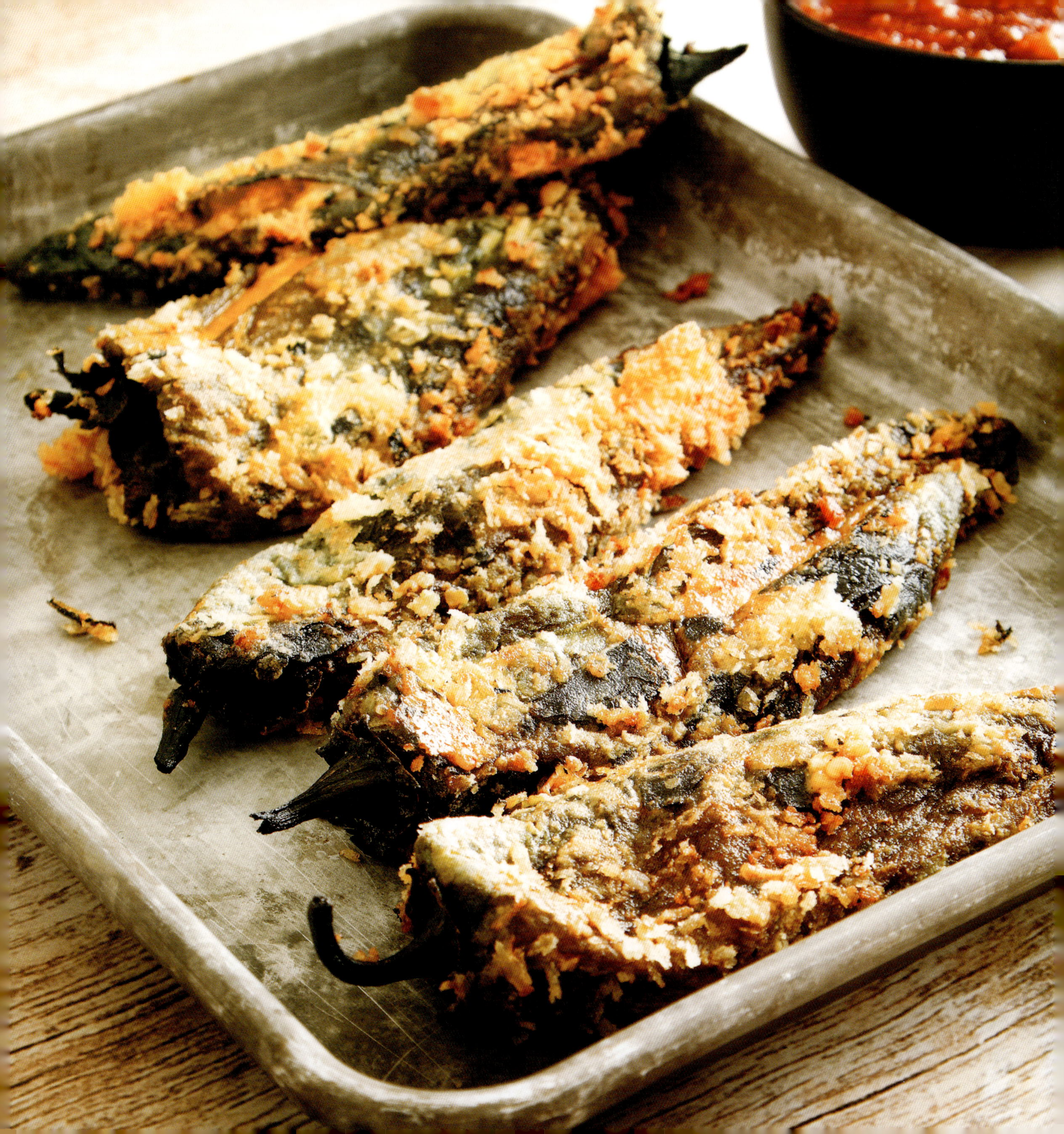

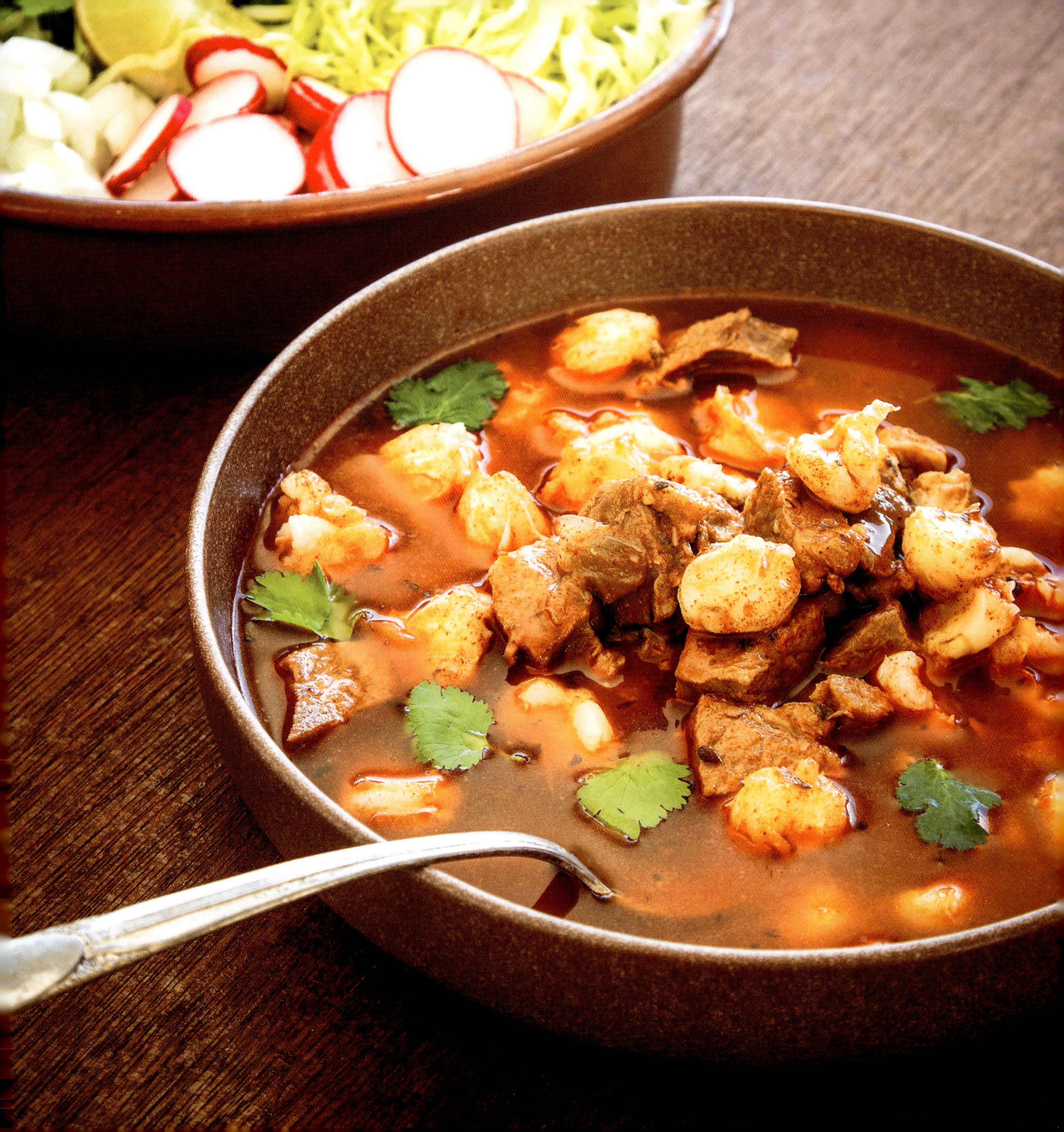

> SANTA ROSA

NEW MEXICAN POSOLE

Silver Moon Cafe ★ MAKES 8 SERVINGS

- 1 pound (455 g) dry hominy (approximately 2 cups)
- 2 quarts (1.9 L) water
- 1 pound (455 g) lean boneless pork shoulder or boneless chicken thighs, cut into bite-size pieces
- 1 onion, cut into 1-inch (2.5 cm) chunks
- 4 cloves garlic, minced
- 3 tablespoons (9 g) New Mexican red chile powder
- 1 tablespoon (18 g) fine salt
- 2 teaspoons dried oregano
- Warm tortillas, for serving
- Lime wedges, for garnishing
- Chopped cilantro, for garnishing

✳ At-Home Tip

For me, posole is all about the garnishes! While the soup cooks, I prepare a platter of thinly sliced cabbage or romaine lettuce, thinly sliced radishes, and diced white onion.

If you want to reduce cooking time, you can use 2 cans (25 ounces, or 710 g each) of hominy, drained and rinsed, in place of the soaked hominy. Simmer the pork and aromatics in 2 quarts (1.9 L) water for 30 minutes, then add the canned hominy for the last 30 minutes of simmering.

Today's Silver Moon Cafe started as McBee's Silver Moon Texaco, a gas station complex that included the Silver Moon Restaurant and Silver Moon Motel. While historical records say the restaurant opened in 1959, a little digging reveals it may have existed even earlier than that. One newspaper article from the same year mentioned that owner Eddie McBee was hoping to "reopen" his café, and a local 1948 newspaper ad mentions a Silver Moon Station.

McBee's gas station and motel eventually evolved into other businesses, but the Silver Moon Cafe (now owned by Keith Ross) remains steadfast as a landmark eatery on Route 66. It's a longtime favorite among locals, truckers, and travelers for its signature New Mexican dishes and American comfort classics, and the restaurant often shares this posole recipe with diners. The spicy New Mexican stew is a ceremonial dish for celebrating life's blessings, and it's traditionally served on Christmas and New Year's Eve.

INSTRUCTIONS

Place the hominy in a medium bowl and cover with 2 inches (5 cm) of water. Soak overnight for at least 8 hours.

The next day, drain and rinse the hominy. Add the hominy and water to a large pot and bring to a boil. Cover with a lid, reduce the heat, and simmer for 1 hour.

Add the pork (or chicken), onion, garlic, chile powder, salt, and oregano and bring to a slow boil. Cover and simmer for about 1 hour over low to medium heat, or until the hominy has burst and is al dente (chewy and tender but not overcooked).

Serve immediately with warm tortillas, garnished, if desired, with lime wedges and cilantro.

La Fonda
On the Plaza
La Plazuela
RESTAURANT
CYNDE ROOF FINE ART

SANTA FE

CHILES RELLENOS DE CAMARÓN
La Plazuela at La Fonda on the Plaza ★ MAKES 3 SERVINGS

SALSA
3 cups (700 ml) water
10 Roma tomatoes, coarsely chopped
1 yellow onion, coarsely chopped
5 cloves garlic, coarsely chopped
8 pieces of toasted chile de árbol
1 bunch cilantro
Salt

CHILES RELLENOS
2 tablespoons (28 ml) neutral oil, plus more for frying
1 yellow onion, finely diced
5 cloves garlic, minced
1 pound (455 g) shrimp, peeled, deveined, and chopped
1 cup (164 g) fresh roasted corn kernels
3 Roma tomatoes, finely diced
2 tablespoons (2 g) chopped cilantro
1 teaspoon ground cumin
1 teaspoon ground black pepper
Salt
1½ cups (112 g) shredded asadero cheese
¾ cup (84 g) grated Oaxaca cheese
2 cups (475 ml) egg whites
3 egg yolks
6 poblano chiles, roasted and peeled (see sidebar)
Chopped cilantro, for garnishing

Here's a bit of trivia for you: The intersection occupied by La Fonda is quite possibly the oldest hotel corner in the country. What's even more impressive is that while La Fonda has stood on that corner for over a century, other adobe inns preceded it—in the same spot—for three hundred years! Early records indicate that an inn, or "fonda," was already operating at that site when Spanish settlers established the city in 1607.

When the last of these inns burned down in 1912, a group of residents formed the Santa Fe Builders Corporation and constructed a new and larger hotel in its place. La Fonda opened in 1922 with a "faux-dobe" style (stucco-covered timber and brick) designed by Isaac Hamilton Rapp, an architect credited with creating the distinctive Santa Fe style.

In 1925, the Atchison, Topeka & Santa Fe Railway purchased the building. Route 66 opened right behind La Fonda the following year, and it was leased to the Fred Harvey Company. With burgeoning demand for hotel rooms, Fred Harvey recruited his longtime designer, Mary Colter, and a young architect, John Gaw Meem, to expand and redesign the structure in the style of Acoma's San Estevan del Rey Mission Church. Mary executed a total interior redesign and—true to her signature—incorporated elements of Spanish and Southwest Native American design in the guest rooms and public spaces. When La Fonda reopened in 1929, it stood as one of the most exceptional Harvey Houses in the country.

La Fonda continued to operate under the Fred Harvey Company until it was sold to Sam and Ethel Ballen in 1968. By then, much of the hotel had fallen into disrepair, Santa Fe had long been bypassed by Route 66, and budget-minded travelers were opting to stay in motor lodges. After nearly fifty years and many building improvements, the Ballen family passed ownership to their longtime friend, Jenny Kimball.

NEW MEXICO | 131

CHILES RELLENOS DE CAMARÓN

CONTINUED

Jenny and a group of local investors purchased La Fonda in 2014 with the aim of resurrecting the historical hotel and preserving its Harvey House legacy. They fully restored La Fonda to the Mary Colter traditions, and many elements of the original design can still be seen throughout the hotel, including the 1920s patio where its restaurant, La Plazuela, now stands.

INSTRUCTIONS

Make the salsa: In a medium pan over medium-high heat, combine the water, tomatoes, onion, garlic, chile de árbol, and cilantro. Bring to a simmer and simmer for about 20 minutes, or until all the vegetables are soft. Remove from heat and let cool slightly. Transfer the mixture to a blender and blend until smooth. Taste and add salt as desired. Set aside.

Make the chiles rellenos: In a large pan over medium-high heat, drizzle the oil and add the onion. Cook for 2 to 3 minutes, until the onion starts to turn translucent. Add the garlic, shrimp, and corn and cook for about 6 minutes, or until the shrimp starts to turn opaque, stirring occasionally. Add the tomatoes, cilantro, cumin, and pepper and cook for 2 more minutes, until the shrimp is cooked through. Taste and season with salt to your liking.

In a small bowl, combine the asadero and Oaxaca cheeses. In another small bowl, whisk the egg whites until foamy. Whisk in the egg yolks until the egg batter is well blended.

Cut a 2-inch (5 cm) slit lengthwise in each poblano pepper and stuff the pepper with the shrimp mixture and the cheese mixture. Do not overstuff; you want the peppers to be able to close.

Line a plate with paper towels. Heat 2 inches (5 cm) of oil in a deep, heavy saucepan to 360°F (182°C). Working in batches, dip a stuffed chile into the egg batter to coat on all sides. Fry each chile for about 4 minutes, or until golden brown, then transfer to the prepared plate to drain.

Garnish with cilantro and serve with the salsa.

At-Home Tip

Since you'll be stuffing them, get the largest poblano peppers you can find.

The easiest way to roast a batch of poblano peppers is to use your oven. Place the peppers on an aluminum foil–lined sheet pan and broil for 10 minutes, flipping halfway through, until the skins are blistered and blackened on both sides. Remove from the oven, cover with aluminum foil, and steam for 10 to 15 minutes. Once they've cooled, carefully peel the skins with your hands.

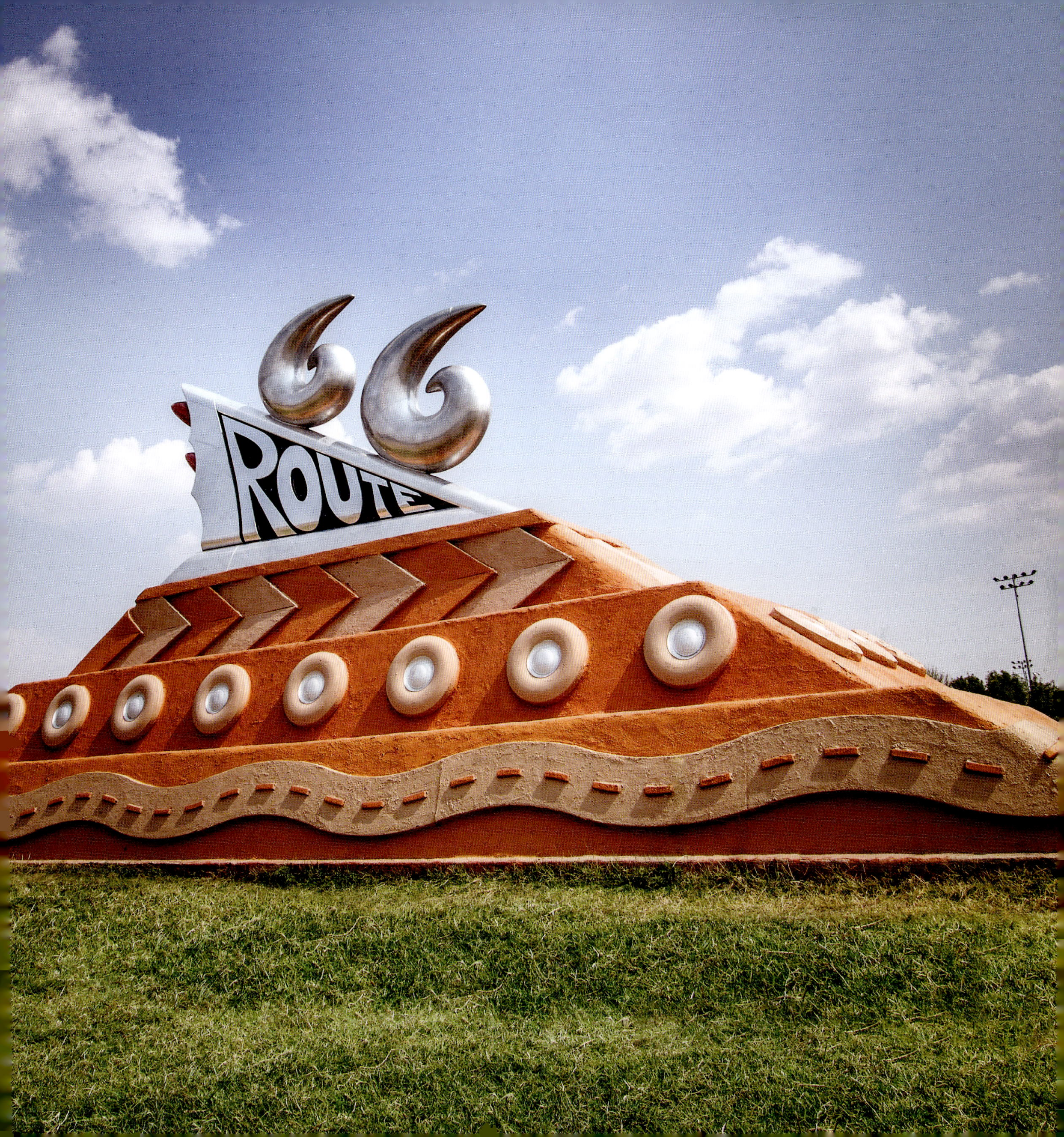
66
ROUTE

ALBUQUERQUE

TATTOOED LADY AND SONORAN DOG
Clowndog Hot Dog Parlor ★ MAKES 1 SERVING

---

1 hot dog bun
1 hot dog, cooked

TATTOOED LADY
Chopped cooked bacon
Flame-roasted jalapeño salsa
Grape jelly
Mustard
Froot Loops® cereal

SONORAN HOT DOG
Chopped bacon
Cooked pinto beans
Flame-roasted jalapeño salsa
Chopped tomatoes
Chopped onions
Mustard
Ranch dressing

With a name like Clowndog, it's no surprise that this Nob Hill restaurant offers a veritable freak show of toppings. Sure, you can get a standard Chicago dog here and more unusual fixings like olives, fried eggs, or even mac and cheese. But where Clowndog really stands out is its assortment of head-scratching toppings: popcorn, chocolate sauce, peanut butter and jelly, and a number of other items that make you wonder who came up with these crazy ideas.

Well, owner Rich Bartel did. Inspired by similar build-your-own-hot-dog places in his hometown of Cleveland, Ohio, Rich opened Clowndog in 2021 with a vast menu that lets you customize your hot dog or choose from one of their premade concoctions. It all starts with a great hot dog—after that, allow your imagination to flow.

The Tattooed Lady sounds like a scary combination, but is surprisingly delicious with its balance of salty, spicy, sweet, and umami. (Don't be shy with the Froot Loops®—the crunch makes it.) And the Sonoran Dog (one of their big sellers) is a savory nod to the Southwest.

INSTRUCTIONS
Assemble your hot dog of choice by piling on the toppings and serve immediately.

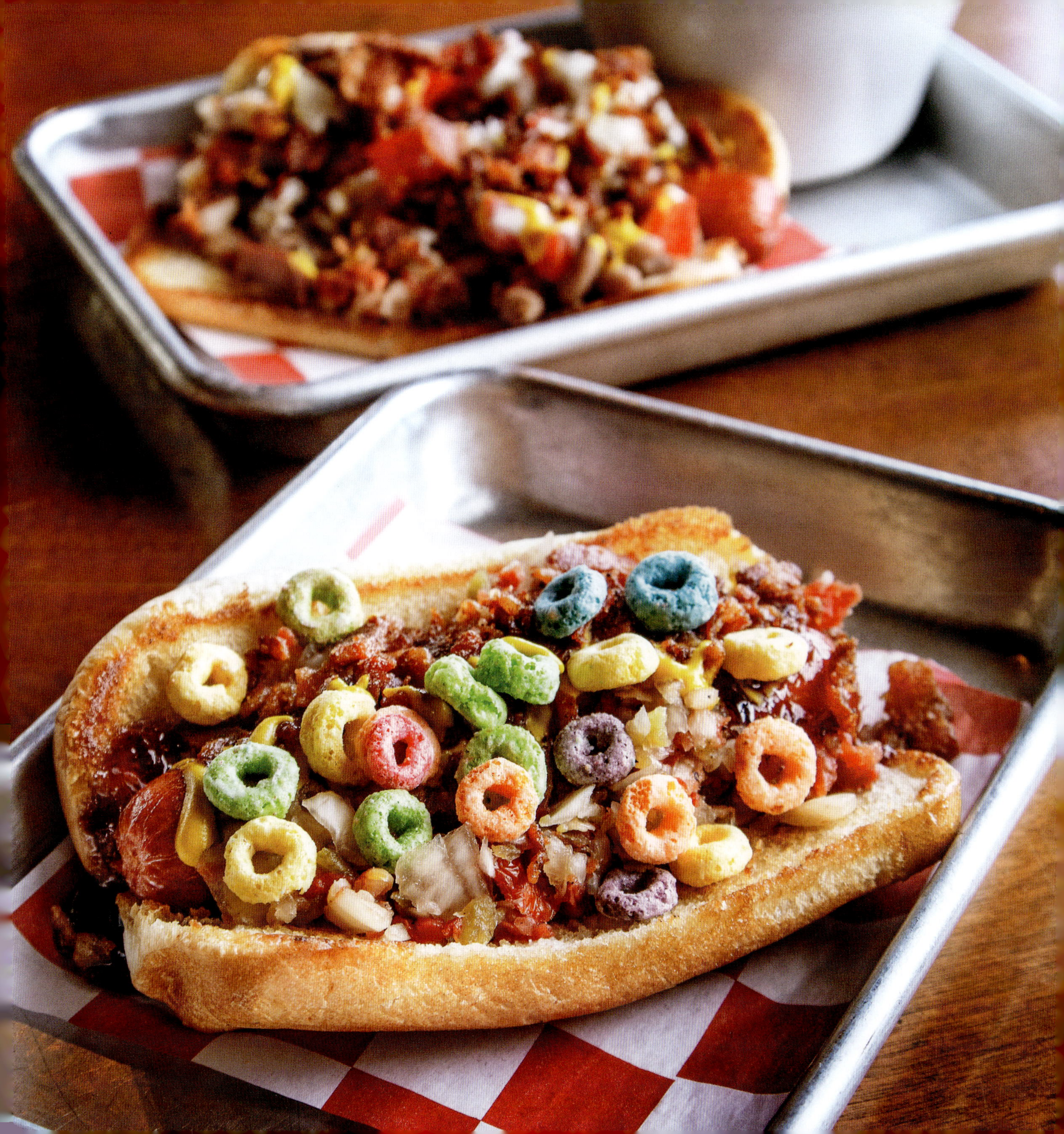

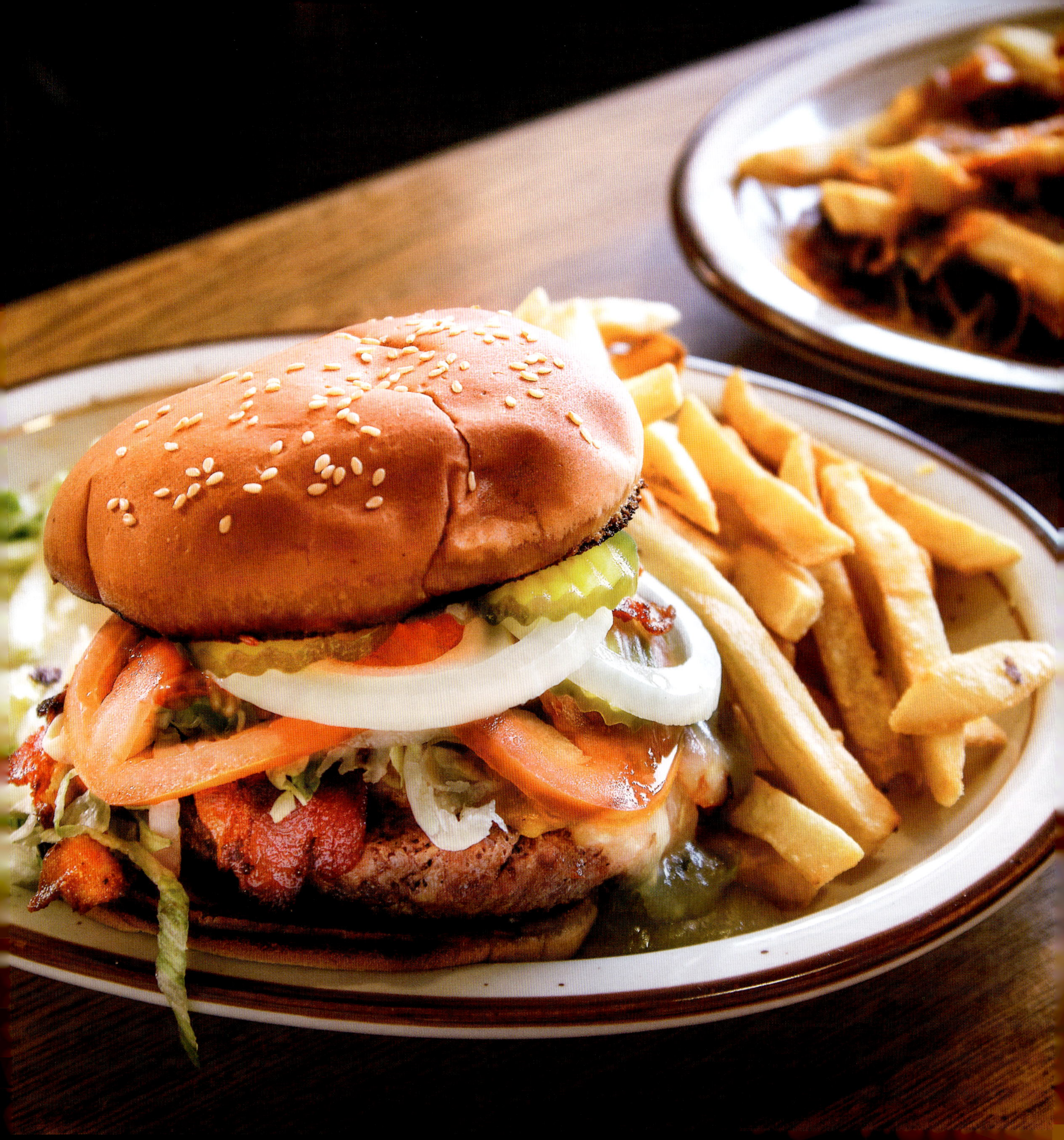

ALBUQUERQUE

SUPER BURGER
Western View Diner & Steakhouse ★ MAKES 2 SERVINGS

12 ounces (240 g) ground 80/20 Angus beef
Salt and ground black pepper
Butter
2 sesame seed hamburger buns, halved
4 slices applewood bacon, cut in half crosswise
2 slices Swiss cheese
2 slices American cheese
2/3 cup (160 ml) green chile sauce, warmed

OPTIONAL TOPPINGS
Lettuce
Pickles
Sliced tomato
Sliced onion

If you dined at Western View when you were a child and came back with your own child decades later, you'll notice that not much has changed. Models of classic cars line the shelves behind the old-school cash register, and photos of vintage Hollywood stars adorn the walls. The diner's age is evident in the weathered wood counter that wraps around the kitchen and the well-worn vinyl-covered booths in the dining room. The original Route 66 mile markers are even still there, albeit hidden in the ceiling now.

Owner Jimmy Anagnostakos (the third in a successive line of Greeks to own the diner) wouldn't change a thing. Western View opened as a roadside Stop and Eat in 1937 and at one point had a filling station in front. It then became the generic Restaurant (yes, that was the actual name) before going through a few other name changes and owners. Jimmy bought the restaurant in 1986 and still works in the kitchen as well as front of the house. He has served four generations of customers and says they keep coming back because his diner is the slice of Americana they've always remembered it as.

INSTRUCTIONS

Hand-form the beef into 2 patties about 1½-inches (4 cm) thick. Sprinkle both sides generously with salt and pepper and set aside.

Melt a pat of butter in a medium skillet over medium heat. Toast the bun halves cut-sides down and toast until the surface is golden brown. Transfer to a plate.

Increase the heat to medium-high. Cook the bacon until crisp. Transfer to a paper towel–lined plate.

In the same hot pan, place the patties and cook undisturbed for 3 to 4 minutes, until the bottoms are browned. Flip the patties, add 1 slice of Swiss and 1 slice of American to each patty, and cook for another 3 to 4 minutes, until done to your liking.

Transfer each patty to a bottom bun. Divide the bacon between the 2 burgers and drizzle green chile sauce. Customize with your preferred toppings, then finish with a top bun and serve.

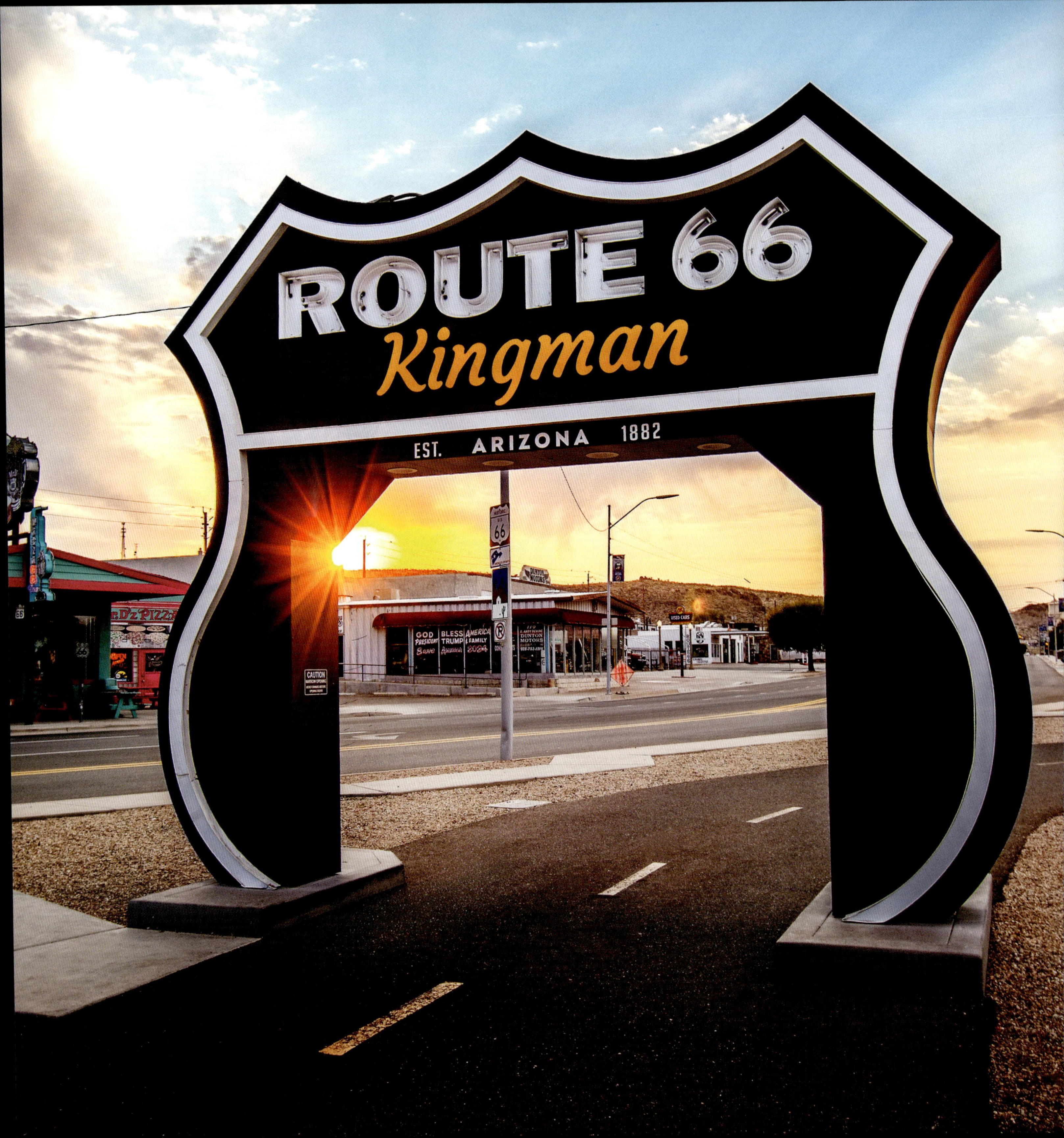
ROUTE 66
Kingman
EST. ARIZONA 1882

SEVEN
ARIZONA

FOR THE NEXT NEARLY FOUR HUNDRED MILES (644 km), Route 66 dips, bends, and winds along a path between the village of Lupton and the Colorado River, opening up the best views on the entire drive. And thanks to the preservation efforts of Angel Delgadillo, the "Guardian Angel of Route 66," Arizona can also claim the longest uninterrupted stretch of the original highway between Seligman and Kingman. The colorful tapestry of landscapes and communities here contribute to the state's multicultural foodways, which reflect a blend of Native American, Mexican, and European influences.

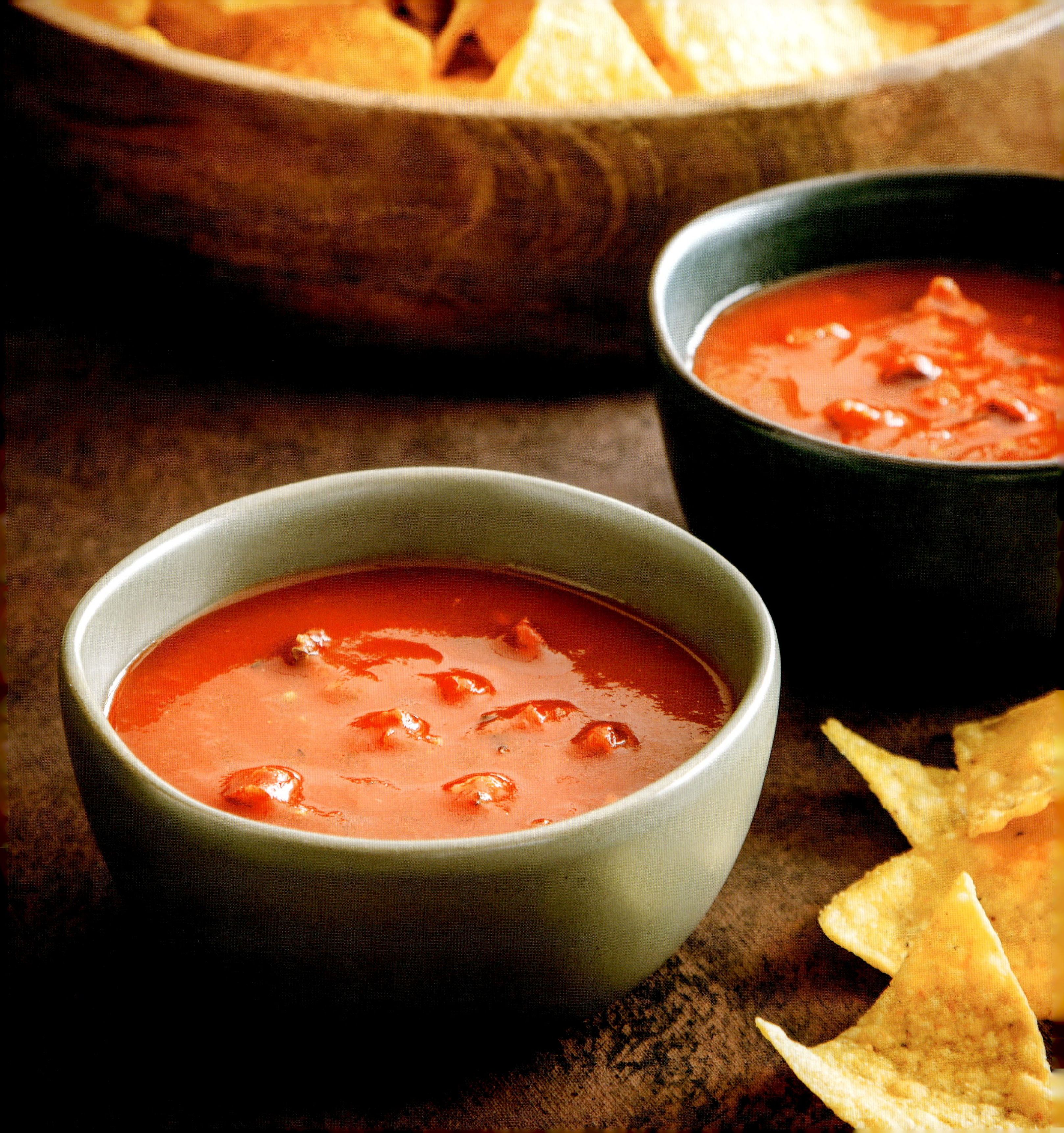

WINSLOW

HOUSE SALSA
Brown Mug Cafe ★ **MAKES 1 QUART (946 ML)**

- 2 cups (475 ml) tomato puree
- 2 cups (475 ml) water
- ¼ cup (16 g) crushed dried pequin chiles
- 1 teaspoon garlic powder
- 1 teaspoon onion powder
- 1 teaspoon fine salt
- 1 teaspoon dried oregano

The brown stucco building that sits across the street from La Posada Hotel (page 142) is a classic hole-in-the-wall with a history that dates back to the 1930s. It was once a bus depot for the Santa Fe Trail System, then a Chinese restaurant in the 1950s.

When Joe and Lucy Ono bought the business in the late 1950s, they renamed it the Brown Mug Cafe. Their daughter Josephine started working in the restaurant straight out of middle school, eventually taking over the family business in the early 1980s with her husband, Joe Perez. In the years that followed, their daughters Paula and Joann would follow in Josephine's footsteps by doing nearly every job in the restaurant from an early age: bussing tables, washing dishes, and cooking up their grandmother's handed-down Mexican recipes.

With the passing of both her parents, Paula Vargas became the third-generation owner in 2021. She and her husband, Martin, still serve the same simple, time-honored food that keeps locals coming back, many decades later. When you want to get away from all the restaurants in town playing "Take It Easy" by the Eagles on repeat, the Brown Mug Cafe is like eating at Grandma's house—in a good way.

INSTRUCTIONS

In a medium bowl, combine all the ingredients until well blended. Let stand for about 2 hours before serving.

★

At-Home Tip

If you're sensitive to spice, start with 1 tablespoon (4 g) of crushed dried chile pequin and taste before adding more.

ARIZONA | 141

WINSLOW

HALIBUT CEVICHE
The Turquoise Room at La Posada Hotel ★ MAKES 4 SERVINGS

- 1 pound (455 g) skinless boneless halibut, cut into ½-inch (13 mm) dice
- 4 ounces (115 ml) fresh lime juice
- 4 ounces (115 ml) fresh orange juice
- 5 tablespoons (55 g) finely diced mango
- 3 tablespoons (27 g) finely diced red bell pepper
- 3 tablespoons (30 g) finely diced red onion
- 2½ tablespoons (25 g) finely diced jalapeño
- 1 teaspoon finely chopped cilantro
- Salt to taste
- Julienned watermelon radish, for garnish
- Tricolored tortilla chips, for serving

La Posada Hotel has the distinction of being the last Harvey House ever built by the Atchison, Topeka & Santa Fe (AT&SF) Railway, and one of only two still operating as a hotel on Historic Route 66—the other one being La Fonda in Santa Fe, New Mexico (page 131). Architect Mary Colter designed the hotel and considered it her masterpiece, as it was the only project where she had a hand in everything, from designing the buildings, interiors, and gardens to selecting the dinner china, maids' uniforms, and furniture.

The hotel opened in 1930, just after the stock market crash, but remained open for just twenty-seven years. It closed to the public in 1957, and AT&SF gutted the building in the early 1960s. When the railway moved out in 1994, they wanted to demolish it.

The landmark was added to the National Trust for Historic Preservation's endangered list, where it got the attention of Allan Affeldt. Once he realized La Posada's fate, he and his wife, Tina Mion, decided to purchase the property in 1997 and take on the monumental task of restoring the Harvey House. (Fun fact: They paid $156,000 for the land, and the building was actually free. But restoration of the historic property was north of $12 million.)

The couple recruited their friend and restaurateur, John Sharpe, to renovate the old dining room—which had once been the finest restaurant in the region—and bring fine dining back to the hotel. The Turquoise Room opened in 2000, named after a private dining car that Mary Colter designed in 1936 on the deluxe Super Chief train. This "train to the stars" carried well-heeled passengers between Los Angeles and Chicago, and the Turquoise Room was a favorite of Hollywood stars and studio chiefs. Its legacy—and that of the original Fred Harvey dining room at La Posada—continues in the new Turquoise Room.

INSTRUCTIONS

Combine the halibut, lime juice, and orange juice in a small nonreactive bowl, cover, and refrigerate for 2 to 4 hours. When the halibut is cooked from the acid as much as you would like, strain the juice into a cup and reserve. Stir in the mango, bell pepper, onion, jalapeño, and cilantro. Add a bit of the reserved juice and season with salt to taste. Spoon into martini glasses. Top with a mound of radish strips and serve with tortilla chips.

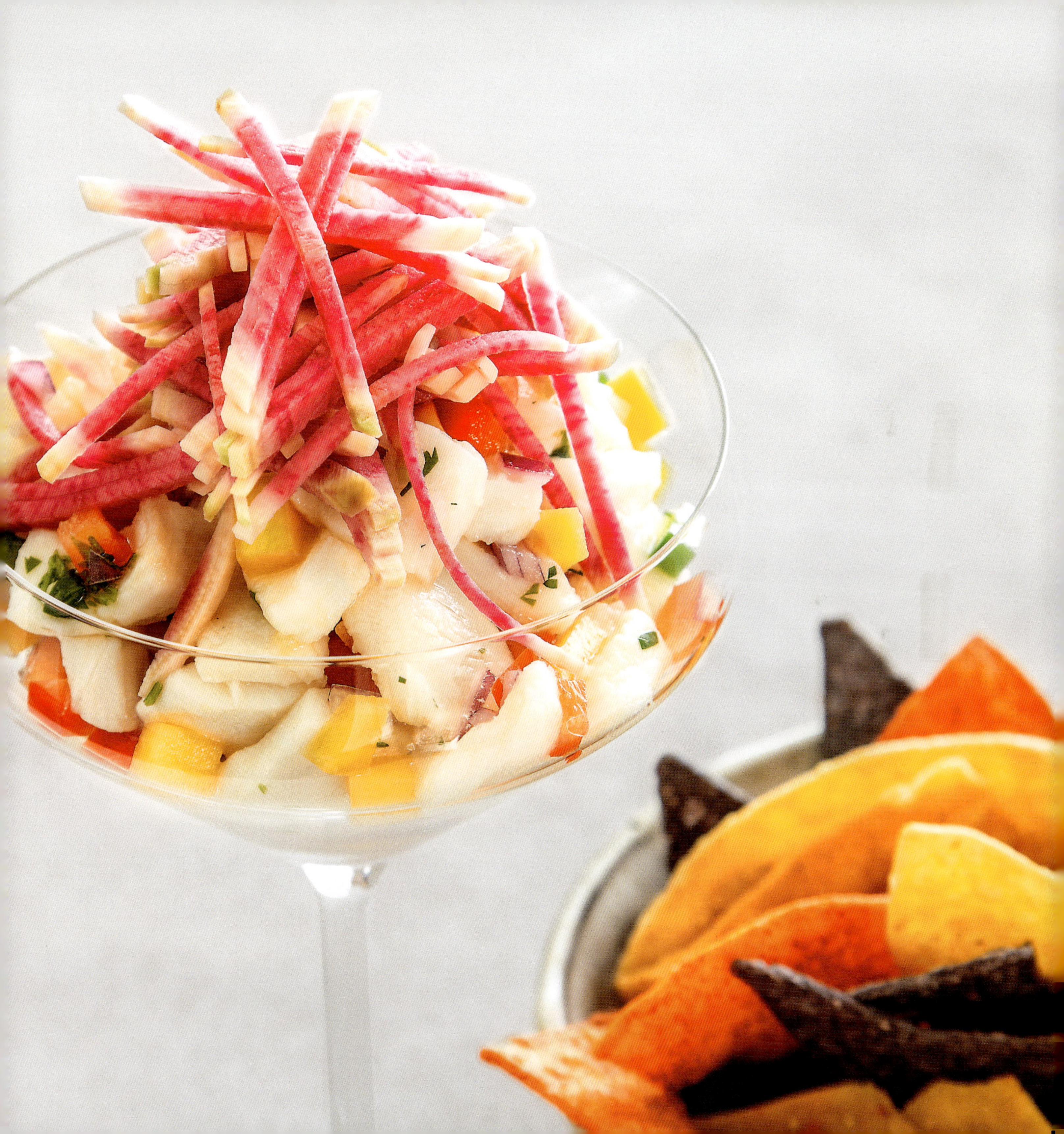

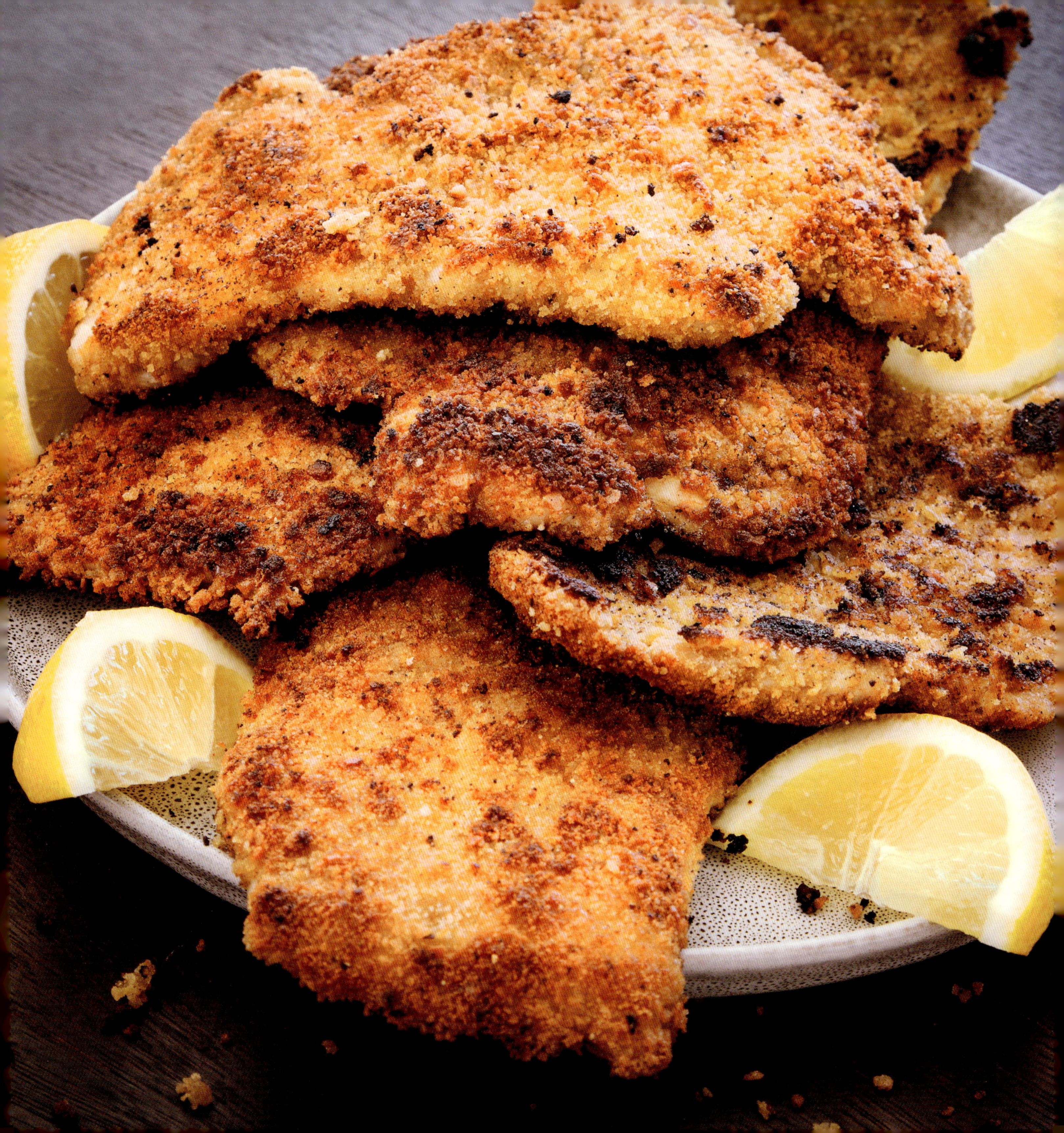

SELIGMAN

PORK WIENER SCHNITZEL

Westside Lilo's ★ MAKES 4 SERVINGS

- 2 pounds (910 g) pork loin or boneless pork chops, trimmed and sliced into ½-inch (13 mm)-thick cutlets
- 2 cups (100 g) German breadcrumbs or (230 g) store-bought breadcrumbs
- 2 teaspoons lemon pepper
- 3 eggs
- Butter or neutral oil, for cooking
- Lemon wedges, for serving

The business that gained a cult following as Westside Lilo's originally opened in 1954 as a hobby shop. By the time Lilo and Pat Russell moved to Seligman in 1962 to start their family, it had become a restaurant, but the building eventually closed in the early 1980s and sat empty for more than a decade.

German-born Lilo had always dreamed of starting a business to share some of her favorite German recipes with locals and travelers. She got her chance in 1996, when she purchased the vacant building and opened Westside Lilo's with the help of her husband and their daughters, Nancy and Brenda. It's a family affair, with all generations having worked in the business (or will soon be working, once they can reach the counter!). Daughter Brenda Bryant now owns and operates the restaurant with her son Rocque.

While the restaurant serves all the classic comfort foods you'd expect to find on Route 66, the house specialties are desserts and Lilo's wiener schnitzel, a dish from her German roots.

INSTRUCTIONS

Place the cutlets in a single layer between 2 sheets of plastic wrap on a cutting board. Pound the cutlets with a meat mallet until ⅛-inch (3 mm) thick.

In a bowl, combine the breadcrumbs and lemon pepper. In another, beat the eggs with a fork.

Dredge both sides of a cutlet into the eggs, letting the excess egg drip back into the bowl before dredging the cutlet in the breadcrumbs. Repeat with all the cutlets.

Line a plate with paper towels. Heat a large nonstick skillet over medium heat and add enough butter or oil to lightly coat. Once hot, add a few cutlets and cook for 3 to 4 minutes on each side, until cooked through. Reduce the heat if the cutlets are browning too quickly. Transfer to the prepared plate and cut into a piece to check doneness; the juices should run clear. Repeat with the remaining cutlets. Serve with lots of lemon wedges.

✳

Remembering Lilo

Lilo Russell passed away just a few months after sharing this recipe with me. I'm honored to include her dish and to have had the pleasure of eating at Westside Lilo's while writing this book, laughing with Lilo on the phone, and telling a bit of her story here. Her warmth and energy will be remembered.

SELIGMAN

RACK OF RACCOON
The Roadkill Cafe ★ MAKES 2 SERVINGS

1 rack St. Louis–style ribs (2½ to 3 pounds, or 1.1 to 1.4 kg), membrane removed
4 cups (946 ml) water
1½ cups (355 ml) barbecue sauce
4 oranges, cut in half

No, this isn't actually raccoon, though a look at the menu at this Seligman pit stop sounds like a bad day on the highway! Among The Roadkill Cafe's specialties are Opossum Blossom, Splatter Platter, No Luck Buck, Thumper Hit the Bumper, and The Chicken That Almost Crossed the Road. Owner Debbie Mejia laughs at the novelty and says patrons stole so many of their menus for souvenirs that the restaurant now sells the same menus in their gift shop.

Debbie and her family moved to Seligman in 1983 to take over a few local businesses that came up for sale. One of those businesses was a small bar called the OK Saloon, where Debbie met her future husband, Bruce Mejia. It was a tough time for the town—forget about the new interstate. The community also had to contend with the Santa Fe Railroad closure, which put Seligman on its deathbed for a decade.

It was during this time that several small-business owners—including Jim and Jean Pope (Debbie's parents) and the now-famous Angel Delgadillo—started petitioning the state of Arizona to designate Route 66 as a historic highway. They succeeded in 1987, which led to a rebranding to attract Route 66 travelers. The Pope family was now running the Historic Route 66 Motel, Historic Route 66 General Store, and Route 66 Automotive and Towing. They enclosed the patio at the OK Saloon in 1997, and The Roadkill Cafe was born. Today, the Popes and Mejias are in their fourth generation of family in one of the most recognizable Mother Road empires along the entire stretch, which continues to grow in the "Birthplace of Historic Route 66."

INSTRUCTIONS

Cut the ribs into sections to fit inside a deep, wide skillet. Place the ribs, water, barbecue sauce, and oranges in the pan. (The water should cover the top of the ribs. If it doesn't, add more water as needed.) Bring to a boil. Reduce the heat to a gentle simmer, cover with aluminum foil or a lid, and cook for about 3 hours, or until the ribs are tender. Discard the oranges before serving.

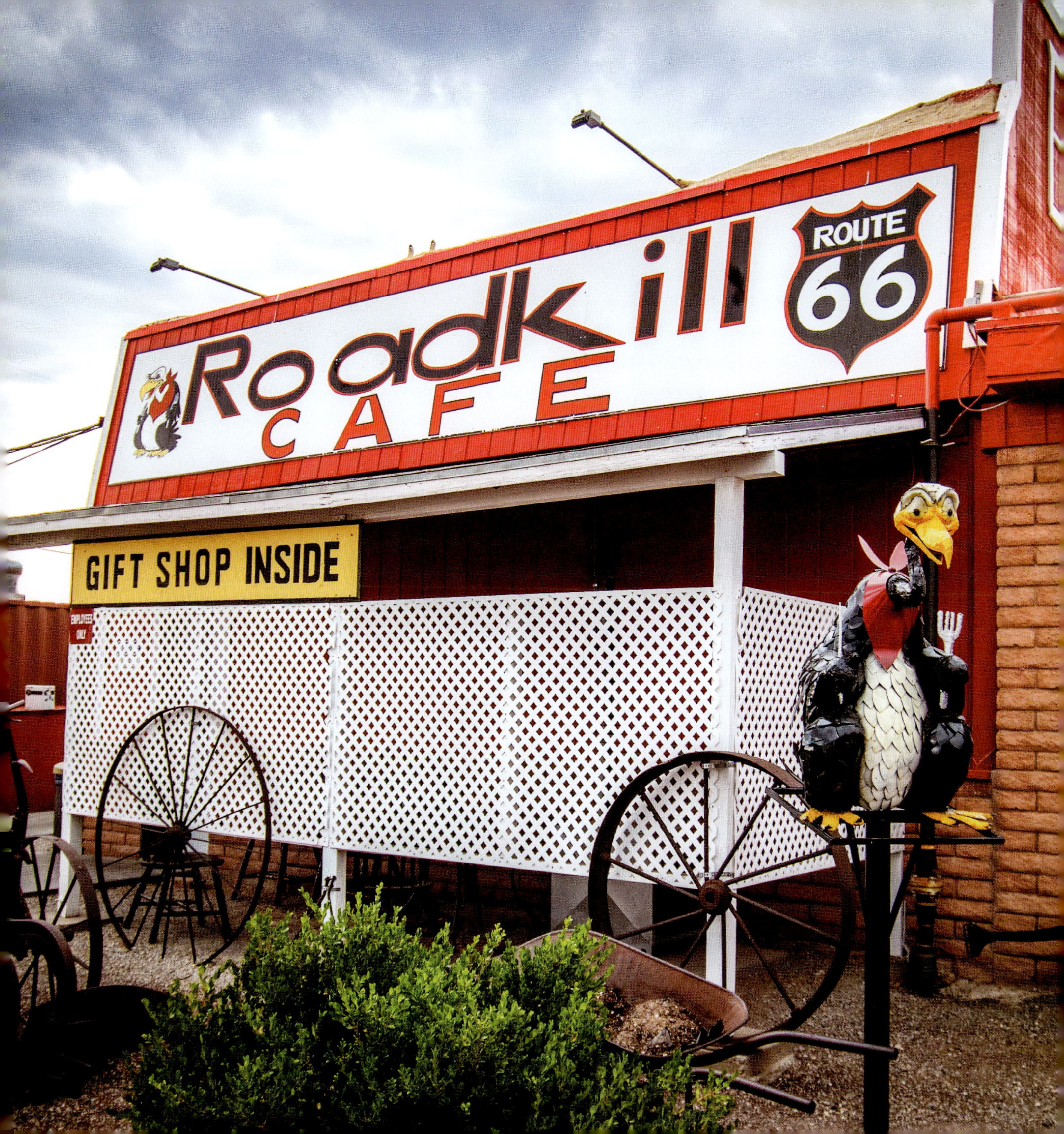
Roadkill
CAFE
ROUTE 66
GIFT SHOP INSIDE

RUTHERFORD'S
ROUTE
66
1941 ROAD TO VICTORY 1945
BUD LIGHT
PLATINUM
SELTZER
Michelob
ULTRA
GOD BLESS
AMERICA

KINGMAN

GREEK SANDWICH
Rutherford's 66 Family Diner ★ **MAKES 1 SERVING**

- ¼ cup (60 ml) balsamic vinaigrette
- ¾ cup (105 g) diced chicken breast
- ¼ cup (45 g) diced tomatoes
- ¼ cup (38 g) chopped artichoke hearts
- ½ cup (22 g) baby spinach
- 2 tablespoons (18 g) crumbled feta cheese
- Butter
- 2 slices sourdough bread
- Garlic powder

✷ The Story Behind the (Other) Sign

A weathered neon sign with remnants of the word "MOTEL" still towers over the Rutherford's 66 building. The sign belonged to the Kingman Motel, which occupied the corner of Andy Devine Avenue and Johnson Avenue from the 1950s through 1960s (and possibly before that). The motel was razed around 1997, and the property has been a vacant lot since.

The story of Rutherford's 66 Family Diner actually begins with Denny's. The popular diner chain originally started as a donut shop and went through several name changes in the 1950s: first as Danny's Donuts, which morphed into Danny's Coffee Shops, which rebranded as Denny's Coffee Shops to avoid confusion with a similarly named restaurant. In 1961, the corporate chain officially became Denny's, and in 1964, Denny's opened its third location in the nation in Kingman, right on Route 66 (now Andy Devine Avenue). After Denny's closed, the Silver Spoon Family Restaurant operated in the iconic boomerang-roof building from 1993 to 2009.

The property sat vacant for a few years before Brent and Tammy Rutherford (then restaurateurs in nearby Bullhead City) decided to buy the building. They opened their restaurant in 2014 on a shoestring budget; at their grand opening, they still even had the old Silver Spoon sign up. But perseverance, fresh-cooked food with quality ingredients, and a focus on the local community carried them through tough times, and the restaurant continues to be a well-loved Kingman staple.

INSTRUCTIONS

In a medium skillet over medium-high heat, combine the balsamic vinaigrette, chicken, tomatoes, artichoke hearts, spinach, and feta. Sauté until the chicken is cooked, stirring occasionally. Remove from heat.

Butter both sides of each slice of bread and sprinkle with a pinch of garlic powder. In a separate skillet over medium heat, toast the bread to a crunchy, crouton-like consistency.

To assemble the sandwich, pile the chicken and vegetable mixture on a slice of bread and top with the remaining slice. Cut the sandwich on a diagonal and serve.

ARIZONA | 149

SANTA MONICA
YACHT HARBOR
SPORT FISHING
BOATING
Cafes
PROHIBITED
ROAD CLOSED

Eight
CALIFORNIA

FEW DESTINATIONS ON ROUTE 66 have evolved as much as California, and it's no surprise. Hundreds of thousands of people escaped to the promised land during the Depression, Dust Bowl, and drought, and many more migrated to the Golden State—from other states, and sometimes other countries—in the decades since. The flavors they introduced from their homelands were also influenced by where they settled, from Southern California–style Mexican fare to seafood with an Asian flair. There's nothing you can't find here as far as food goes, and in the final three hundred miles (483 km) of Route 66, from Needles to Santa Monica, the diversity of cuisines is as rich as the patchwork of landscapes you traverse.

AMBOY

ALBERT'S HAM SANDWICH
Roy's Motel & Cafe ★ MAKES 1 SERVING

- 3 tablespoons (42 g) Best Foods® Real Mayonnaise
- 2 slices white bread (or 1 roll French bread, sliced in half lengthwise)
- 3 slices honey-baked ham
- 2 slices tomato
- 4 slices dill pickle
- Iceberg lettuce, torn to fit sandwich
- Mezzetta® Hot Chili Peppers, for serving

Route 66 lore is full of stories about the rise and fall of small towns that dotted the old highway, but none are more intriguing than the story of Amboy, a tiny mining town.

In 1924, Roy and Velma Crowl (and their daughter, Betty) arrived in Amboy after their car broke down on the way to Los Angeles. Unable to pay for their car repair, they stayed—for a while. In 1938, Roy purchased four acres (2 hectares) of land. He then teamed up with his son-in-law, Herman "Buster" Burris, to build a 24/7 gas and service station, and the business later expanded to include a café, auto repair garage, and overnight cabins. By the 1950s, Roy's Garage and Cafe employed 10 percent of the town's population.

The Googie-style boomerang sign was erected in 1959 to advertise Roy's Motel & Cafe, visible for miles on Route 66. Roy and Velma retired at that time and passed the business on to Betty and Buster, who operated Roy's until 1978. By that point, Amboy was in rapid decline. The 1972 opening of Interstate 40 diverted all traffic north. Roy's, a post office, and a chloride plant became the only remaining businesses in town.

In 1995, New York photographer Timothy White leased the entire town from Buster and eventually bought it for $710,000 as a potential filming location. He soon found out that running a remote town was tough. After a failed eBay auction to sell the town and its eventual foreclosure in 2005, Timothy relinquished control to Bessie, Buster's widow (and his second wife), who put the town up for sale. A private investor named Albert Okura stepped in, acquiring 950 acres (384 hectares) for $425,000 in cash.

Albert owned a successful chain of regional fast-food restaurants; he won the bid for Amboy because he pledged to save the ghost town. A Route 66 enthusiast, Albert planned to revitalize the town, but a lack of modern infrastructure made the process slow going. He reopened the gas station in 2008, followed by a mini mart. The iconic neon sign was restored and relit in 2019.

After Albert's death in 2023, his son Kyle took ownership of Amboy. Cottages are under construction next to Roy's, and the original motel lobby has been partially restored. Plans are underway to open a café. When asked how this book could honor his dad's legacy, Kyle offered Albert's favorite ham sandwich—a recipe that's as American as his story.

INSTRUCTIONS

Spread the mayonnaise evenly on one side of each slice of bread. Layer the ham, tomato, dill pickles, and lettuce on one slice of bread, then top with the remaining bread. Serve with the chili peppers on the side.

CALIFORNIA

BARSTOW

STRAWBERRY MARGARITA PIE
Chiquita Rosita's ★ MAKES 8 SERVINGS

CRUST
3 cups (360 g) mini twist pretzels
¼ cup (72 g) fine salt
½ cup (112 g) butter, melted

FILLING
1 pound (455 g) hulled strawberries, divided
1½ teaspoons granulated sugar
1 teaspoon lemon juice
½ cup (120 ml) sweetened condensed milk
¼ cup (60 ml) tequila
2 tablespoons (28 ml) triple sec
2 tablespoons (28 ml) lime juice
4 ounces (115 g) whipped topping (such as Cool Whip)

Whipped cream, for serving
Thinly sliced strawberries, for serving

If you've driven along Main Street (originally Route 66), you've likely seen the mural spanning a long, beige stucco building with "Rosita's—Est. 1954" painted on the side. That Rosita's no longer exists, at least not as the restaurant that Rosa Griego first opened. The business began as Griego's Market in 1948, and a restaurant was added in 1954. Rosa eventually phased out the grocery side in 1957 and promoted her daughter, Mary Alice, and son-in-law, Genaro "Jerry" Guardado, as her partners in 1971.

When a vacant building down the street caught Jerry's eye, the three owners decided to make the purchase in 1974. They transformed the building into a hacienda-style restaurant, and the Guardados' five children were all part of the business at some point. One of their sons, Jerry Jr., became the fourth partner in the business in 1991, and later his daughter Anastasia stepped up to help run the restaurant.

Ironically, sixty-six years after opening Rosita's Restaurant on Route 66, the family decided to shut it down and sell the building. But Jerry Jr. and Anastasia couldn't stay away for *too* long; the duo eventually opened a smaller location on Main Street in 2023. Called Chiquita Rosita's (*chiquita* meaning "small" in Spanish), the restaurant brings back some of their grandmother's (and great-grandmother's) recipes but also the newer generations' favorites, like their signature margaritas. If you can't decide between ordering dessert or another drink, how about both in one boozy bite?

INSTRUCTIONS

Make the crust: Blend the pretzels in a blender until they become powdery. Transfer to a large bowl and combine with the salt. Stir in the melted butter until incorporated. Firmly press the mixture evenly across the bottom and up the sides of a 9-inch (23 cm) pie pan.

Make the filling: Blend 4 ounces (115 g) (about one-quarter) of the strawberries with the sugar and lemon juice until smooth. Thinly slice the remaining strawberries and set aside.

In a separate bowl, combine the strawberry puree, condensed milk, tequila, triple sec, and lime juice. Fold in the whipped topping. Pour into the pie crust and smooth out the top. Arrange the sliced strawberries in a single layer on top.

Freeze for at least 4 hours. Serve with whipped cream and more strawberries on top.

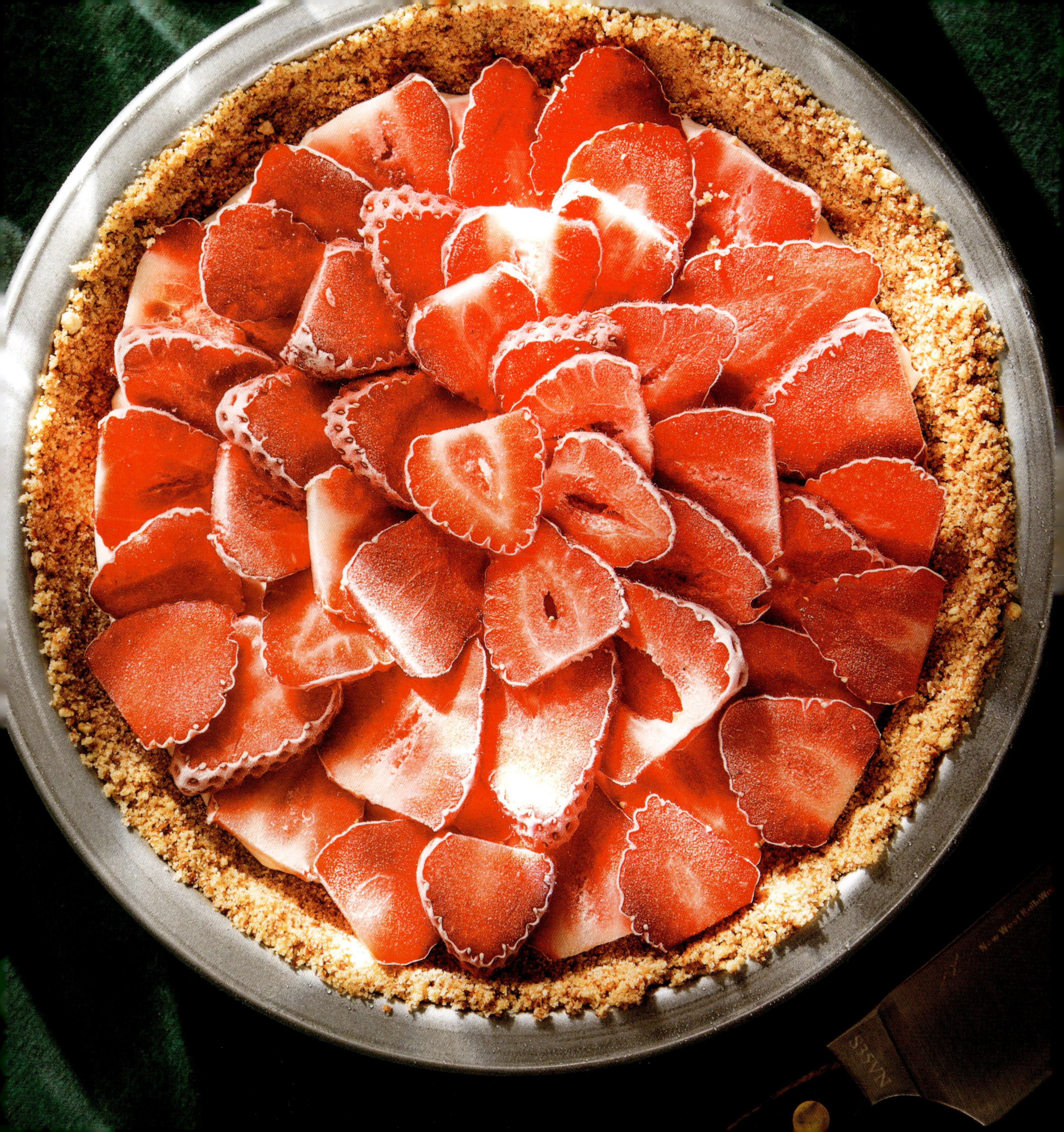

100 Years of Service
FAIR OAKS
PHARMACY
SODA FOUNTAIN
Fair Oaks AVE 800
NO U TURN
BIKE ROUTE

SOUTH PASADENA

CHOCOLATE MALT
Fair Oaks Pharmacy & Soda Fountain ★ MAKES 2 SERVINGS

6 ounces (175 ml) chocolate syrup
2 ounces (28 ml) milk
2 ounces (28 g) malted milk powder
1 pint (473 ml) vanilla ice cream
Whipped cream, for topping
Cherries, for topping

✳ Fun Facts

Chocolate milkshakes and malts were always made with vanilla ice cream and chocolate syrup—never with chocolate ice cream. Because of this, they were often called "black and white" milkshakes or malts.

The biggest misconception about malts is that they differ from milkshakes in their texture and consistency. But that isn't true! The main difference between the two is the flavor itself: A malt tastes like the WHOPPERS candy you usually get at the movie theater.

An entrepreneur of her time, Gertrude Ozmun, a real estate speculator, purchased the corner lot on Fair Oaks Avenue and Mission Street in 1914 for $14,000. She believed it would be a safe investment in the city and built the iconic building (then known as South Pasadena Pharmacy) in 1915. In the 1920s and 1930s, it became Raymond Pharmacy and a soda fountain was added, making it a popular pit stop for travelers on the new Route 66 alignment. The mom-and-pop business changed ownership again in the 1940s and finally settled in as Fair Oaks Pharmacy.

The pharmacy and soda fountain has always been family owned and operated, and today it's run by the Shahniani family. Mom Zahra, a pharmacist, prepares prescriptions in the back while her sons Brandon and Ash are involved in the day-to-day management.

The entire building looks and feels like a vibrant, old-timey convenience store—a true time capsule! This is a place where you can pick up medication, grab a retro toy and some old-fashioned candy for your kids, and indulge in what's possibly the landmark's biggest draw: a near-limitless selection of custom sodas, ice cream, milkshakes, and malts, which the soda jerks combine and concoct to their customers' delight.

INSTRUCTIONS
In a cup, stir together the chocolate syrup, milk, and malted milk powder until the powder is fully hydrated and all the ingredients are combined. Add the chocolate mixture and the ice cream to a blender and blend until smooth. Pour into tall glasses and top each glass with whipped cream and a cherry before serving.

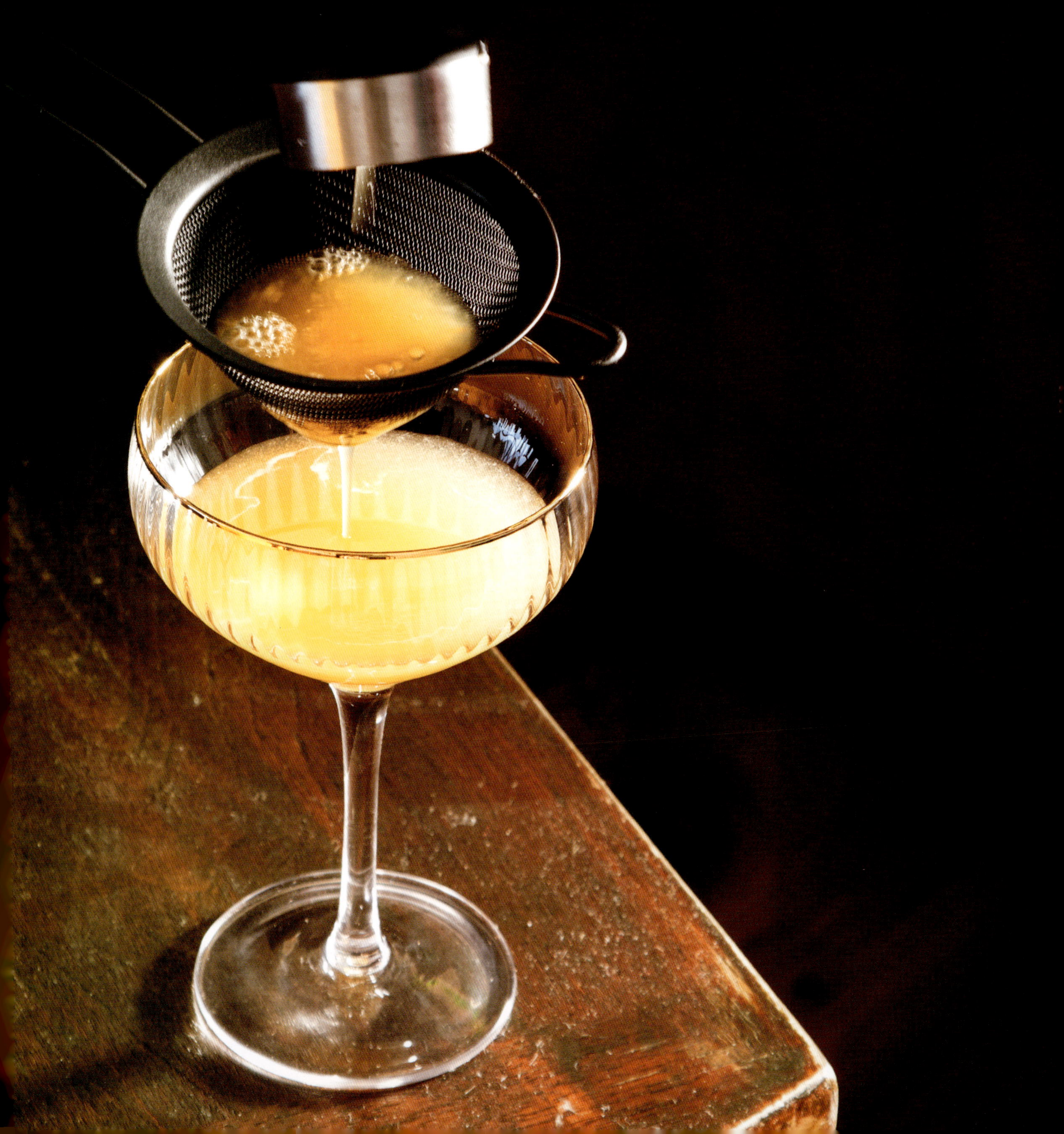

HIGHLAND PARK

SMOKE AND PEACHES
La Cuevita ★ MAKES 1 SERVING

¾ ounce (21 ml) lemon juice
¾ ounce (21 ml) white peach puree
½ ounce (15 ml) agave nectar
1 ounce (28 ml) Tanteo habanero tequila
1 ounce (28 ml) La Tierra de Acre Cenizo mezcal

The 1930s-era building on North Figueroa Street—one of the prime examples of Route 66 hiding in plain sight in Los Angeles—has lived many lives. At one time it was a watch store and a stamp shop; in the 1960s it was a notorious biker bar called Richard's Hofbrau; in 2003 it became the dark, divey bar Little Cave; and renovations in 2011 uncovered a vintage sign under the facade for Highland Hofbrau, whose time in history is still a little murky.

Following renovations, Little Cave transformed into La Cuevita (a literal Spanish translation of its name), and the neo-Gothic theme gave way to an old-world Mexican grotto bar with a focus on traditional agave spirits. While the neighborhood tavern got a slightly different name after its makeover, it isn't hard to find—the glowing red neon sign above the door still says Little Cave. The quirky sign (which owner and 1933 Group partner Bobby Green found in a thrift store) happens to also have a past life: It originally came from a 1970s through 1980s gay bar in Silver Lake called Paul's Little Cave.

INSTRUCTIONS
Add all the ingredients to a cocktail shaker and shake until well blended. Double strain into a Nick and Nora glass and serve.

At-Home Tip

To double strain, place a Hawthorne strainer over the cocktail shaker. Hold a fine-mesh strainer over your glass and slowly pour the contents of the cocktail shaker into the basket of the mesh strainer.

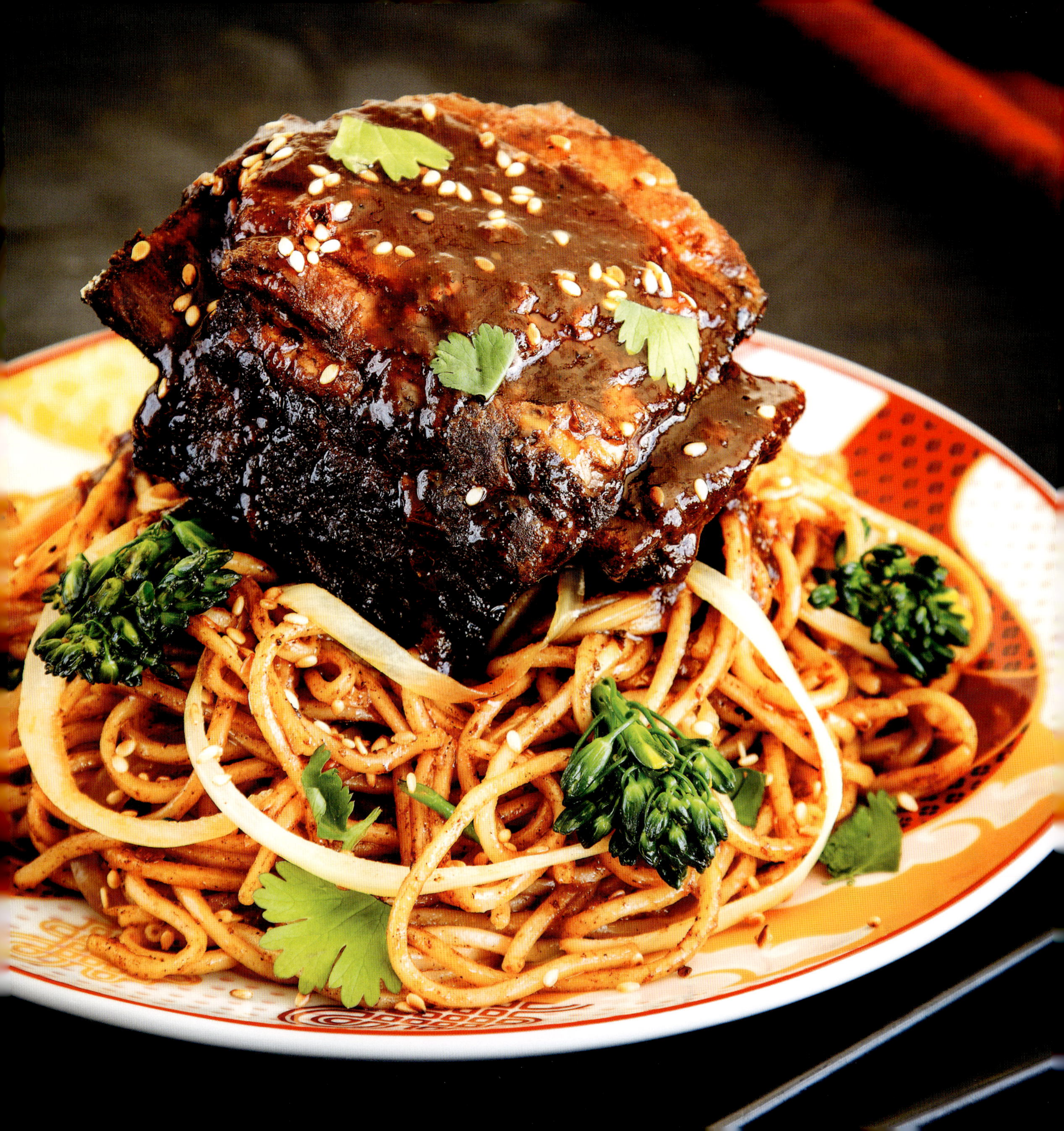

STICKY SHORT RIB NOODLES

The Formosa Cafe ★ MAKES 4 SERVINGS

Nonstick cooking spray

SHORT RIBS
1 tablespoon (15 ml) neutral oil
2 pounds (910 g) beef short ribs
Kosher salt
1 teaspoon curry powder
1 teaspoon Chinese five-spice powder

SAUCE
2 cups (475 ml) beef broth
1 cup (250 g) Texas-style barbecue sauce
2 tablespoons (28 ml) apple cider vinegar
1 tablespoon (16 g) chili paste (such as sambal oelek)
1 tablespoon (15 g) black bean sauce
1 tablespoon (8 g) grated fresh ginger (or 1 teaspoon ground ginger)
1 tablespoon (6 g) Chinese five-spice powder
2 teaspoons curry powder
3 tablespoons (60 g) honey

NOODLES
6 ounces (170 g) uncooked egg noodles
1 tablespoon (15 ml) neutral oil
½ cup (80 g) diced yellow onion
½ cup (36 g) sliced broccolini stems

Toasted sesame seeds, for garnish
Chopped cilantro, for garnish

The structure that occupies the corner of Santa Monica Boulevard (a.k.a. Historic Route 66) and Formosa Avenue began its chapter a century ago—first as a humble lunch counter called the Red Post Cafe in the 1920s, and then as the infamous celebrity haunt Formosa Cafe in 1939. Nested across the street from the movie studios, it was a favorite watering hole of old Hollywood stars as well as a mobster or two. (In fact, Bugsy Siegel's floor safe, tucked under one of the restaurant's signature red booths, is now encased in glass for all to see.)

But Hollywood was also a source of agitation: The Formosa was nearly demolished in 1991 to create a parking lot for the movie studios. The building escaped that fate, only to be shuttered in 2016 after a remodel gone awry. Backlash over the loss of the iconic, lacquered red-and-black interior led local preservationists to bring the restaurant and bar back to its former glory. In 2019, the Formosa reemerged with an extensively restored space that pays homage to its Chinese and Hollywood roots.

STICKY SHORT RIB NOODLES
CONTINUED

INSTRUCTIONS

Lightly coat a slow cooker with nonstick cooking spray.

Make the short ribs: Heat a large skillet over medium-high heat and drizzle in the oil. Season the short ribs with a pinch of salt, curry powder, and Chinese five-spice powder Sear the short ribs in the hot oil until both sides are browned. Transfer the short ribs to the prepared slow cooker.

Make the sauce: Deglaze the skillet with beef broth, scraping and stirring in all the browned bits with a spatula. Whisk in the barbecue sauce, apple cider vinegar, chili paste, black bean sauce, ginger, Chinese five-spice powder, and curry powder until blended.

Pour the mixture over the short ribs in the slow cooker, cover with a lid, and cook for 6 hours on high heat, or until the meat is fork-tender and falling apart. Remove the meat from the slow cooker, transfer to a platter, and cover with foil to keep warm.

Transfer the sauce to a small saucepan over medium heat. Add the honey and cook until the sauce is thickened and reduced by half.

Make the noodles: Cook the egg noodles according to the package directions. Drain and set aside.

Heat a large skillet over medium-high heat and swirl in the oil. Add the onion, broccolini, and cooked noodles and stir to combine. Pour in some of the thickened sauce and toss to evenly coat all the vegetables and noodles.

To serve, divide the noodles among 4 bowls. Top each bowl with short ribs and a drizzle of sauce and garnish with a sprinkle of sesame seeds and cilantro.

WEST HOLLYWOOD

WOK FRIED RICE WITH PORK BELLY
The Formosa Cafe ★ MAKES 4 SERVINGS

FRIED RICE SEASONING
1 teaspoon kosher salt
1 teaspoon ground white pepper
1 teaspoon mushroom bouillon

FRIED RICE
2 tablespoons (28 ml) neutral oil
8 ounces (225 g) diced pork belly
2 tablespoons (28 ml) pork broth
½ cup (80 g) diced onion
½ cup (60 g) diced celery
1¼ cups (89 g) broccolini stems
½ cup (55 g) shredded carrot
¾ cup (72 g) sliced scallions, plus more for garnish
1 tablespoon (10 g) minced garlic
1 tablespoon (6 g) minced ginger
4 cups (744 g) day-old cooked white rice
Nonstick cooking spray
1 egg
Fried shallots, for garnish

In the 1940s, Hong Kong–born chef Lem Quon started running the kitchen at the Formosa, dishing out greasy Cantonese comfort food for his celebrity guests. He entered a partnership with owner Jimmy Bernstein in 1945, eventually taking ownership of the restaurant in 1976 after Jimmy's death. The business remained in the family for generations with Lem's grandson, Vince Jung, operating the Formosa until it closed in 2016.

When the Formosa reopened with a new look and new management under the 1933 Group (who had also preserved other Route 66 icons, including La Cuevita, page 159, and Tail o' the Pup, page 164), it stayed true to Quon's vision. Chinese food still rules the menu under Executive Chef Dan Huerta, but with modern takes on familiar classics.

INSTRUCTIONS

Make the seasoning: Combine all the ingredients for the fried rice seasoning in a small bowl and set aside.

Make the fried rice: Heat a wok over high heat and swirl in the oil. Add the pork belly and cook until golden brown. Stir in the pork broth and cook until it's fully absorbed by the meat. Mix in all the vegetables, garlic, and ginger, and cook for about 1 minute. Add the rice and stir to combine. Sprinkle in the fried rice seasoning and toss to evenly coat all the rice. Remove the wok from heat.

Lightly coat a small skillet with cooking spray and heat over medium heat. Fry the egg sunny-side up, until done to your liking.

Serve the pork belly fried rice with the fried egg on top and garnish with scallions and fried shallots.

WEST HOLLYWOOD

THE ROUTE 66 PUP
Tail o' the Pup ★ MAKES 1 SERVING

---

1 hot dog, grilled

1 Martin's Famous top-sliced potato roll, steamed

Chili, warmed (use your favorite)

Diced onions

House mustard (see sidebar)

Jalapeño spread (see sidebar)

Cooked french fries

House Mustard

Tail o' the Pup makes their own mustard blend with yellow, spicy, whole-grain, and honey Dijon mustards.

Jalapeño Spread

To make your own jalapeño spread that tastes just like Pup's, combine 1 cup (225 g) mayonnaise, 1 minced jalapeño pepper, ¼ cup (4 g) chopped cilantro, 2 teaspoons lime juice, and 2 teaspoons lemon juice. Use what you'd like and store the rest in an airtight container in the fridge for up to 2 weeks.

Tail o' the Pup was built in 1946 and designed by architect Milton J. Black, at a time when programmatic architecture was popular around the country. The novelty style is characterized by building designs that mimic another item, usually—but not always—the item that the business specializes in. So yes, Pup (as the hot dog stand is known) looks like a hot dog! The stand was originally located at 311 North La Cienega Boulevard and owned by Frank Veloz and Yolanda Casazza, a famous husband-and-wife American ballroom dance team. The stars eventually divorced and sold the restaurant to Eddie Blake and his son Dennis in 1976, and for a time, it was known as Eddie Blake's Tail o' the Pup.

It was nearly demolished in the 1980s to make room for a hotel, but public outcry led to the restaurant being moved a couple blocks away to 329 North San Vicente Boulevard instead. Over the years, the hot dog stand appeared in many movies, TV shows, magazines, and album covers, but even fame couldn't stop another real estate developer from scooping up the land. The restaurant closed in 2006, and the iconic building was moved into storage, where it sat for a decade.

In 2018, the 1933 Group purchased the Pup from Jay and Nicole Miller (Eddie's grandson and his wife). The new owners brought it back to life, found a new location on a stretch of Route 66 known as Santa Monica Boulevard, and reopened the restaurant in 2022.

INSTRUCTIONS

Place the hot dog in the roll. Layer a few spoonfuls of chili, a sprinkling of onions, the mustard, and the jalapeño spread over the hot dog. Top with a handful of fries.

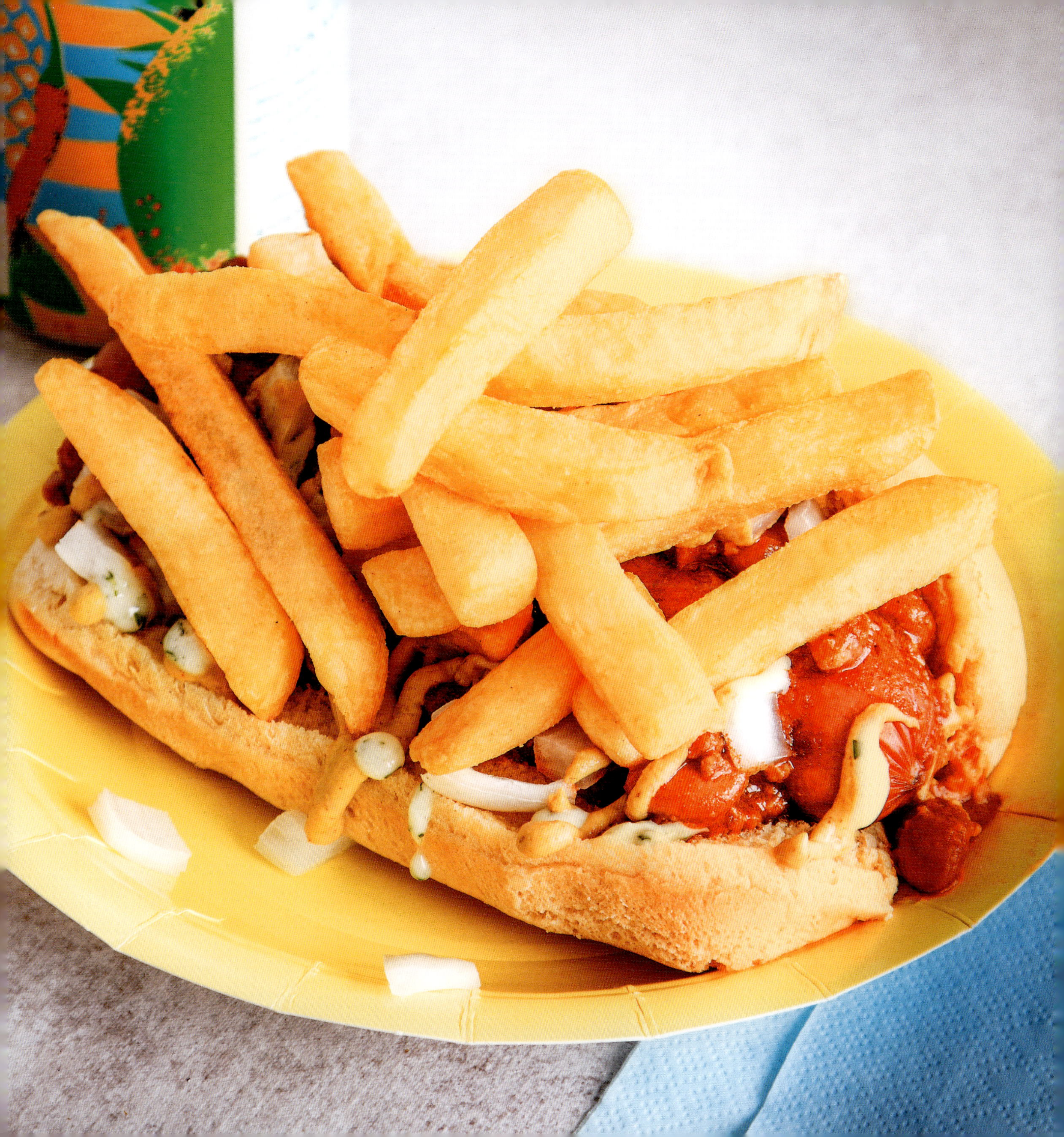

SANTA MONICA

GRANDMA'S CHICKEN SOUP

Mel's Drive-In ★ MAKES 6 SERVINGS

Chicken bones from a 4-pound (1.8 kg) chicken

12 cups (2.8 L) water

1 whole chicken (3 to 4 pounds, or 1.4 to 1.8 kg), giblets removed

½ white onion

2 bay leaves

4 tablespoons (72 g) chicken base, divided

4 ribs celery, sliced

2 carrots, sliced

8 ounces (225 g) uncooked fusilli pasta

Chopped green onions, for garnish

Chopped parsley, for garnish

Situated at the official end of Route 66 on the corner of Lincoln and Olympic boulevards, Mel's Drive-In is a familiar name to diners. David "Mel" Weiss and Harold Dobbs opened the first drive-in restaurant in San Francisco in 1947, pioneering the carhop concept. It didn't take long for that first restaurant to turn into eleven Mel's locations in the Bay Area, with the original restaurant gaining fame in the George Lucas film *American Graffiti*. The chain sold in 1972, but in 1985, Steven Weiss had an itch to bring back the good times and convinced his father to reopen Mel's.

A family rift soon caused the business to split: Mel would continue on as The Original Mels, while Steven would create Next Generation Mel's and operate as Mel's Drive-In. Steven and his partners opened on Route 66 in Santa Monica in 2018, taking over the iconic Googie-style building that once housed The Penguin Coffee Shop—thus the penguin preserved atop Mel's neon sign.

The "Grandma" in this recipe is actually Mel's mom, and grandma to the third generation of the Weiss family who currently co-own the business. It's the same classic recipe they've been serving for nearly eighty years!

INSTRUCTIONS

Put the chicken bones in a stockpot and cover with water. Bring to a gentle boil and boil for 1 hour. Remove and discard the bones.

Add the chicken, onion, bay leaves, and 3 tablespoons (54 g) of the chicken base, and boil for 45 minutes, or until the chicken is done cooking. Transfer the chicken to a cutting board and chop into bite-size pieces. Strain the broth into another pot.

Bring the broth to a boil again and skim the fat off the surface. Add the celery and carrots and continue boiling for about 15 minutes, or until the vegetables are tender. Stir in the remaining 1 tablespoon (18 g) chicken base and the chopped chicken, reduce the heat, and keep warm.

In a separate saucepan, cook the pasta according to the package directions until al dente.

To serve, add some pasta noodles to a bowl and pour the hot soup over it. Garnish with a handful of chopped green onions and parsley.

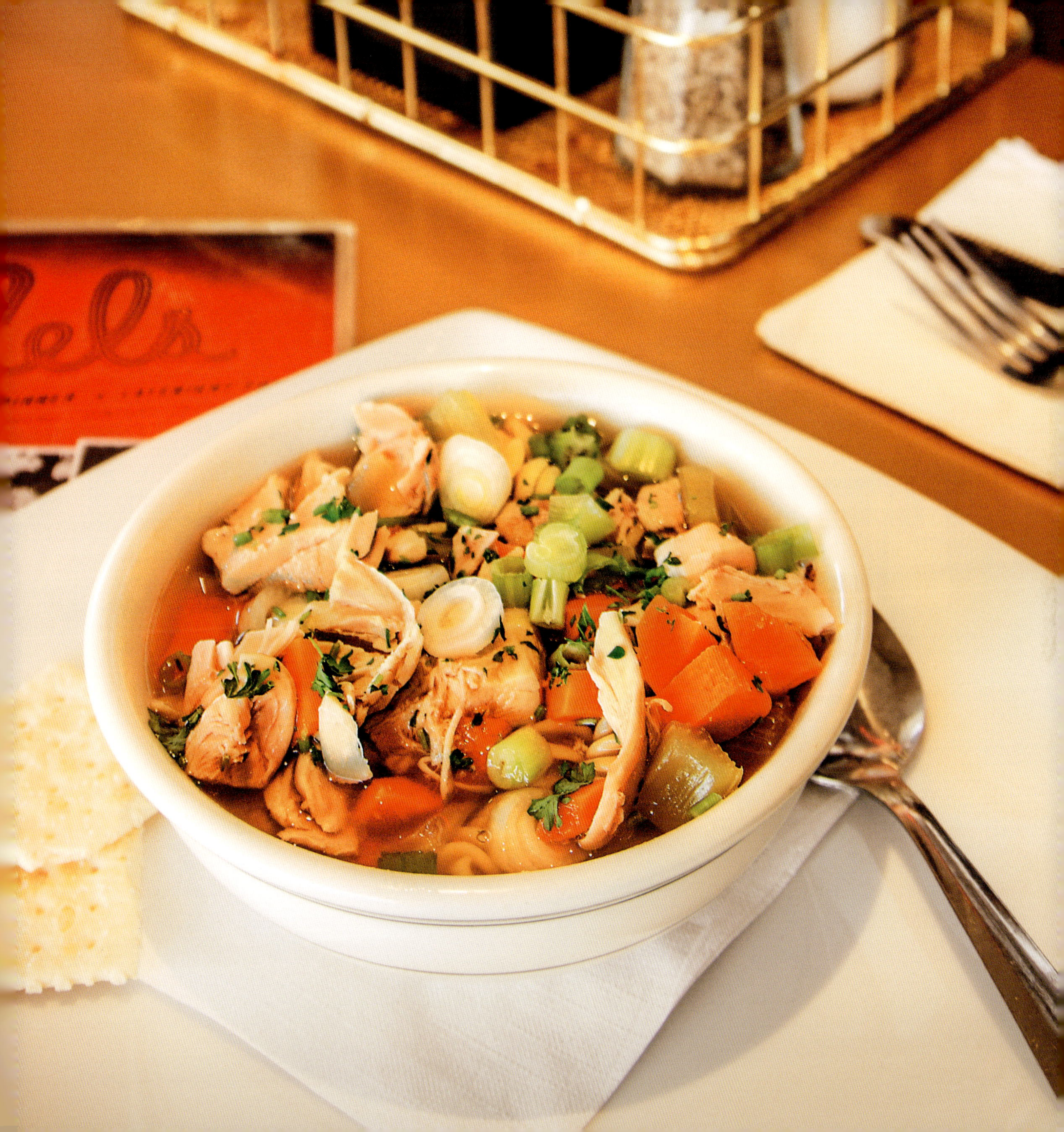

THE
LOBSTER
RESTAURANT
Ocean
DIAGONAL CROSSING OK
DO NOT
ENTER
ONE WAY
CROSS
ON
WALK
SIGNAL
ONLY

SANTA MONICA

KHEE TO MY SUCCESS
The Lobster ✶ MAKES 1 SERVING

Lime wedge
Thai basil leaf
Lychee fruit
1 ounce (28 ml) fresh lime juice
1 ounce (28 ml) lychee syrup
½ ounce (15 ml) agave
5 drops yuzu juice
2 ounces (60 ml) KHEE "38" Soju (see sidebar)

As you near the symbolic end of Route 66 on the Santa Monica Pier, you see a two-story cantilevered building perched at the entrance next to the famous neon sign. Its wraparound windows offer one of the most iconic views in Southern California: the lively pier with its illuminated Ferris wheel and the Pacific Ocean, all the way up the Malibu coastline.

But The Lobster didn't always look like that. The original restaurant opened in 1923 as a humble 900-square-foot (84-square-meter) building with thirty stools outside, selling the fresh catch of the day. Dishwasher-turned-owner Mateo Castillo took the helm in the 1950s and turned the quintessential seafood shack into a beloved local diner. The Lobster had a good run until it shut its doors in 1985, and the shack sat empty for a decade, becoming an eyesore on the bustling waterfront.

In 1995, a group of local investors came together to begin the process of renovating, reviving, and reinventing the historic restaurant. They expanded the space while incorporating the original structure in the new footprint and finally reopened in 1999.

Today, the menu under Chef Govind Armstrong is much more than just the fresh catch of the day (and much more than lobster). If the dizzying array of seafood—from caviar and Santa Barbara uni to wild Dungeness crab and charred octopus—has you feeling flustered, start with this popular cocktail.

INSTRUCTIONS

Prepare a cocktail skewer with a lime wedge, Thai basil leaf, and lychee.

In a cocktail shaker, pour the lime juice, lychee syrup, agave, yuzu juice, and soju over ice and shake vigorously. Strain the mixture into a chilled martini glass and garnish with the prepared skewer before serving.

✶
At-Home Tip
If you don't have KHEE "38" Soju, you can substitute any delicately floral soju with subtle fruit tones.

CALIFORNIA | 169

SANTA MONICA

SEARED MUSHROOMS WITH SCALLION-GINGER DRIZZLE

The Lobster ★ MAKES 2 TO 4 SERVINGS

DRIZZLE
1 bunch scallions, trimmed and thinly sliced
½ cup (48 g) minced ginger
¼ cup (60 ml) neutral oil
½ cup (120 ml) tamari
1 tablespoon (15 ml) sherry vinegar
Splash of mirin
Salt and ground black pepper

MUSHROOMS
2 maitake mushrooms (3½ ounces, or 100 g each), lightly trimmed and split in half lengthwise
Salt and ground black pepper
1 teaspoon neutral oil

Toasted sesame seeds, for garnish
Chopped cilantro, for garnish

Maitake mushrooms, with their wild and feathery appearance, are also known as hen-of-the-woods, though they're easily sourced in better supermarkets. This is a simple side dish—essentially a maitake "steak"—that looks far more impressive on a plate than the time it actually takes to make. (And it's so good that you might even be tempted to serve it as a vegetarian entrée!)

INSTRUCTIONS

Make the drizzle: In a medium bowl, combine all the drizzle ingredients. Taste and adjust the seasoning with salt and pepper, as desired.

Make the mushrooms: Season the mushrooms with salt and pepper. In a medium pan over medium-high heat, swirl the oil and gently arrange the mushrooms in a single layer. Place a cooking weight on the mushrooms and cook for about 3 minutes, or until the bottom is golden brown and caramelized. Using tongs, carefully flip the mushrooms and cook for 2 to 3 minutes, until soft and browned all over.

Transfer the mushrooms to a serving plate, drizzle with the sauce, and sprinkle with sesame seeds and cilantro. Store any remaining sauce in the refrigerator for up to 3 weeks for another use.

At-Home Tip

The cooking weight flattens the mushroom and gives it more surface area for a better sear. You can use a grill press, a bacon press, a brick wrapped in foil, or a heavy cast-iron pan.

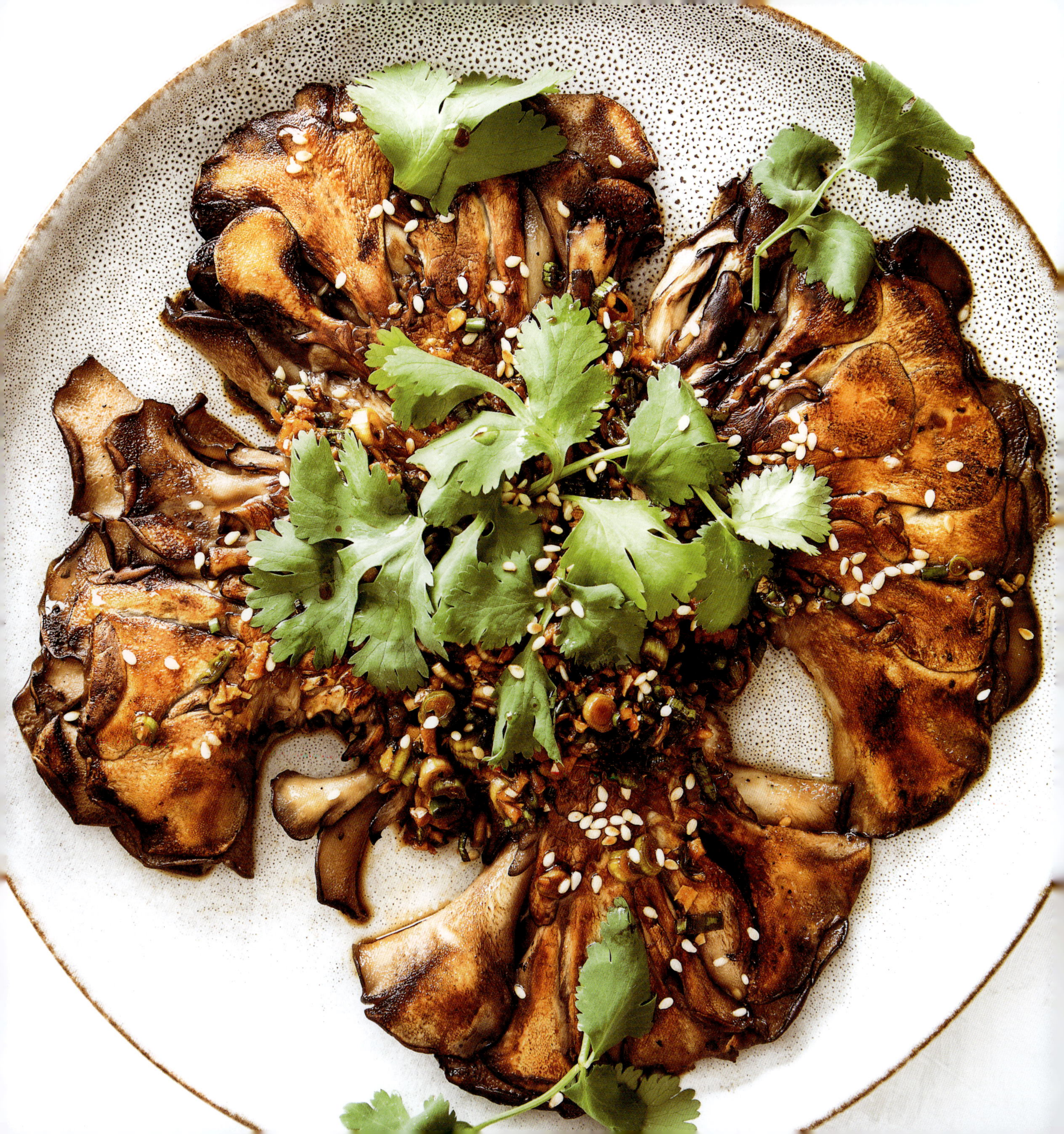

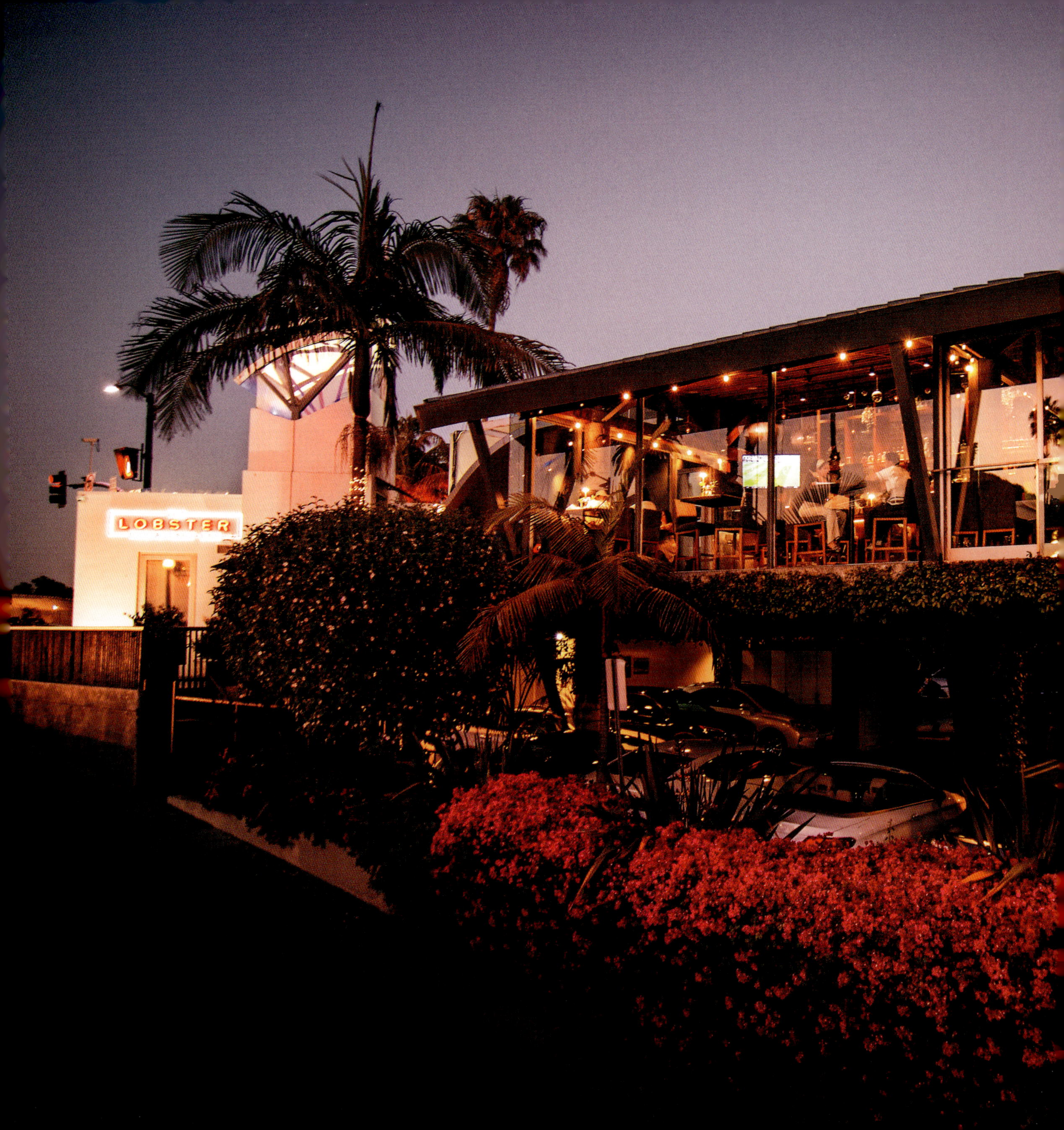
LOBSTER

SANTA MONICA

GRILLED MAINE LOBSTER WITH LEMON GARLIC HERB BUTTER

The Lobster ★ MAKES 2 SERVINGS

Salt, for boiling

1 live Maine lobster (3 pounds, or 1.4 kg)

2 tablespoons (28 ml) warm melted butter

2 tablespoons (28 ml) olive oil

3 teaspoons (30 g) minced garlic, divided

Zest of ½ lemon

1 tablespoon (4 g) chopped parsley

½ teaspoon chopped fresh thyme

½ teaspoon chopped fresh oregano

3 tablespoons (45 ml) clarified butter

1 tablespoon (15 ml) fresh lemon juice

Fresh lemon wedges, for serving

With a name like The Lobster, expectations are high. And once you try the restaurant's signature crustacean dish in all its luxurious drama, propped on a plate with a crock of drawn butter, you'll understand why a lot of people come here for their lobster fix.

INSTRUCTIONS

Prepare a charcoal grill over medium-high heat (about 400°F [200°C]).

Bring a large pot of salted water to a boil. Meanwhile, humanely kill the lobster by storing it in the freezer for 25 minutes to anesthetize it and quickly placing it headfirst into a pot of boiling water. Cook for 2 minutes. Transfer to an ice bath and cool until the internal temperature (measured in the thickest part of the tail, through the underside) reaches 40°F (4°C).

In a small bowl, combine the melted butter, oil, 2 teaspoons garlic, lemon zest, parsley, thyme, and oregano and set aside for seasoning. In a separate bowl, combine the clarified butter, lemon juice, and remaining 1 teaspoon garlic and set aside for serving.

Remove the lobster claws where they meet the body and crack them with the back of a knife to allow heat to penetrate while grilling. Using a cleaver, split the lobster in half lengthwise through its head and tail. Remove the vein and discard any undesired coral (lobster roe) or tomalley. Brush the flesh and cavity with the seasoned butter and sprinkle with salt and pepper.

Rake or push the coals to one side of the grill. Arrange the claws, body, and tail, flesh-side down, on the grate opposite the coals. Cook for about 4 minutes. Using sturdy tongs, lift from under the tail and gently flip the lobster to the shell side and cook for another 4 minutes. Continue to flip the lobster every 4 minutes and cook for a total of 15 to 25 minutes, until the flesh is opaque. (The claws will take 1 to 3 minutes longer.)

Serve the lobster with the clarified butter mixture and plenty of fresh lemon wedges.

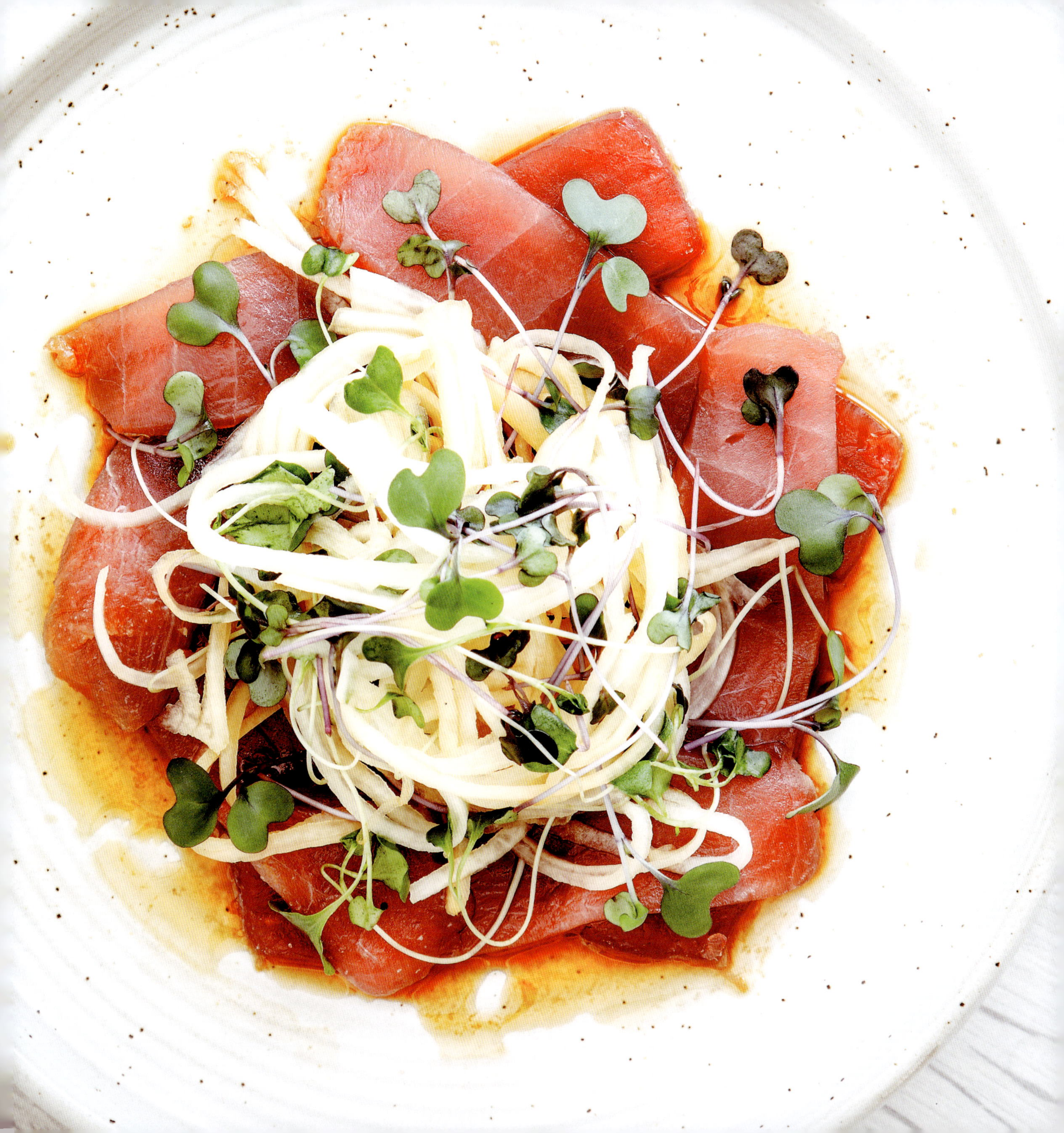

SANTA MONICA

AHI TUNA CRUDO WITH KOHLRABI
The Misfit ✱ MAKES 2 SERVINGS

6 to 7 slices Ahi tuna fillet, sliced ¼-inch (6 mm) thick (about 2¾ ounces, or 78 g)

3 tablespoons (45 ml) ponzu sauce, divided

1 cup (135 g) julienned kohlrabi or (116 g) daikon

3 tablespoons (6 g) microgreens

If you were to take the Will Rogers Highway all the way to its end in Santa Monica, you'd pass the twelve-story Clock Tower Building, which, for forty years, held the record for the tallest building in the skyline. As the city's first high-rise, the Art Deco landmark (capped with a four-faced terra cotta clock for which it's named) was originally called the Bay Cities Guaranty Building and designed by renowned architecture firm Walker & Eisen. It was built in 1929 and commissioned by John Rishell, founder of the Bay Cities Guaranty and Loan Association, for his company headquarters. Talk about bad timing—it hardly had any time to fulfill its intended function before the stock market crashed.

After the company collapsed, the city introduced a special ballot proposal to buy the new building and turn it into City Hall. The proposal was resoundingly defeated by Santa Monica citizens, and the building has remained an office tower ever since. In subsequent decades, it was also known as the Crocker-Citizens National Bank Building and Crocker Bank Building before becoming the Clock Tower Building.

When The Misfit moved into the ground floor in 2011, it took over a space that was previously a traditional French brasserie. Owner Bob Lynn wanted to try something new, based on the idea that he would rather eat in a bar than drink in a restaurant (think: better than bar food, with an all-day happy hour). And the name? It's inspired by the people of Los Angeles and all their quirks. Bob loves that openness: "When you're really yourself, we're all misfits in a way. We're all different."

INSTRUCTIONS

Arrange the tuna slices in a circular pattern around the center of a small plate with about 2 inches (5 cm) of empty plate in the center, leaving space for the kohlrabi mixture. Drizzle 2 tablespoons (28 ml) ponzu over the tuna, letting it run evenly over the plate. In a small bowl, toss the kohlrabi and microgreens with the remaining 1 tablespoon (15 ml) ponzu until evenly coated. Mound the mixture in the center of the plate and serve immediately.

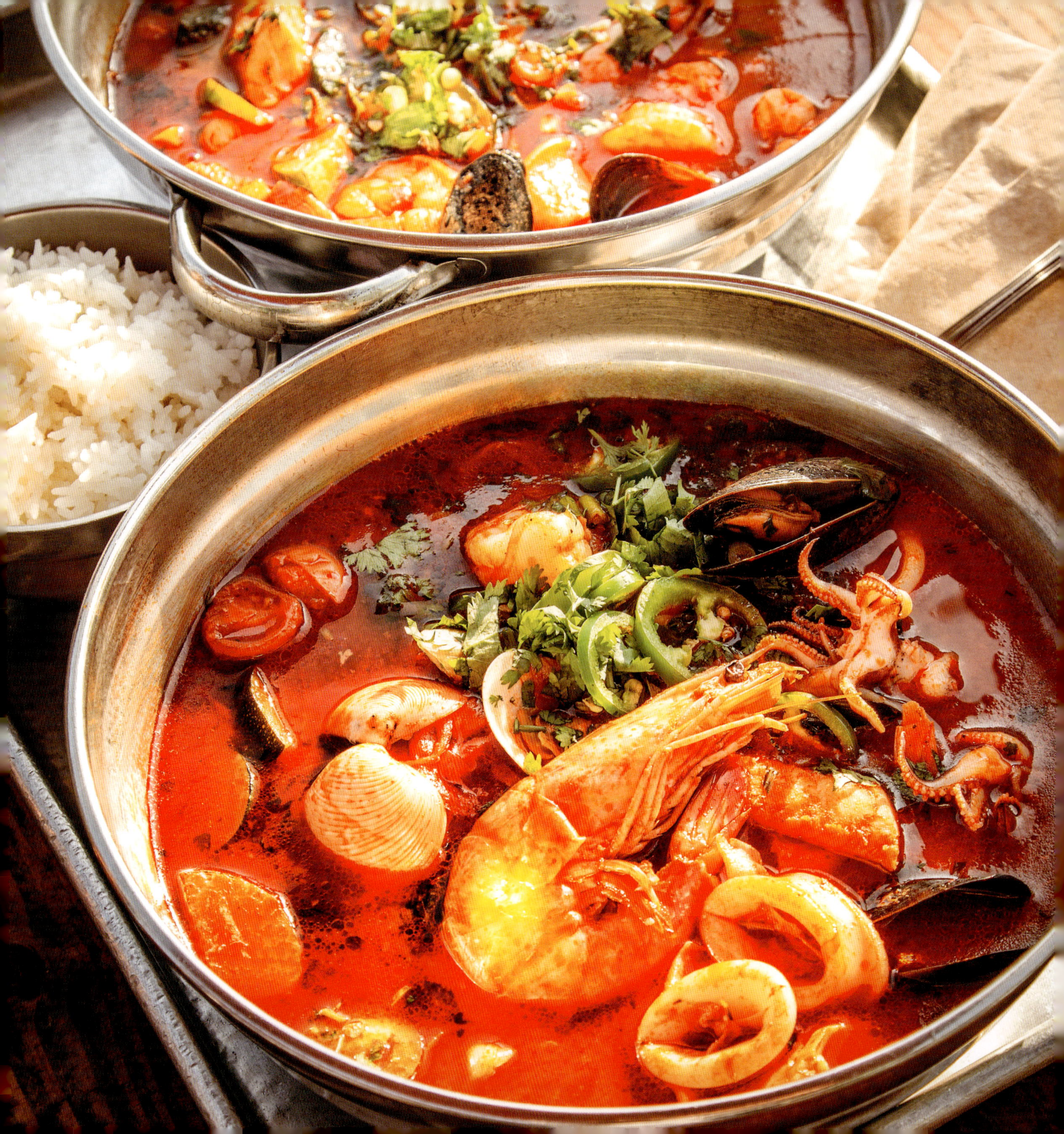

SPICY SEAFOOD SOUP

The Albright ✶ **MAKES 1 SERVING**

SANTA MONICA

FISH STOCK
1 tablespoon (15 ml) olive oil
6 ribs celery, sliced
4 tomatoes, diced
2 carrots, peeled and diced
1 yellow onion, diced
4 jalapeños, sliced
1 cup (150 g) chopped garlic
1 teaspoon fine salt
1 teaspoon ground black pepper
1 cup (235 ml) white cooking wine
3 pounds (1.4 kg) fish bones
1 cup (64 g) fresh oregano leaves
¼ cup (8 g) fresh thyme leaves
5 quarts (4.7 L) water

SOFRITO
1 shallot, minced
2 cloves garlic, minced
Olive oil

SOUP
2 tablespoons (28 ml) olive oil
1 cup (120 g) diced zucchini
¾ cup (113 g) halved cherry tomatoes
4 ounces (115 g) Atlantic cod, cut into 4 long strips
5 littleneck clams
5 Prince Edward Island black mussels
3 white shrimp, peeled and deveined with tail on
2 small head-on shrimp
2 calamari rings
2 calamari tentacles

Sliced jalapeño, for garnish
Chopped cilantro, for garnish
½ cup (93 g) steamed white rice, for serving

Few people can say they grew up on the Santa Monica Pier and *still* call it home—but Yunnie Kim Morena can. Her parents emigrated from Korea when she was young. Her dad, Yong Kim, loved fishing and was looking for a way to support his family in their new life. When a business opportunity on the pier came along in 1977, he opened SM Pier Seafood, becoming a go-to spot for local fishermen who came for the family's home cooking. The restaurant moved to a larger space in 1983 (after a hurricane wiped out a third of the pier) and finally settled into its current location in the mid-1990s.

After Yong's passing in 2008, his wife, Hae Ju, took over the restaurant. She eventually retired in 2013, so Yunnie and her husband, Greg Morena, stepped in, revamped the space, and rebranded as The Albright.

Much of the original character was preserved so regulars still feel at home, but the warm, modern vibe beckons a new generation of pier visitors. The updated menu stays true to their fish shack roots, and this spicy seafood soup is particularly meaningful to the family. It pays homage to a longtime recipe, *maeuntang* (Korean fish stew), that Yunnie's mom used to serve at the original restaurant. Use a very large soup bowl for this restaurant-size serving!

So why "Albright" as a name? It's a nod to the nautical Albright knot and symbolizes the tying together of two generations in a family business.

CALIFORNIA | 177

SPICY SEAFOOD SOUP
CONTINUED

INSTRUCTIONS

Make the fish stock: Heat the oil in a large pot over medium-high heat. Add the celery, tomatoes, carrots, onion, and jalapeños and cook, stirring occasionally, until the vegetables start to soften, 4 to 5 minutes. Add the garlic, salt, and pepper and stir to incorporate all the ingredients.

Pour in the cooking wine, then add the fish bones, oregano, and thyme. Simmer for 2 to 3 minutes, then add the water and bring to a boil. Turn off the heat and let the stock cool completely. Strain, then set aside 3 to 4 cups (700 to 946 ml) of stock (depending on how brothy you like your soup) and refrigerate the remaining stock for up to 3 days for use in other recipes. (The stock can be made up to 3 days in advance.)

Make the sofrito: Mix the shallot and garlic together in a small bowl. Stir in just enough olive oil to form a thick, chunky consistency. Set aside 1 tablespoon (15 ml) of the mixture and store the rest in the refrigerator for up to a week for use in other recipes.

Make the soup: In a medium saucepan, heat the oil over medium-high heat. Add 1 tablespoon (15 ml) sofrito, the zucchini, and the tomatoes and cook until the vegetables soften and start to brown, about 4 minutes. Add all the seafood and cook until the shrimp just start to turn opaque but are still raw inside, about 2 minutes. Pour in the reserved fish stock and bring to a boil. Continue to boil for 3 to 4 minutes, until all the seafood is fully cooked. Remove from heat and ladle the soup into a large bowl.

Garnish with jalapeño and cilantro and serve the soup with steamed rice.

End of the Trail

HISTORIC
CALIFORNIA
US
66
ROUTE
END

66 To Cali

HISTORIC
CALIFORNIA
US
66
ROUTE

Where's the Real End
OF ROUTE 66?

There's a sign on the Santa Monica Pier. There's a mural behind Mel's Diner and an official-looking sign on the corner of Lincoln and Olympic boulevards. There's even a bronze plaque marking the end of the Will Rogers Highway in Palisades Park, which some sources claim is really the western terminus of Route 66.

So who's right?

Like much of Route 66, the answer follows some twists and turns.

From 1935 to 1963, the endpoint was—legally—where The Penguin Coffee Shop (now Mel's Diner) once stood, as a highway could not "dead end" a traveler. Thus Route 66 traveled along Santa Monica Boulevard and turned down Lincoln to connect to Highway 1.

During this same period, the US Highway 66 Association campaigned to have the highway renamed as the Will Rogers Highway, and to move its endpoint to Palisades Park on Ocean Avenue and Santa Monica Boulevard. Warner Brothers had shot a movie about the life of Will Rogers, and to help promote the movie, the US Highway 66 Association and Ford Motor Company drove along Route 66 from St. Louis to Santa Monica, placing memorial markers at each state line. The final marker was placed in 1952 at a pseudo "state line" in the park, right next to the Pacific Ocean.

When the decommissioning of Route 66 began in California in 1964, its endpoint could've been either of these... or anywhere else.

But far-flung travelers coming from inland or from other countries want to keep going until they can touch the Pacific. It feels anticlimactic to stop at a busy intersection.

Which is why, in an effort to end the epic journey on a high note, a brilliant marketing move recognized the official terminus as the Santa Monica Pier. To honor the pier's centennial in 2009, the Route 66 Alliance, Santa Monica Convention and Visitors Bureau, Santa Monica Pier Restoration Corp., and 66 to Cali (a Route 66 souvenir company) erected a new sign to designate the pier as the end of the trail. Since Caltrans no longer had a say in the matter, the move was a local "official" relocation of the western terminus of an "officially" defunct highway.

The sign looks out over the Pacific in a symbolic display of what was once (and still is) a destination for countless road-trippers over the last century. Both sides are labeled "End" so that travelers ask, "If it ends here, where does it go?"

Because after all, the Route 66 of today is about the journey as much as the destination.

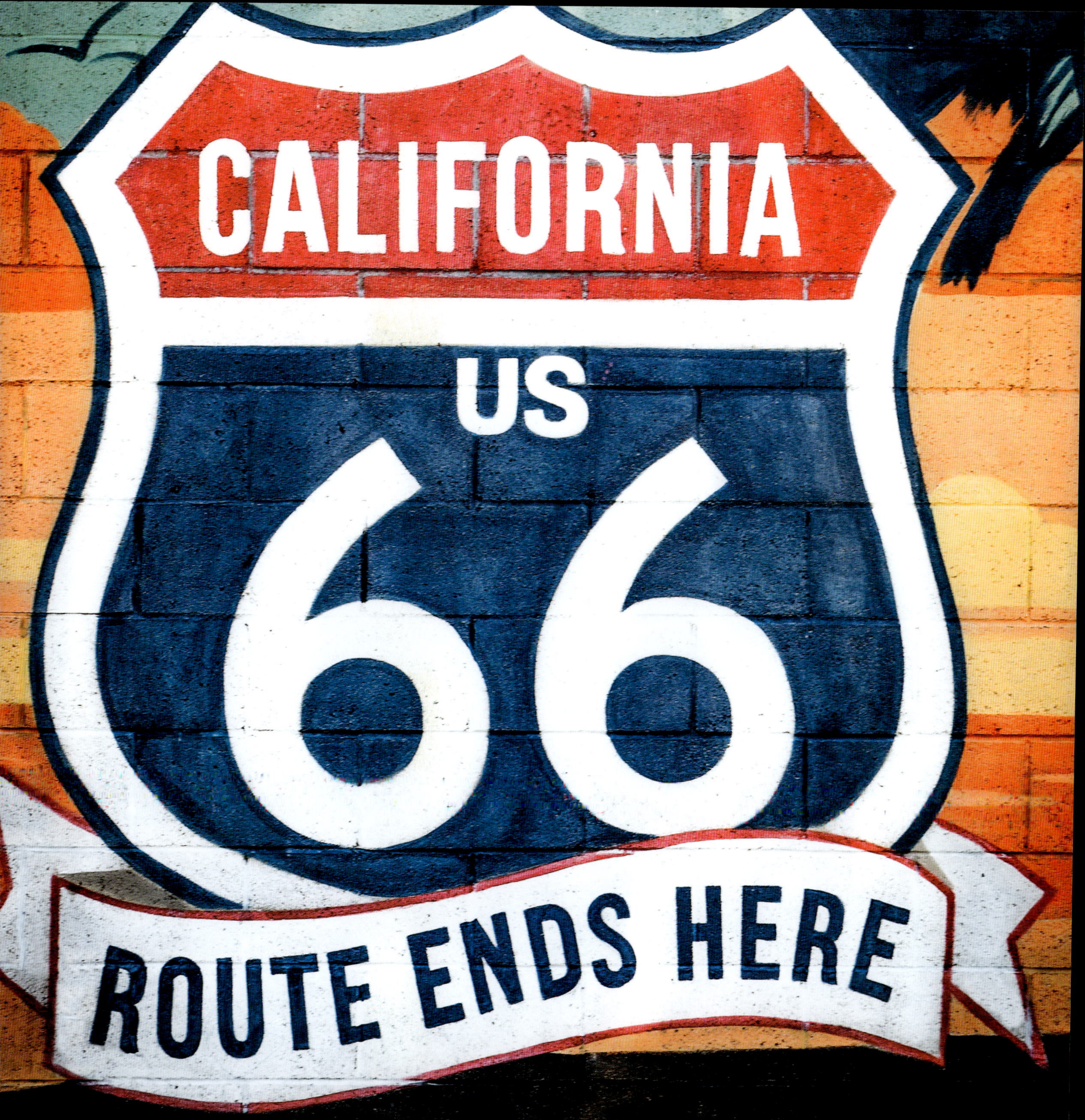
CALIFORNIA
US
66
ROUTE ENDS HERE

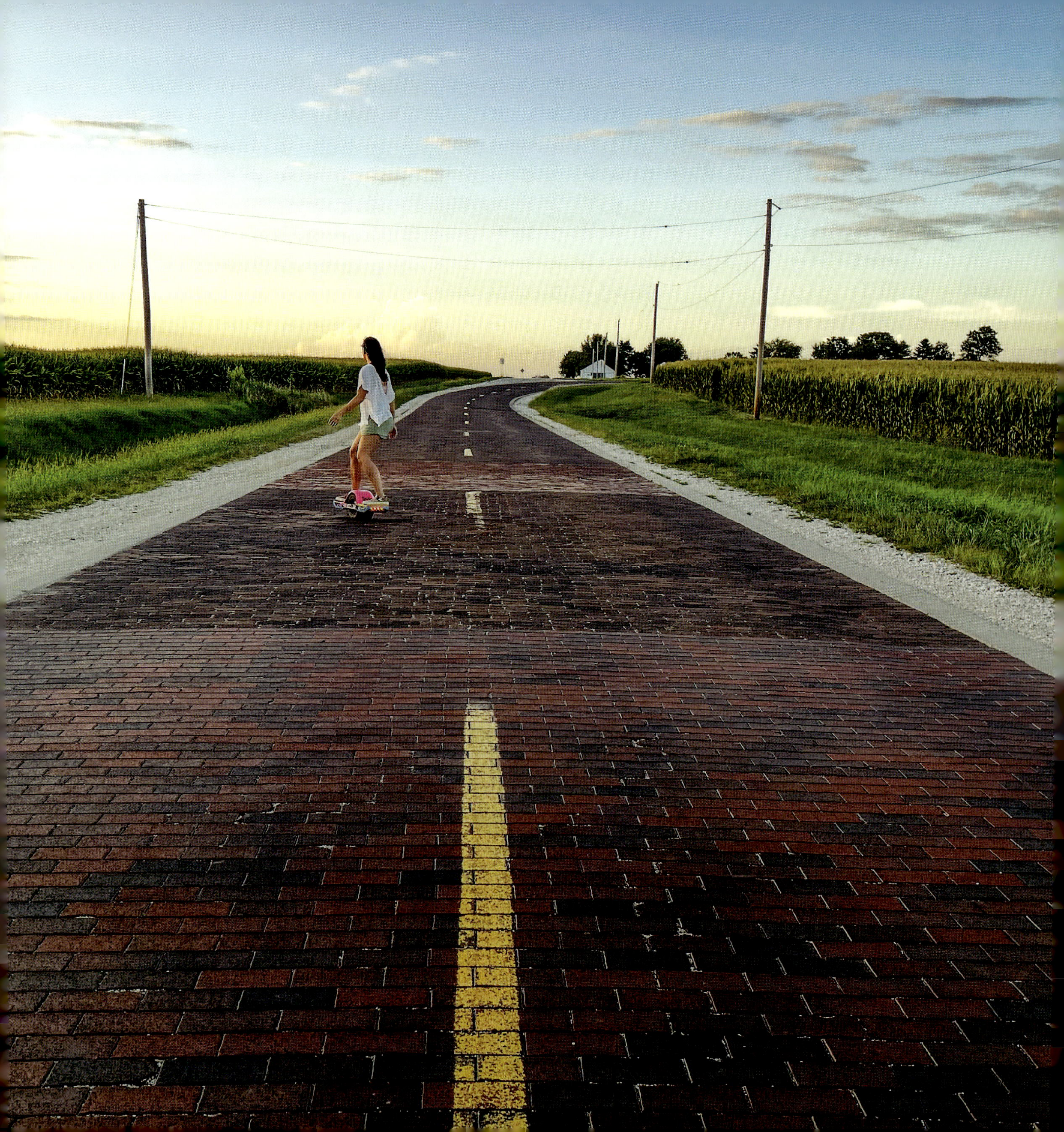

ACKNOWLEDGMENTS

TURNING AN IDEA INTO A BOOK is no small feat, and this project, in particular, was my most challenging—and most rewarding—yet. I wasn't sure I could adequately capture the essence of Route 66 in a limited amount of space, and there were so many more restaurants I wish I could've featured, but I'm grateful for the opportunity and hope I did justice to this small slice of American history.

A very special thanks to all the small-business owners and their chefs, their staff, and their families who generously gave their time and shared their recipes in all sorts of ways: on the phone, via text, through email, or on good old-fashioned paper. (The handwritten recipe on a guest check is probably my favorite—and so Route 66.) Some of the most memorable meals on my trip were equally about the food and the people I got to spend time with—including the people who were serving me. They are truly good, hardworking folks whose stories need to be told and passed on, and I'm honored to be a voice in their chapter.

I owe a heap of thanks to my former editor of eleven years, Thom O'Hearn, who pitched *me* on this book idea, and to my team at Quarto Publishing, whom I've worked with for the past thirteen years, for their trust and guidance with every book I've written.

My family is my "why," and my kids are two of the best reasons for everything. Without them, the journey certainly wouldn't have been as fun—or nearly as hilarious. I'm the luckiest to be loved by them, and I'm so happy I get to be their mama. Gemma and Ember, *you* are my greatest adventure.

And of course, they wouldn't be here were it not for their doting dad and my talented photographer, fearless navigator, epic adventure partner, and best friend—a.k.a. my husband—Will Taylor, who truly brought these pages to life with his lens. Thank you for always having my back and for your positive energy, your incredible patience, and your mad driving skills that took us on a seven-thousand-mile (11, 265 km) road trip of a lifetime. I love you more than all the stars.

(Yes, it took us seven thousand miles [11,265 km] to explore Route 66 and everything there and back . . . because that's how we roll.)

And for all the people who have bought, shared, reviewed, and cooked from my books over the years and continued to spread the word about them—THANK YOU. A thousand times over. Creating something that's earned a place in your home and helped feed your families is a privilege I don't take for granted.

ABOUT THE AUTHOR

LINDA LY grew up in a family that lived for good food and great road trips, which inspired her lifelong love of cooking and traveling—a love that has influenced her writing on her award-winning blog, *Garden Betty*, and several farm-to-table and outdoor cookbooks, including *The No-Waste Vegetable Cookbook*, *The National Parks Cookbook*, *The Backyard Fire Cookbook,* and bestseller *The New Camp Cookbook*.

Linda lives on a sprawling homestead in Bend, Oregon, where she obsesses over plants and tends to a flock of chickens with her husband, Will, and their ever-curious, ebullient daughters, Gemma and Ember. The family is always seeking out their next adventure as they go Onewheeling, snowboarding, mountain biking, hiking, paddling, and exploring the country in their twenty-four-foot (7 m) Minnie Winnie named Wanda (as in "wanda lust").

Her favorite part of writing *The Route 66 Cookbook*—besides trying new foods—was getting to meet and talk with hundreds of people across the country and seeing America from a fresh perspective. She also loved swimming in Grand Falls (Joplin) and walking through the amazing gardens at Gary's Gay Parita (a must-stop in Ash Grove, Missouri, in late summer).

Read more at www.gardenbetty.com.

ABOUT THE PHOTOGRAPHER

FROM AN EARLY AGE, WILL TAYLOR was captivated by photography and took pictures with anything he could get his hands on, from disposable cameras to his parents' vintage Rolleiflex. But it was the ten years spent "living the life" in Lake Tahoe, California, and being surrounded by spectacular scenery every day that ignited his passion for storytelling and motivated him to make a career out of photography.

For the past thirty years, Will's assignments in landscapes, lifestyle, fashion, and food have taken him around the world and have appeared in dozens of publications, including his wife Linda's cookbooks.

When he's home in Central Oregon, he likes to spend as much time as possible outside, whether it's building and tinkering in the yard or playing in the Cascades and showing his two little girls the joys of chasing sunsets off the beaten path.

Will's favorite part of Route 66 was driving through what felt like an open-air museum of advertising relics, from the Burma Shave signs and Muffler Men to the gas pumps and neon marquees. His favorite meal was at Lola's (page 33) . . . followed by a Chicago dog at Carl's Ice Cream in Normal, Illinois.

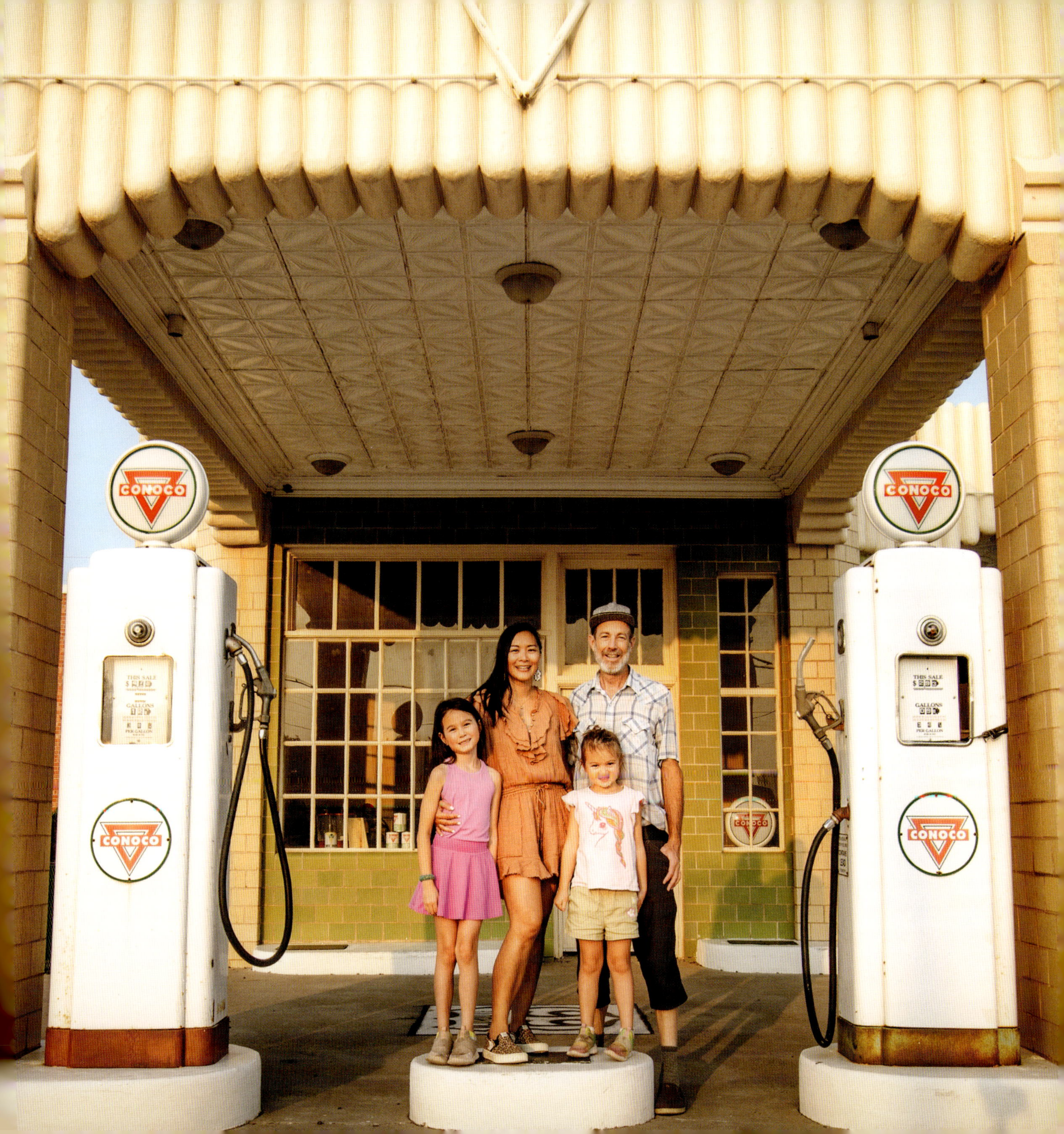
CONOCO
CONOCO
CONOCO
CONOCO
CONOCO

CONTRIBUTORS

ILLINOIS

Lou Mitchell's Restaurant & Bakery
565 W. Jackson Blvd.
Chicago, IL 60661
(312) 939-3111

The Berghoff
17 W. Adams St.
Chicago, IL 60603
(312) 427-3170

Mercat a la Planxa at The Blackstone
636 S. Michigan Ave.
Chicago, IL 60605
(312) 447-0955

Dell Rhea's Chicken Basket
645 Joliet Rd.
Willowbrook, IL 60527
(630) 325-0780

Lola's
210 N. Ladd St. Unit 1
Pontiac, IL 61764
(815) 277-1074

Maldaner's Restaurant
222 S. 6th St.
Springfield, IL 62701
(217) 522-4313

Docs Just Off 66
133 S. 2nd St.
Girard, IL 62640
(217) 627-3491

The Ariston Cafe
413 Old Route 66 North
Litchfield, IL 62056
(217) 324-2023

Jubelt's Bakery & Restaurant
303 North Old Route 66
Litchfield, IL 62056
(217) 324-5314

Weezy's Route 66 Bar & Grill
108 Old US Route 66
Hamel, IL 62046
(618) 633-2228

MISSOURI

Crown Candy Kitchen
1401 St. Louis Ave.
St. Louis, MO 63106
(314) 621-9650

Carl's Drive-In
9033 Manchester Rd.
Brentwood, MO 63144
(314) 961-9652

Historic Big Chief Roadhouse
17352 Manchester Rd.
Wildwood, MO 63038
(636) 458-3200

Weir on 66
102 W. Washington St.
Cuba, MO 65453
(573) 885-3004

Missouri Hick Bar-B-Que
913 E. Washington Blvd.
Cuba, MO 65453
(573) 885-6791

St. James Winery
540 State Route B
St. James, MO 65559
(800) 280-9463

Hoppers Pub
318 Historic 66 East
Waynesville, MO 65583
(573) 774-0135

College Street Cafe
1622 W. College St.
Springfield, MO 65806
(417) 351-4255

Rise & Grind Coffee Station
11861 State Highway 96
Miller, MO 65707
(417) 452-4545

The Carthage Deli
301 S. Main St.
Carthage, MO 64836
(417) 358-8820

KANSAS

Streetcar Station Coffee Shop
515 S. Main St. #1219
Galena, KS 66739
(620) 783-5554

Nelson's Old Riverton Store
7109 SE Highway 66
Riverton, KS 66770
(620) 848-3330

Bricks & Brews Woodfire Grill & Pub
1531 Military Ave.
Baxter Springs, KS 66713
(620) 304-2056

Monarch Pharmacy and Soda Fountain
1601 Military Ave.
Baxter Springs, KS 66713
(620) 856-3030

OKLAHOMA

Clanton's Cafe
319 E. Illinois Ave.
Vinita, OK 74301
(918) 256-9053

El Rancho Grande Mexican Food
1629 East 11th St.
Tulsa, OK 74120
(918) 584-0816

Doctor Kustom Bistro
1102 S. Lewis Ave.
Suite C
Tulsa, OK 74104

Rock Cafe
114 W. Main St.
Stroud, OK 74079
(918) 968-3990

Pops 66
660 W. Highway 66
Arcadia, OK 73007
(405) 927-7677

Classen Grill
5124 Classen Circle
Oklahoma City, OK 73118
(405) 418-4161

Green Chile Kitchen
12 E. Main St.
Yukon, OK 73099
(405) 265-4346

Sid's Diner
300 S. Choctaw Ave.
El Reno, OK 73036
(405) 262-7757

Lucille's Roadhouse
1301 N. Airport Rd.
Weatherford, OK 73096
(580) 772-8808

Country Dove Gifts & Tea Room
610 W. Third St.
Elk City, OK 73644
(580) 225-7028

TEXAS
The Big Texan Steak Ranch
7701 Interstate 40
Amarillo, TX 79118
(806) 372-6000

The GoldenLight
Cafe & Cantina
2906 SW 6th Ave.
Amarillo, TX 79106
(806) 374-9237

Mama Jo's Pies & Sweets
922 E. Main St.
Vega, TX 79092
(806) 282-7699

Midpoint Cafe
305 Historic Route 66
Adrian, TX 79001
(806) 536-6379

NEW MEXICO
Del's Restaurant
1202 East Historic Route 66
Tucumcari, NM 88401
(575) 461-1740

Silver Moon Cafe
2545 Historic US Route 66
Santa Rosa, NM 88435
(575) 472-3162

La Plazuela at La Fonda
on the Plaza
100 E. San Francisco St.
Santa Fe, NM 87501
(505) 995-2334

Clowndog Hot Dog Parlor
3624 Central Ave. SE
Albuquerque, NM 87108
(505) 255-0052

Western View Diner
& Steakhouse
6411 Central Ave. NW
Albuquerque, NM 87105
(505) 836-2200

ARIZONA
Brown Mug Cafe
308 E. 2nd St.
Winslow, AZ 86047
(928) 289-3958

The Turquoise Room
at La Posada Hotel
305 E. Second St.
Winslow, AZ 86047
(928) 289-2888

Westside Lilo's
22855 Old Highway 66
Seligman, AZ 86337
(928) 422-5456

The Roadkill Cafe
22830 Old Highway 66
Seligman, AZ 86337
(928) 422-3554

Rutherford's 66
Family Diner
2011 E. Andy Devine Ave.
Kingman, AZ 86401
(928) 377-1660

CALIFORNIA
Roy's Motel & Cafe
87520 National Trails Highway
Amboy, CA 92304
(760) 733-1066

Chiquita Rosita's
760 E. Main St.
Barstow, CA 92311
(760) 256-1058

Fair Oaks Pharmacy
& Soda Fountain
1526 Mission St.
South Pasadena, CA 91030
(626) 799-1414

La Cuevita
5922 N. Figueroa St.
Los Angeles, CA 90042
(323) 255-6871

The Formosa Cafe
7156 Santa Monica Blvd.
West Hollywood, CA 90046
(323) 794-1106

Tail o' the Pup
8512 Santa Monica Blvd.
West Hollywood, CA 90069
(310) 579-1213

Mel's Drive-In
1670 Lincoln Blvd.
Santa Monica, CA 90404
(310) 392-0139

The Lobster
1602 Ocean Ave.
Santa Monica, CA 90401
(310) 458-9294

The Misfit
225 Santa Monica Blvd.
Santa Monica, CA 90401
(310) 656-9800

The Albright
258 Santa Monica Pier
Santa Monica, CA 90401
(310) 394-9683

ROUTE 66 ASSOCIATIONS

Route 66 Association of Illinois
www.il66assoc.org

Route 66 Association of Missouri
www.missouri66.org

Kansas Historic Route 66 Association
www.facebook.com/kshistoricroute66

Route 66 Association of Kansas
www.facebook.com/KansasRoute66Association

Oklahoma Route 66 Association
www.oklahomaroute66.com

Old Route 66 Association of Texas
www.rt66oftexas.com

New Mexico Route 66 Association
www.rt66nm.org

Historic Route 66 Association of Arizona
www.historic66az.com

California Historic Route 66 Association
www.route66ca.org

National Historic Route 66 Federation
www.national66.org

Czech Route 66 Association
www.r66.cz

188 | THE ROUTE 66 COOKBOOK

INDEX

agave/agave nectar
    Khee to My Success, 169
    Smoke and Peaches, 159
Ahi Tuna Crudo with Kohlrabi, 175
Albert's Ham Sandwich, 152–153
apples
    Apple Strudel, 24–25
    Green Chile Apple Pie, 105
artichoke hearts
    Greek Sandwich, 149

bacon
    Bang Bang Burger, 64
    Dátiles con Almendras, 27
    Heart-Stopping BLT, 51
    Super Burger, 137
    Tattooed Lady and Sonoran Dog, 134
bananas
    The Elvis Ugly Crust Pie, 122
Bang Bang Burger, 64
Beans and Corn Bread, 72
beef
    Bang Bang Burger, 64
    Chef's Special Pastel, 91–92
    Goldenlight Cafe Chili, 117
    Goulash, 76
    Onion Fried Burger, 106
    Roast Beef Sandwich, 79
    Sticky Short Rib Noodles, 161–162
    Super Burger, 137
    The Vernon—The Ultimate Route 66 Burger, 67
beef base/broth
    about, 15
    French Onion Soup, 54
    Sticky Short Rib Noodles, 161–162
Beef Rub and Rib Rub, 61

black bean sauce
    Sticky Short Rib Noodles, 161–162
Blackberry Wine Cake, 63
BLT, Heart-Stopping, 51
Bobby's Egg Custard Pie, 120
Bodegas Tradición
    Smoke-Filled-Room Cocktail, 28
Bread Pudding, Root Beer, 99
broccolini
    Sticky Short Rib Noodles, 161–162
    Wok Fried Rice with Pork Belly, 163
Butter Spritz Cookies, 41–42
buttermilk
    Beans and Corn Bread, 72
    Calf Fries, 87
    Lucille's Jalapeño Fried Pork Chops, 109

cabbage
    Dátiles con Almendras, 27
    Weezy's Coleslaw, 45
cachaça
    Chef's Special Pastel, 91–92
calamari
    Spicy Seafood Soup, 177–178
Calf Fries, 87
carrots
    Cream of Chicken and Wild Rice Soup, 57
    Grandma's Chicken Soup, 166
    Spicy Seafood Soup, 177–178
    Weezy's Coleslaw, 45
    Wok Fried Rice with Pork Belly, 163
celery
    Chile Colorado, 89
    Grandma's Chicken Soup, 166
    Spicy Seafood Soup, 177–178
    Wok Fried Rice with Pork Belly, 163

cheese
    Bang Bang Burger, 64
    Chef's Special Pastel, 91–92
    Chiles Rellenos de Camarón, 131–132
    Dátiles con Almendras, 27
    Del's Rellenos, 126
    Goldenlight Cafe Chili, 117
    Greek Sandwich, 149
    Green Chile Grit Cakes, 100
    Mashed Potatoes, 114
    Morel Mushroom Pie, 35
    Roast Beef Sandwich, 79
    Strawberry Whipped Cheesecake, 38–39
    Super Burger, 137
    The Vernon—The Ultimate Route 66 Burger, 67
    The Voodoo Child Pizza, 81
Chef's Special Pastel, 91–92
chicken
    Cream of Chicken and Wild Rice Soup, 57
    Crispy Chicken Adobo Wings, 33
    Grandma's Chicken Soup, 166
    Greek Sandwich, 149
    New Mexican Posole, 129
    Posole, 103–104
chicken base/broth
    about, 15
    Beans and Corn Bread, 72
    Cream of Chicken and Wild Rice Soup, 57
    Grandma's Chicken Soup, 166
    Green Chile Grit Cakes, 100
    Posole, 103–104
Chicken Livers, Sautéed, 30–31
Chile Colorado, 89
chile/chili powder
    Goldenlight Cafe Chili, 117
    Goulash, 76

New Mexican Posole, 129
Chiles Rellenos de Camarón, 131–132
chocolate
    French Silk Pie, 110
    Heavenly Hash, 48
chocolate sauce/syrup
    Chocolate Malt, 157
    Docs S'mores Sundae, 36
    Egg Cream, 83
cilantro
    Chef's Special Pastel, 91–92
    Chiles Rellenos de Camarón, 131–132
clams
    Spicy Seafood Soup, 177–178
cocoa powder
    The Elvis Ugly Crust Pie, 122
cod
    Spicy Seafood Soup, 177–178
Coleslaw, Weezy's, 45
cooking vessel sizes, standard, 12

corn
    Chiles Rellenos de Camarón, 131–132
cornmeal
    Beans and Corn Bread, 72
    Calf Fries, 87
    The Voodoo Child Pizza, 81
Cream of Chicken and Wild Rice Soup, 57
Crispy Chicken Adobo Wings, 33
Cucumber and Onions, 58
Curly-Q Dog, 53

Dátiles con Almendras, 27
Del's Rellenos, 126
Docs S'mores Sundae, 36

Egg Cream, 83
eggs
    about, 15
    Bobby's Egg Custard Pie, 120
    Chef's Special Pastel, 91–92
    Chiles Rellenos de Camarón, 131–132
    Del's Rellenos, 126
    The Elvis Ugly Crust Pie, 122
    Grilled Thick French Toast, 22
    Morel Mushroom Pie, 35
Elvis Ugly Crust Pie, The, 122

fish and seafood
    Ahi Tuna Crudo with Kohlrabi, 175
    Chiles Rellenos de Camarón, 131–132
    Grilled Maine Lobster with Lemon Garlic Herb Butter, 173
    Halibut Ceviche, 142
    Spicy Seafood Soup, 177–178
flour
    about, 15
    measuring, 12
French fries
    The Vernon—The Ultimate Route 66 Burger, 67
French Onion Soup, 54
French Silk Pie, 110

garlic
    Chef's Special Pastel, 91–92
    Chiles Rellenos de Camarón, 131–132

Goldenlight Cafe Chili, 117
Grilled Maine Lobster with Lemon Garlic Herb Butter, 173
New Mexican Posole, 129
Posole, 103–104
Spicy Seafood Soup, 177–178
Wok Fried Rice with Pork Belly, 163
gelatin, berry-flavored
    Blackberry Wine Cake, 63
ginger, fresh
    Seared Mushrooms with Scallion-Ginger Drizzle, 170
    Sticky Short Rib Noodles, 161–162
Goldenlight Cafe Chili, 117
Goulash, 76
Grandma's Chicken Soup, 166
Greek Sandwich, 149
green chile sauce
    Super Burger, 137
green chiles
    Del's Rellenos, 126
    Green Chile Apple Pie, 105
    Green Chile Grit Cakes, 100
Grilled Maine Lobster with Lemon Garlic Herb Butter, 173
Grilled Thick French Toast, 22
Grit Cakes, Green Chile, 100

Halibut Ceviche, 142
ham
    Albert's Ham Sandwich, 152–153
    Beans and Corn Bread, 72
Heart-Stopping BLT, 51
Heavenly Hash, 48
herbs, about, 12
hominy
    New Mexican Posole, 129
    Posole, 103–104
hot dogs
    Curly-Q Dog, 53
    The Route 66 Pup, 164
    Tattooed Lady and Sonoran Dog, 134
House Mustard, 164
House Salsa, 141

190 | THE ROUTE 66 COOKBOOK

ice cream
   Chocolate Malt, 157
   Docs S'mores Sundae, 36
ingredients, about, 14–15

Khee to My Success, 169
kitchen scales, 14
Kohlrabi, Ahi Tuna Crudo with, 175

Licor, 43
   Smoke-Filled-Room Cocktail, 28
Lobster with Lemon Garlic Herb Butter,
   Grilled Maine, 173
Lucille's Jalapeño Fried Pork Chops, 109
lychee syrup
   Khee to My Success, 169

malted milk powder
   Chocolate Malt, 157
mango
   Halibut Ceviche, 142
marinara sauce
   The Voodoo Child Pizza, 81
marshmallows/marshmallow cream
   Docs S'mores Sundae, 36
   Heavenly Hash, 48
Mashed Potatoes, 114
measuring flour, 12
mezcal
   Smoke and Peaches, 159
Mom's Yeast Rolls, 69–70
Morel Mushroom Pie, 35
mushrooms
   Morel Mushroom Pie, 35
   Seared Mushrooms with Scallion-Ginger
      Drizzle, 170
mussels
   Spicy Seafood Soup, 177–178

New Mexican Posole, 129
nuts
   Apple Strudel, 24–25
   Blackberry Wine Cake, 63
   Dátiles con Almendras, 27
   French Silk Pie, 110

Green Chile Apple Pie, 105
Heavenly Hash, 48
Poor Man's Pecan Pie, a.k.a. Oatmeal Pie, 94
Strawberry Whipped Cheesecake, 38–39

onions
   Beans and Corn Bread, 72
   Chef's Special Pastel, 91–92
   Chile Colorado, 89
   Chiles Rellenos de Camarón, 131–132
   Crispy Chicken Adobo Wings, 33
   Cucumber and Onions, 58
   Dátiles con Almendras, 27
   French Onion Soup, 54
   Grandma's Chicken Soup, 166
   Halibut Ceviche, 142
   Morel Mushroom Pie, 35
   New Mexican Posole, 129
   Onion Fried Burger, 106
   Posole, 103–104
   The Route 66 Pup, 164
   Sautéed Chicken Livers, 30–31
   Spicy Seafood Soup, 177–178
   Sticky Short Rib Noodles, 161–162
   Tattooed Lady and Sonoran Dog, 134
   Wok Fried Rice with Pork Belly, 163
orange juice
   Halibut Ceviche, 142

pasta and noodles
   Goulash, 76
   Grandma's Chicken Soup, 166
   Sticky Short Rib Noodles, 161–162
Peaches, Smoke and, 159
peanut butter
   The Elvis Ugly Crust Pie, 122
pepperoni
   The Voodoo Child Pizza, 81
peppers, bell
   Chile Colorado, 89
   Halibut Ceviche, 142
peppers, chile
   Chef's Special Pastel, 91–92
   Chile Colorado, 89
   Chiles Rellenos de Camarón, 131–132

Halibut Ceviche, 142
House Salsa, 141
Jalapeño Spread, 164
Lucille's Jalapeño Fried Pork Chops, 109
Spicy Seafood Soup, 177–178
Peychaud bitters
   Smoke-Filled-Room Cocktail, 28
phyllo dough
   Apple Strudel, 24–25
pickles
   Albert's Ham Sandwich, 152–153
   Onion Fried Burger, 106
pie crusts
   Bobby's Egg Custard Pie, 120
   The Elvis Ugly Crust Pie, 122
   Green Chile Apple Pie, 105
   Morel Mushroom Pie, 35
   Poor Man's Pecan Pie, a.k.a. Oatmeal Pie, 94
pie pans/plates, 14
Pizza, Voodoo Child
   The, 81
ponzu sauce
   Ahi Tuna Crudo with Kohlrabi, 175
Poor Man's Pecan Pie, a.k.a. Oatmeal Pie, 94

INDEX | 191

pork
    Chile Colorado, 89
    Lucille's Jalapeño Fried Pork Chops, 109
    New Mexican Posole, 129
    Pork Wiener Schnitzel, 145
    Wok Fried Rice with Pork Belly, 163
Posole, 103–104
Potatoes, Mashed, 114

Rack of Raccoon, 146
ribs
    Rack of Raccoon, 146
    Sticky Short Rib Noodles, 161–162
rice
    Cream of Chicken and Wild Rice Soup, 57
    Crispy Chicken Adobo Wings, 33
    Spicy Seafood Soup, 177–178
    Wok Fried Rice with Pork Belly, 163
Roast Beef Sandwich, 79
Root Beer Bread Pudding, 99
Route 66 Pup, The, 164
rye
    Smoke-Filled-Room Cocktail, 28

salami
    The Voodoo Child Pizza, 81
salt/salting, 12, 15
Sautéed Chicken Livers, 30–31
seafood. *See* fish and seafood
Seared Mushrooms with Scallion-Ginger
    Drizzle, 170
shallots
    Dátiles con Almendras, 27
    Spicy Seafood Soup, 177–178
sheet pans, 12
shrimp
    Chiles Rellenos de Camarón, 131–132
    Spicy Seafood Soup, 177–178
Smoke and Peaches, 159
Smoke-Filled-Room Cocktail, 28
sour cream
    Mashed Potatoes, 114
    Strawberry Whipped Cheesecake, 38–39
Späetzle, 97
spices, about, 12

Spicy Seafood Soup, 177–178
spinach
    Greek Sandwich, 149
stand mixers, 14
Sticky Short Rib Noodles, 161–162
strawberries
    Strawberry Margarita Pie, 154
    Strawberry Whipped Cheesecake, 38–39
Super Burger, 137

tamari
    Seared Mushrooms with Scallion-Ginger
        Drizzle, 170
Tattooed Lady and Sonoran Dog, 134
techniques, 12
tequila
    Smoke and Peaches, 159
    Strawberry Margarita Pie, 154
Thai chili sauce
    Bang Bang Burger, 64
thermometers, 14
tomatoes
    Albert's Ham Sandwich, 152–153
    Chile Colorado, 89
    Chiles Rellenos de Camarón, 131–132
    Goldenlight Cafe Chili, 117
    Goulash, 76
    Greek Sandwich, 149
    Heart-Stopping BLT, 51
    House Salsa, 141
    Roast Beef Sandwich, 79
    Spicy Seafood Soup, 177–178
    Tattooed Lady and Sonoran Dog, 134
tools, 12, 14
triple sec
    Strawberry Margarita Pie, 154
Tuna Crudo with Kohlrabi, Ahi, 175

vegetable broth
    Green Chile Grit Cakes, 100
vermouth
    Smoke-Filled-Room Cocktail, 28
Vernon—The Ultimate Route 66 Burger, The, 67
Voodoo Child Pizza, The, 81

waffle cones
    Docs S'mores Sundae, 36
Weezy's Coleslaw, 45
wine, Marsala
    Sautéed Chicken Livers, 30–31
wine, white
    about, 15
    Dátiles con Almendras, 27
    French Onion Soup, 54
    Spicy Seafood Soup, 177–178
Wok Fried Rice with Pork Belly, 163

yuzu juice
    Khee to My Success, 169

zucchini
    Spicy Seafood Soup, 177–178